# PRAISE FOR *TEN WAYS TO CHANGE THE WORLD IN YOU*

"What really distingu[...] [...]resents real world cases of you[...] [...]. These aren't just ideas—they're success stories."
—Ben Jervey, environmental journalist

"Everywhere I go around the planet, I find young people, fresh from college, leading the new green movement. With savvy and heart, they're making a real difference—and as this book shows, you can too!"
—Bill McKibben, 350.org

"Libuse Binder has a heart as big as the world. *Ten Ways to Change the World in Your Twenties* is imperative reading for young people committed to helping the planet, and one another, toward a more enlightened future. Read this book!"
—Mark Matousek, author of *When You're Falling, Dive* and *Ethical Wisdom: What Makes Us Good?*

"*Ten Ways to Change the World in Your Twenties* won't only teach you how to change the world, it will get you exhilarated about doing so. Libuse Binder is a passionate advocate and activist, and she writes in fun, accessible prose that's never preachy, that speaks to any generation—whether you're in your 20s or your 80s—about how to live mindfully, and have a blast while doing so."
—Melissa Kirsch, author of *The Girl's Guide to Absolutely Everything*

"Binder drives home one of the most important messages of the green movement for those of us in our 'Roaring Twenties':

You don't have to sacrifice what you love to do (or eat!) to live a more eco-conscious lifestyle. We all seem to be heading towards a place where living our lives fully and caring for the earth intersect, and Binder's book is a compass pointing in that direction. *Ten Ways* breaks down a wide variety of ideas into real tips that I can actually see myself (or any other twentysomething) doing. I can open the book at random and find an activity that I'd not only be interested in, but can get started that same day."

—Jennifer Berry, public and strategic relations manager, Earth911.com

"Having a positive impact doesn't have to be complicated, but sometimes the biggest obstacle is knowing where—and how—to start. *Ten Ways* is a great resource to help people who are just starting out know how to start making a difference."

—Meg Busse, director, Nonprofit Transitions Program at Idealist.org.

# 10
# WAYS TO
# CHANGE
## THE WORLD
## IN YOUR
# 20S

# 10
# WAYS TO CHANGE THE WORLD IN YOUR 20S

## Libuse Binder

SOURCEBOOKS, INC.®
NAPERVILLE, ILLINOIS

Published by Sourcebooks, Inc.
P.O. Box 4410, Naperville, Illinois 60567-4410
(630) 961-3900
Fax: (630) 961-2168
www.sourcebooks.com

Library of Congress Cataloging-in-Publication Data

Binder, Libuse.
  Ten ways to change the world in your twenties / by Libuse Binder.
    p. cm.
  1. Lifestyles--United States. 2. Social change. 3.
Environmentalism. 4. Green movement. 5. Youth--Conduct of life.
I. Title.
  HQ2044.U6.B55 2009
  303.48'40842--dc22
                           2009030714

Printed and bound in the United States of America.
VP 10 9 8 7 6 5 4 3 2 1

*For Steve, an architect of dreams*

# CONTENTS

# ACKNOWLEDGMENTS

This book is the result of the efforts of many and the encouragement of even more, and I am grateful to all who took a leap of faith with this project. Like me, they believe in the importance of empowering the next generation of leaders to create a better future for us all, and in their support for this book they have proven my faith justified.

When this project began, I was just one person looking to make something more of my twenties. Yet, it did not take long to find a plethora of personalities to provide humbling and inspirational examples of this generation's potential. All of the twentysomething world changers who enthusiastically and candidly shared their experiences reaffirmed my belief in our ability to bring about change when those committed to a positive idea take action. Whether their story appears in the book or not, I am thankful to everyone who patiently shared their wisdom and answered my many questions, including Edward Alderson, Jack Algiere, Shannon Algiere, Nancy Diaz Bain, Eben Bayer, Stephanie Bernstein, Julie Bottjen, Lauren Brossy, Amanda Brown, Stacey Clarkson, Amanda Cooper, Brady Dunklee, Kristen Eddings, Maisha Everhart, Christine Farnham, Lindsey

Franklin, Simon Frost, Cass Ghiorse, Nigel Fellman Greene, Mark Hanis, Scott Harrison, Ben Jervey, Mechelle Jones, Blake Johnston, Sarah Kalloch, Allison Letts, Christine Letts, Jordan Levy, Jacob Lief, Kali Lindsey, Meredith Lobel, Daniel Lurie, Rachel Meeropol, Jody Myrum, Stacie Okosky, Joshua Onysko, Sheila Paule, Camvan Phu, Neesha Rahim, Janelle Robbins, Elizabeth Robinson, Steve Rosenthal, Kristen Sager, Kam Santos, David Segal, Quinn Sidon, Jeffrey Alexander Simeon, Josh Solomon, Jon Steinman, Nolan Treadway, Basil Tsimoyianis, Ellen Shortill, and Tom Szaky.

What good fortune that this book found itself in the hands of my editor, Shana Drehs, whose insight, encouragement, and expertise have guided me through this process. Her perceptive comments always hit the mark, and she steered the book in the right direction with clarity, vision, and wit.

I am also grateful for the efforts of the entire team at Sourcebooks who lent their talents to this book, including Sara Kase, Erika Koff, Carrie Gellin, Heather Moore, Barbara Hague, and Regan Blinder.

I could not have asked for a better champion of *Ten Ways* than my agent, Michelle Brower. She has been steadfast in her belief in this project since the beginning. I am indebted to her for such steady guidance, enthusiasm, and support, as well as her indispensable sense of humor.

A special debt of gratitude is owed to Mark Matousek who, as a teacher, mentor, and friend, was as encouraging as he was generous in connecting me to those who could help. *Ten Ways* began its transformation from idea to book due in large part to his unwavering faith in my dream.

Friends and family generously and enthusiastically shared resources, organizations, and initiatives, and suggested many people for me to interview. All who came across my path in the last few years ran the risk of being drawn into my next experiment in lower impact living, and I am grateful to this merry band who, from seasonal cooking, to draft reading, to marathon canning sessions, were up for any adventure I presented. Among those folks, I'd like to especially thank the Babcock, Binder, Petit, and Uydess clans, Denise Benitez, Jennifer Berry, May Boeve, Jessica Boylston-Fagonde, Elena Brower, Joe Burmeister, Meg Busse, Dana Covello, Anne DeMelle, Brendan DeMelle, Raquel Fagan, Andrew Frishman, Anne Frost, Louise Gava, Trey Granger, Marah Hardt, Gretchen Hess, Melissa Kirsch, Ellen McCormick, Amy Minella, Leigh Needleman, Meredith Noll, Robin Posey, Jessica Rudder, Josie St. Peter, Lorraine Shea, Alexis Steinman, Lesley Steinman, and Sara Whalen.

Thanks to all those who graciously agreed to read drafts of this book at every stage of the process including Shannon Connors, Seth Fischer, Laura Goodwin, Charlotte Owen, Erin Prendergast, Jen Rhoads, Erin Richmond, Raegan Russell, Larry Uydess, and Terry Wolverton. Your perspectives and insights lent themselves to a richer, more accurate finished product, and this book is immeasurably better because of you.

And, finally to my husband, Steve Uydess, who read and offered suggestions on every version of the manuscript. He has been in my corner from the beginning and continues to nourish me with his good cooking and bad puns.

To everyone else who offered words of encouragement along the way, each one of you helped to bring this book to life. To those of you about to change the world and those of you who already have, whether or not I have included you by name, you have my thanks and the thanks of future generations who do not yet know of the gifts your work will bestow to them.

# INTRODUCTION

My work is loving the world.

*Mary Oliver*

Who says twentysomethings can't change the world? Right now a twenty-eight-year-old woman is working to prevent violence against women in Ethiopia, a twenty-one-year-old college student in Pennsylvania is directing the Student Anti-Genocide Coalition, and a twenty-five-year-old woman is running an organic farm with her twenty-three-year-old partner. Right now they are using their talent and energy to change the world. Whether you are already one of these people and would like to do more or you are just trying to figure out what you can do to make the world a better place, you will find hundreds of ideas and suggestions within the pages of this book.

Welcome to the Roaring Twenties. A decade, like its historical counterpart, filled with fun, adventure, and carefree living. Of course, you will recall where that attitude landed our country just as the big Three-O was approaching. Yet your trip through the twenties need not resemble a hedonistic material and spiritual binge doomed to end in disaster. In fact, it should be especially gratifying to know that you can enjoy yourself and make a difference at the same time. If you've picked up this book, you've already shown that you care about what is going on in the world and that you want to make a difference. You might be ready to do something about the problems in your backyard, or you might want to involve yourself with global issues in ways that will have both immediate and long-term effects. You want to use your talents, skills, and interests to change the world for the better, and perhaps, most importantly, you don't want to throw away your youth doing it. Well, the good news for the former is that you can and, for the latter, you don't have to.

There are currently thousands of national and local organizations and businesses that are committed to causes such as sustainable living, health care, fair trade, green energy, socially responsible investing, corporate responsibility, and humanitarianism. When you think about all that's out there, it can get a little overwhelming. Think of this book as your go-to, has-all resource. Each chapter offers ways to approach a particular world-changing venture, such as how to find the right volunteer placement for yourself. In addition, each chapter contains a step-by-step guide to accomplishing some of the ideas suggested. You'll find easy-to-implement ideas, descriptions of a variety of nonprofit organizations, and inspirational stories. You can search by topic or by level of time commitment, approximate cost, or degree of lifestyle change that you're comfortable with.

But you may be asking, "With all of these options, how do I choose what to do? How can I discover what excites me? How can I be most *effective*? How do I focus? Oh, and by the way, did I mention that I still need to find a job and figure out where I want to live?" Indeed, you may be experiencing many drastic changes in your life—graduating from college, embarking on a new career (or several!), falling in and out of love, negotiating office politics, getting married, moving far from home, and possibly even buying a house or starting a family.

While the overachievers among you may be asking, "Seriously, is that all?" the majority of you may feel overwhelmed by your new roles as independent adults. No matter where you fall on this spectrum, these years have the potential to be some of the most exciting ones of your life. Although this book is titled *Ten Ways to Change the World in Your Twenties*, it is not limited to any age group. Indeed, for those of you in your teens, twenties, and thirties, your legacy is yet to be determined. Your page in the history books is still blank. Events in the last decade in such varied places as New Orleans, Darfur, and Iraq clearly show us that you are inheriting the earth at a critical juncture. Although you are faced with environmental and humanitarian issues of a scope never before seen, your timing is perfect. You are old enough to care, innovative enough to find solutions, and energetic enough to take action. You are the next generation of leaders, ambassadors, and trendsetters, and you are armed with intelligence and ingenuity. You have incredible power.

But where to start? This business of changing the world can be overwhelming. If you are reading this book, you have already taken the critical first step: caring. Still, you are likely wondering how exactly you are supposed to convince politicians to change laws and policies, the general public to curb their consumption and pollution habits, and your parents to support your pursuits, lucrative or not. The bottom line is, how do you make sure that your voice—your one little voice of the future—is heard?

The answer is that you just need to speak. Sorry for the letdown, but it really is that simple. And a major goal of this book is to show you just how many simple ways there are for you to make yourself heard. If this book does anything, I hope it will convince you that each of us has the power to shape our future. After all, we determine the latest fashions and the hottest music, so shouldn't we also decide who gets to represent us in office and which companies should be making record profits? While some transformations seem to take longer than others, most dramatic changes are the product of countless, seemingly insignificant steps.

While this book does not have all the answers to the world's woes (I do need to think about a sequel, after all!), by working together, implementing ideas, and coming up with collaborative, creative solutions, we can change the world. Creating a better world is a constant work in progress—as are you and I—and I invite you to use the space at the end of this book to chronicle your triumphs and challenges as you set out to change the world. And who knows? You may need the material for your memoir once you become famous.

You can read straight through from start to finish or pick a chapter that piques your interest. The goal of each chapter is to help educate you about a given issue or method, provide some resources and creative solutions, and explore the effects of these solutions through the examples of those already making a difference. These chapters will also help clarify such common practical quandaries as "Paper versus plastic?" "Does my vote really make a difference?" "Omnivore or vegetarian?" and often most importantly, "This sounds great, but how can I do it on the cheap?"

Here is an overview of what you will find in each chapter:

### Chapter 1: Ways to Get Excited and Involved—Discover Your Unique Viewpoint by Exploring the Resources around You

Your twenties are an important time to think about where your interests lie and how your actions and decisions impact the world around you. In chapter 1, you will find ways to discover your passions by discerning the causes you care about most and learning about ways to evaluate organizations that address these issues.

### Chapter 2: Ways to Live, Give, and Thrive through Volunteering—Self-Discovery Need Not Be a Selfish Process

Once you have found causes worthy of deeper exploration, consider one of the most effective ways to make an impact and to find your passion: volunteering. This chapter will profile unique international, national, and local volunteer programs, as well as a variety of volunteer vacations. A volunteer position already exists that is ideal for your needs, interests, and skills; chapter 2 will give you candid information and advice to help you find it.

### Chapter 3: Ways to Be the Life of Your Party—Support Political Actions That Reflect Your Values

The goal of this chapter is to shed more light on your daily connection with public policy decisions and to provide ideas for becoming more educated about and involved in government and community policymaking. Issues like your health insurance (or lack thereof), your grandparents' retirement, and food safety are all matters of public debate, and you have the power to make good things happen in these areas. This chapter includes important actions such as voting, and it also explores many other easy ways for you to get involved with the political process: writing a persuasive letter, challenging and/ or supporting politicians, and various steps you can take to change a particular policy or law.

### Chapter 4: Ways to Be a Green Giant—Practical Ideas for Leading an Eco-active Lifestyle

This chapter will focus on changing habits in order to be more environmentally responsible, including many small, everyday measures you can take to conserve natural resources, protect habitats, and decrease your contribution to global warming.

### Chapter 5: Ways to Lose Waste Fast—Reduce Your Footprint and Simplify Your Life

If green is the new black, then simplicity is the new green. Chapter 5 offers strategies for reduction, the crown jewel in the Three R Triumvirate (reduce, reuse, recycle).

### Chapter 6: Ways to Make Your Money Talk and Companies Listen—Harness the Power of Your Dollar by Supporting Ethically and Environmentally Sound Businesses

Chapter 6 explores how to uncover and understand the ethical and environmental practices of different companies as well as how consumers can communicate their desires/concerns to companies by harnessing the power of their dollars. We can drive the market with our demand for fairly traded, recycled and recyclable, low-impact, efficient, and responsibly manufactured products (not necessarily all at the same time, but you get the idea!).

### Chapter 7: Ways to Eat What You Want without Eating *That*—The Triumphs of Good Taste for the New Low-Impact, Seasonal Omnivore

Whether you are a locavore, omnivore, or strict carnivore like my cat, chapter 7 will be your easy-to-digest guide to the healthier, safer consumption of delicious food.

### Chapter 8: Ways to Throw (or Attend!) a Party with a Purpose—A Step-by-Step Guide to Throwing Parties That Can Change the World

A party is a great place to raise awareness about a cause you believe in. This chapter offers directions for planning all sorts of events, from a small bash with your buddies to an elegant, invite-only benefit.

### Chapter 9: Ways to Travel Lightly (and Cheaply!) Everywhere You Go—Expand Your Horizons by Heading for...Well, the Horizon

Whether your travel takes you to the ends of the earth or simply to the opposite end of your block, chapter 9 offers resources designed to help you decrease your environmental footprint while increasing your understanding of the diverse issues facing people all over the globe.

**Chapter 10: Ways to Turn Your Passion into Promise—Turn Your Interests into Your Vocation**

This chapter serves as the professional's guide to changing the world, aimed at anyone who is passionate about making a difference, not just earning a paycheck.

## Ratings Explained

Nobody wants to set out on a task only to find out it's going to break the bank or eat up all of his or her spare time. To that end, each way will be rated on a scale of one to five based on the three factors that often matter most: time 🕐, cost $, and lifestyle impact 🏠. With the rating scale as a guide, you can easily choose ideas that match your commitment. Registering to vote doesn't require money or a major commitment. Donating to charities is just a click away, but it may well cost you money. Joining the Peace Corps, meanwhile, is a major investment of time and a huge lifestyle change. I will mark each according to the lowest possible investment, but you are welcome to give more time, money, or dedication than what is indicated.

A handy appendix at the end of the book also sorts each category numerically. If you want to know all of the things you can do on a tight budget or short timeframe or if you're looking for some recommendations for friends and family who are afraid they'll have to give up their worldly belongings and forage for food to make a difference, this is a great place to start. Conversely, if you don't know what to do with all that money you just inherited, or if you have a semester to travel, or if your parents, racked with guilt, are ready to sell their Hummer and return to their hippie lifestyles, you're also in luck.

Let this book serve as a jumping-off point for you to create the kind of world you want to live in, and let it guide you as you decide how much time and effort to commit to each world-changing effort. If we commit to focusing on fixing things that matter most to us, the world will surely be a better place. Be creative as you chart your own path. And remember that each time you shop conscientiously, send an email to your senator, prepare a sustainable meal, or throw a "green" party with a purpose, you affirm your power to transform everyday activities into world-changing affairs. No one expects you to have all the answers, but this book is a good place to start figuring out what you think needs to change and what you are willing to do to make a difference. More than anything, this book will show you that making a difference is not a chore that's being assigned to you but rather an opportunity to do what you love. No matter what our personal passions (sports, art, music, archaeology, video games, ornithology), we all have felt the joy of losing ourselves in something we love. My goal is to help you find where your passions, abilities, and intentions meet. From there it's simply a matter of doing what comes naturally—and marveling at the changes that follow.

# Chapter 1

# WAYS TO GET EXCITED AND INVOLVED

*Discover Your Unique Viewpoint by Exploring the Resources around You*

In the unlikely story that is America, there has never been anything false about hope.

*Barack Obama*

## IN THIS CHAPTER

- Jump-Start Your World-Changing Efforts

- Be an Informed Activist

- How to Look for Third-Party Credibility

- Ideas for Investing in the Future

- *Ways* Guide to Getting Involved Right Now

- Ready to Do More?

## JUMP-START YOUR WORLD-CHANGING EFFORTS

As we stand at this crossroads, it is clear that the tide is swiftly turning toward hope, action, and a collective interest in a better world. With record youth-voter turnout in the 2008 election, we see that change as the result of our actions is possible, and we are energized and excited about this potential. So what are your goals, exactly? The answer for everyone will be different, but now is the time to embark on explorations about how to spend your valuable time on this planet. Seize this moment to choose your own adventure.

As soon as people hear about this book, the most common (and heartening) question is, "What can I do?" My response is always, "What are you interested in?" Changing the world is deeply personal; at its core it is the quest to identify what matters most to you. What do you want for yourself, your community, and for the world? Do you want to help children learn to read? Do you want to save monkeys? Do you want to help fight malaria? Do you want to teach monkeys to read or fight malaria? Your options are limited only by your willingness to believe in your ability to make a difference. To be sure, many of you are grappling with circumstances that limit you in some practical sense, whether they are financial burdens, health restrictions, or time constraints that you do not fully control. I am not here to deny that such realities exist, but as you will see throughout this book, people of all stripes and backgrounds have been able to do remarkable things despite, and sometimes because of, these obstacles. So while I can't tell you exactly how to go about changing the world, I can offer many suggestions to help you answer these questions by finding interesting and creative ways to start exploring your most precious inheritance: the world.

## Get the Ball Rolling  🕐=1 💲=1 🏢=1

This business of "making a difference" often seems overwhelming, and the information superhighway can often lead to a feeling of overload. Every day I wade through the barrage of news from around the world and action updates from the charities that I support. Like many of you, I often find that the volume of statistics and anecdotes available in my inbox, mailbox, and living room is staggering. My stack of books and research is now so tall that my husband uses it for cover when he sneaks off to play video games. From global warming to poverty and disease, the list of challenges we face seems to grow faster than we can track.

But within this confluence of good intentions, fluctuating priorities, and shortages of time, it is important to remember (and I will continue to remind you) that we have already taken the first step: we care. I wouldn't have started writing my **Weekly Way** blog and this book—and you wouldn't be reading this book—if that were not the case. One of the best aspects of being in your twenties is increased autonomy: what you do with your day (or at least part of it) is up to you, so start making proactive decisions about how you will spend it. Besides, doing what you love now could help prevent a midlife-crisis freak-out when you're fifty. In an effort to avoid overwhelming you, here goes: Just start. Go ahead and pull the trigger! Too many people spend too much time getting ready or aiming.

Begin by using the rating system in this book to help you find the most convenient suggestions these chapters have to offer. Take a simple action or two every day or a few times a week, even if you don't think it matters much. Don't worry, I will spare you the corny talk about how a journey of a thousand miles starts with a single step, or how a waterfall begins with a single drop, or how, by working together, a school of tiny piranhas can skeletonize a cow. Still, even babies must crawl before they run, and they have to get up off their little bellies to do even that much.

Once these actions become second nature and you develop some momentum, you will probably find yourself looking for more to do and learn. But consider this your fair warning: knowledge and activism, like power, Facebook, and Sour Patch Kids, are addictive, so be prepared for a life of personal growth and positive contributions to your local or global community. While the world has occasionally changed in enormous and rapid ways (ask the dinosaurs), most big changes are the product of millions of little changes. You are one of those millions, and the momentum of your efforts is what will keep the changes coming. Get started by trying a few or all of the ideas detailed later in this chapter, see what works best for you, and let me know how it goes.

## Ten Ways in Ten Days

1. **Watch a movie.** More specifically, check out a documentary or feature film about an issue or cause you are interested in. This is a great way to learn the basic facts, and perhaps the movie will inspire you to explore further. *An Inconvenient Truth* spurred millions to take action to stop global warming. The implicit message of many documentaries is that knowledge conveys power. Now that you know more, you can lend your voice to a movement of change. Many documentaries suggest steps to do just that. **See the list on page 17** for more movie recommendations.

2. **Sign the One Declaration.** According to the **One campaign,** One is "Americans of all beliefs and every walk of life—united

as One—to help make poverty history." Join a campaign of over 2.4 million people who have already signed "an historic pact for compassion and justice to help the poorest people of the world overcome AIDS and extreme poverty." Once you sign the online pact, spend a few more minutes on the website to see how you can work within your community to help end poverty. For more ways to help those in need, check out **chapter 2**.

3. **Register to vote.** This is the first step to getting involved politically and having your voice heard. If you have already registered to vote, then make sure you vote in every election. Local elections, despite the lack of fanfare, often impact you as much as or more than national elections, so stay involved at every level. For more ways to fire up your inner politician, check out **chapter 3**.

4. **Find something else you can reuse or recycle.** We all know about recycling aluminum cans, plastic, and glass. But you can also recycle printer cartridges, cell phones, batteries, and plastic bags. Many grocery stores offer plastic-bag recycling receptacles and a cash refund if you bring your own bag. If you are ready to stop using plastic bags once and for all, check out the website for **Reusable Bags.** Before you recycle or discard anything, see if there is a creative way to reuse it first. For more suggestions about how to lead an eco-active lifestyle, check out **chapter 4**.

5. **Replace a bulb.** According to the Environmental Protection Agency (EPA), "If every home in America replaced just one incandescent light bulb with an Energy Star–qualified CFL (compact fluorescent light bulb), in one year it would save enough energy to light more than three million homes. That would prevent the release of greenhouse gas emissions equal to that of about eight hundred thousand cars."[1] How's that for easy? Of course, you can replace more than one bulb, which will save you more money and make up for any slackers out there. For more energy-saving tips, check out **chapter 5**.

6. **Give a green gift.** Face it. With all of the occasions to celebrate throughout the year, you will eventually have to pony up and give somebody a gift. Use the opportunity to raise awareness about the wide array of products made by environmentally and socially responsible companies by giving a gift from one of them. Not sure where to start looking for such gracious fare? Check out **EcoExpress, Earth Mama Angel Baby, Organic Bouquet, or Equal Exchange.** Also consider giving a gift certificate to your favorite organic restaurant or tickets to a concert; this way very little is consumed, and the present is an experience instead of an object. For more ways to support ethical businesses (and find cool gifts!) see **page 175 in chapter 6**.

7. **Try local, sustainably grown food.** Check out **LocalHarvest** to find farmers' markets, community-supported agriculture groups (CSAs)/farm shares, grocery stores, co-ops, and restaurants that supply and use local and organic products. For many more ways to be a low-impact eater, see **page 197 in chapter 7**.

8. **Host a mini pledge drive.** When you have decided on an organization or cause you would like to support, invite some friends over and plan a short presentation about your chosen cause. Ask friends to bring a small donation rather than the usual host/hostess gift (for instance, a small donation instead of a case of beer). Once they are sufficiently fired up, ask them to spread the word further by committing to email or discuss the issue with at least five more people. For many more ideas about how to throw a party with a purpose, see **page 215 in chapter 8**.

9. **Become a carbon-neutral traveler.** Or at least carbon-sensitive. Check out **TerraPass** and use its emissions calculator to determine, reduce, and finally offset your carbon footprint by investing in green energy initiatives. For more ideas to help you travel lightly, see **page 233 in chapter 9**.

10. **Check out the *Ten Ways* website.** The "Businesses Making a Difference" and "Organizations Making a Difference" pages offer links to and descriptions of many of the companies and organizations mentioned throughout the book. The list is updated frequently to reflect new resources and companies. Try one of the products, join one of the organizations, or even apply for a job or internship today.

## BE AN INFORMED ACTIVIST

Not the pompous, condescending kind but the wise, gentle kind, like Yoda or Gandalf, who seem merely to be reminding people of what they already know to be true. After all, nobody likes to be told what to do, but if presented in the right way, a gentle suggestion about recycling or purchasing socially responsible products is almost always welcome among friends.

Before preaching to the choir or converting the heathens, you actually need to know what you are talking about. A crappy argument is an unconvincing one, and while personal insults and sarcasm might be a self-satisfying form of entertainment, neither will do much to move an issue forward. If you want to effectively influence people, advocate for a cause you care about, or enlighten someone about green consumption habits, volunteering opportunities, or energy-efficient practices, you'd better do your homework first. There are many ways to fire up those neurons, and there are endless issues to explore. Don't panic. Start slow and stay true to yourself. You will find the path and actions that are right for you.

### Listen  🕐=1  💲=1  🏢=1

At the core of any good dialogue is not the ability to talk louder than your colleagues in discourse; rather, it is the ability to listen calmly to diverse perspectives. Be curious, because the day you run out of curiosity is the day you start to become boring to the rest of us. Ask questions about the world around you, and pay attention to the answers.

You can always learn more by listening to other points of view, especially those you disagree with. It is hard to find common ground without understanding where people are coming from. Spend as much time as possible listening to what other people have to say, even when you are sure of your stance. After all, if you are going to bring a message to people, understanding and appreciating their positions is the first step in persuading them to accept yours.

The more you listen to differing points of view, the more clearly you will be able to articulate your own. Pay attention to yourself, your local community, and the world around you. Be open to change. The smartest people in the room are often the ones with the least to say. They aren't talking because they are listening, and when they do decide to speak, you can bet everyone else will be paying attention.

### Okay, I'm Hooked. What about a Book? 🕐=3 💲=2 ⊞=1

Reading a book is one of the easiest ways to expand your knowledge without forking over thousands of dollars for a formal education. By all means, if school makes sense for you, do that, too; however, there is a wealth of free information available from a variety of sources, and there are many ways to develop knowledge about a topic. I'm a big fan of reading books and newspapers, watching films and television, and researching topics on the Web. In the age of text, instant, and broadcast messaging, reading is still one of the best things you can do with your time.

So go feed that brain, and learn a little more in the process. I have listed some of my favorites in a variety of genres in the sidebar. Many of the titles mentioned were useful in researching this book, and all of them taught me something new, further sparked my interest, and inspired me to take action. While this book is intended to encourage and facilitate activism, perhaps one of the others listed in this section will help you find your passion. Of course, this is by no means a definitive list; it's just a good place to start.

## Books—Still a Good Way to Learn Stuff

There are countless books about almost every contemporary topic imaginable (like *Men Who Knit and the Dogs Who Love Them*. Perfect for the man who has everything…except a sweater for his dachshund). While this may sound overwhelming at first, many of the best-written books make it to the top of the best-seller lists immediately, so it's not always necessary to wade through tons of books to find the good ones. It is easy to find sources that inform with wit, humor, and interesting anecdotes. Just an hour spent browsing online, in a bookstore, or at the library will likely yield several books about your area(s) of interest.

**Human rights and cultural issues:** Samantha Power's book *A Problem from Hell* can seem an intimidating tome at over 600 pages, but this book is *the* primer for those interested in international human rights abuses. It is such a compelling read that Mark Hanis was inspired to drop everything in order to found the Genocide Intervention Network (see his success story on **page 12**). While many human rights atrocities such as genocide are still not receiving the attention they should, *Not On Our Watch* by Don Cheadle and John Prendergast offers a good overview of these types of situations as well as what you can do about it. Paul Hawken's book *Blessed Unrest* is also an inspiring read about innovative actions organizations and individuals around the world are taking to address environmental and social justice issues. For more about how to pump up your humanitarian efforts, **read chapter 2**.

**Living on minimum wage:** Barbara Ehrenreich's book *Nickel and Dimed: On (Not) Getting By in America* describes her year spent trying to make ends meet on the minimum wages that many try to live on every day.

**Political action:** Books on this topic abound from John F. Kennedy's *Profiles in Courage* to Barack Obama's *The Audacity of Hope.* To find the political and/or philosophical books for you (often the two go hand in hand), pay attention to the politicians, thinkers, and philosophers that you find interesting. Then see if they have written a book—chances are they probably have. See **page 54 in chapter 3** for more suggestions about how to get more informed and involved with a full spectrum of political issues.

**Living the green life:** Whether you live in New York City or not, *The Big Green Apple: Your Guide to Eco-Friendly Living* by Ben Jervey offers many tips to help you live life in a darker shade of green. Ben was in his twenties when he wrote this book (see his success story in **chapter 10 on page 265**), and he is in touch with both an urban lifestyle and the realities of living green on a budget. *Green Living* by the editors of *E Magazine* is another good compilation of suggestions on the topic. For lots of tips on living the good, green life, check out **chapter 4.**

**Climate change:** *An Inconvenient Truth* by Al Gore is everywhere for good reason, but for another easy-to-understand explanation of the global warming situation, check out *The Weather Makers* by Tim Flannery or *Fight Global Warming Now* by Bill McKibben and the Step It Up campaign team. For tips on what you can do about global warming and other environmental issues, see **page 104 in chapter 4 and 121 in chapter 5.**

**Where does it all come from—*and* where does it all end up?** If you want to read more about our consumption habits and what happens to all the trash we generate as a result, a perusal of

*Cradle to Cradle: Remaking the Way We Make Things* by William McDonough and Michael Braungart and *Garbage Land* by Elizabeth Royte will take you through production processes from start to finish. For ideas on how to reduce your overall consumption *and* waste, see **page 137 in chapter 5.**

**The powerful consumer:** The consumer holds the keys to the manufacturing kingdom. Websites like **Amazon** and **TripAdvisor** operate under the assumption that if enough of us want something, chances are good that we will eventually get it. This power paradigm is evident in the flood of "green" and "socially responsible" products entering the marketplace during the past decade. Some of the best books on this topic include *The Wal-Mart Effect: How the World's Most Powerful Company Really Works—and How It's Transforming the American Economy* by Charles Fishman, *What Matters Most: How a Small Group of Pioneers Is Teaching Social Responsibility to Big Business, and Why Big Business Is Listening* by Jeffrey Hollender, and *Big Green Purse: Use Your Spending Power to Create a Cleaner, Greener World* by Diane MacEachern. These money folks seem to be fans of lengthy subtitles, but don't let that deter you—these books are informative and easy to understand. For more tips on harnessing the power of your dollar, check out **chapter 6.**

**Low-impact eating:** *Plenty* by J.B. Mackinnon and Alisa Smith and *Animal, Vegetable, Miracle* by Barbara Kingsolver both chronicle efforts to eat locally for a year. *Plenty* takes place in an urban setting, and Kingsolver and family base their operations on a rural farm in southern Appalachia. While you may not ever commit to such strict rules for your own food consumption, the stories told in both of these books are as inspiring as they are informative. *Omnivore's Dilemma* by Michael Pollan explores what we put in our bellies and how these choices affect not only us but also the diverse animal and plant ecosystems that supply our food. For many more tips on mindful eating, check out **chapter 7.**

## Don't Just Take My Word for It 🕐=2 💲=1 🏠=1

Many of you may already have a stack of books at the ready from your gluttonous trips to the local bookstore or library (yes, that's me, too). Others of you may love to read but have a hard time committing to a whole book without some hint of its quality. Regardless of your affiliation as bibliophile or bibliophobe, let the Internet help you by joining **Goodreads**. Think of it as a social networking site for people who stay inside reading all day. (I kid, of course. We also leave the house to return and pick up books and, occasionally, to eat.) Goodreads offers a free service that lets readers keep track of the books they are reading (and want to read), peruse writer recommendations and reviews, and share pearls of wisdom with friends. Regular visits to this site will not only improve your literary IQ, but they will also ensure that you never go book hungry again.

# SUCCESS STORY

## Taking on Genocide from the Ground Up

Mark Hanis read a book in college that made him take action in support of the anti-genocide movement, but he had been conscious of human rights issues long before college. All four of Mark's grandparents survived the Holocaust, and he grew up surrounded by those who had a fierce determination that the Holocaust not be forgotten. After reading several newspaper articles about the genocide in Darfur in college, he decided to do more extensive research. When he read the Pulitzer Prize–winning book *A Problem from Hell* by Samantha Power, he realized that despite the international community's many post-Holocaust efforts, it had failed to stop genocides throughout the twentieth century and into the twenty-first. In response to this inaction, the political science major became determined to publish an op-ed letter that would encourage the U.S. government and the public to support the building of a permanent anti-genocide coalition.

Since he knew that college students rarely get op-eds published in major newspapers, he devoted his time to finding a prominent co-author. He emailed every PhD in Holocaust studies and African studies, and he attempted to contact every influential figure he could think of from Colin Powell to Bill Gates.

Hanis finally got results when he contacted Gayle Smith, who at the time was the senior director for African affairs at the National Security Council. Smith didn't want to simply author the op-ed; she wanted to make Hanis's idea a reality. She met with members of the African Union and proposed a peacekeeping initiative that at the time was unprecedented. "Our goal was to have individuals fund civilian protection programs for people facing genocide," Hanis says of the unconventional strategy. The members of the African Union were hesitant about taking money from private funds because it was something that had never been done before, but eventually they agreed.

Undeterred by the initial reluctance, Hanis and his friends opened a bank account and began fundraising. Before he knew it, the twenty-two-year-old had a major campaign with a core base of supporters initially established through social networking websites and word of mouth. "We asked people to raise money, write letters to members of Congress and the president, send emails, and go to the office of their representatives and push them to pass key policies."

The organization grew from there, and today the **Genocide Intervention Network** (GI-NET) has a yearly operating budget of 2.4 million dollars, and its nationwide grassroots efforts and training programs have helped support a growing anti-genocide movement. With an intelligent, strategic approach to ending genocide, the intensely committed team members at GI-NET have become very effective citizen lobbyists. Here are some of their many accomplishments:

- Established over a thousand student chapters through the student-led division of GI-NET, STAND
- Helped pass divestment legislation in twenty-seven states and encouraged over sixty colleges and sixteen cities to divest as well
- As a result of divestment education efforts, activated thirteen companies to pull out of Sudan or alter behaviors to be part of the solution
- Helped write, pass, and implement federal legislation—the Sudan Accountability and Divestment Act
- Raised over three million dollars, with a portion of the money going directly toward protection of displaced Darfuris and Burmese and mobilization of a permanent anti-genocide constituency
- Created the first anti-genocide hotline (1-800-Genocide), which allows people all over the country to call their representatives, senators, or the White House; for each option they pick, callers are given up-to-date talking points and then connected to a specific leader's office.

Hanis says that you don't have to work for a group like his in order to make a difference, and he encourages people to educate themselves on the issues, to advocate, and to donate. "The more information you know, the more effective you will be. The more you understand where a bill is in the House or Senate, the more effectively you will be able to advocate for it. We have to stop treating genocide like a humanitarian crisis; it is a political one, and if we treat it that way, we can end it." Hanis is committed to continuing the work he has started and expanding the efforts of GI-NET to address other areas of mass atrocities (like Burma, the Congo, and Sri Lanka). He also encourages citizens in the United States and internationally to get involved. According to Hanis, "In our age, there is no such thing as keeping out of politics."

## See What Those Pundits Have to Say ●=2 💲=1 ▦=1

I'm addicted to the news. In a world where planes fly into buildings, people I don't trust have access to bombs, and a good part of an entire U.S. city was swept under water in 2005, I feel the need to check the news at least once a day. As the title of Thomas Friedman's 2005 book explains, the world is indeed flat, in the sense that events in faraway lands have the potential to directly affect us all. What this idea makes plain is that the argument for isolationism is moot; our fate is inextricably tied to that of the rest of the world, and we must honor and explore these connections to thrive.

You can feed this addiction in several ways. My format of choice is the newspaper; I am partial to the *New York Times*, which is now available for free on the Web. In addition, I like magazines with diverse perspectives such as the *Utne Reader* or *The Economist*. I also recommend picking up a local daily, because it's a good way to get a feel for regional issues and to get better acquainted with your surroundings and what matters most to your neighbors.

## Become a Blog Hog ●=2 💲=1 ▦=1

There are blogs on almost every topic imaginable. From how to change the world (shameless plug) to how to knit your own Star Wars figures, a blog (or many) probably exists on the subject. This prospect is both exciting and daunting: How do you know which ones to trust? Which ones should you read on a regular basis, and which ones should you skim every so often? In addition to my favorite tip for many of these types of explorations—ask people you trust which blogs they read—you can also start your search with **Technorati**, which is *the* directory of blogs. You can search by topic or authority (to see who else is linking to these blogs—guilt or cred by association), as well as read reviews. Visit

Technorati to find popular blogs on topics that interest you. Two blogs that offer a consistent and interesting roundup of the day's news are the **Huffington Post** and the **Daily Beast**. Depending on where you live, you can usually find a site that offers a local news roundup on a daily or weekly basis. In the Pacific Northwest, where I currently live, we have the **Sightline Institute,** which is "a not-for-profit research and communication center whose mission is to bring about sustainability, a healthy, lasting prosperity grounded in place." Simply put, each Monday through Friday I get an email with an update that offers links to the top regional news stories of the day.

## Moving Pictures, Please! 🕐=1 💲=1 ▦=1

Perhaps sitting in a chair staring at a computer screen until your eyes glaze over isn't your thing. Maybe you prefer sitting on a couch staring at a television until your eyes glaze over. Either way, you've got options. While watching television may not immediately change the world, you'll want to be up to date on current issues if you are going to be a world changer, not to mention a potential opinion influencer. What's more, five minutes spent watching today's news should reveal enough injustice to serve as a sufficient call to action.

Television, especially cable television, and weekend television on the major networks, has more pundits than you can shake a stick at. Nightly news is another easy way to stay informed, but keep in mind that, like newspapers, networks also have political slants, and unlike the pundits, they may not be as forthright regarding their biases. For a show that strives to present multiple sides of an issue, I am partial to PBS's *NewsHour* with Jim Lehrer. I also rely on "hard-hitting" reports from *The Daily Show* and *The Colbert Report* for my daily dose of news delivered with a sarcastic punch.

# Some Hot-Topic Documentaries to Check Out

Here are some outstanding documentaries that cover diverse topics from health care to global warming:

*A Crude Awakening: The Oil Crash*—an in-depth look at the world's dependence on oil and the long-term implications of this habit

*The Blue Planet*—the aquatic counterpart to the *Planet Earth* series, an epic documentary about the world's oceans

*The Business of Being Born*—an examination of common birthing practices in the United States as well as the resurgence of midwifery

*Constantine's Sword*—a history of Christianity's lower points and an exploration of the consequences of absolutism in faith

*Darfur Now*—a documentary following the plight of six people trying to stop the genocide in Darfur

*The Fog of War*—Robert McNamara discusses his role as Secretary of Defense during the Vietnam War and the moral dilemmas that come with conflict

*For the Bible Tells Me So*—an exploration of the debate over homosexuality among and within the various sects of Christianity in the United States

*Girlhood*—an examination of the U.S. justice system, shown through the experiences of two female juvenile prison inmates

*The Ground Truth*—soldiers back from Iraq recount their experiences on the battlefield as well as their struggle to reacclimate back home

*Lake of Fire*—a candid and graphic documentary examining the abortion debate

*Lost Boys of Sudan*—a moving documentary on a tragic topic

*March of the Penguins*—a story of survival in the Antarctic, set around the lives of emperor penguins

*Outfoxed: Murdoch's War on Journalism*—a critical commentary on the man behind the ever-popular FOX News Channel: they report, you decide

*Planet Earth*—quite possibly the most awesome nature documentary series available, thanks to footage of rare and exotic animals and revolutionary new filming technology

*Rize*—how youth on L.A.'s South Side created new styles and forms of dance as a social and emotional outlet

*Sicko*—Michael Moore's exploration of the American healthcare system

*Super Size Me*—Morgan Spurlock's eye-opening and humorous month spent eating nothing but food from McDonald's

*Wal-Mart: The High Cost of Low Price*—a look at what happens to towns when Wal-Mart stores move in

*When the Levees Broke*—Spike Lee's documentary about the events leading up to and following Hurricane Katrina

*Who Killed the Electric Car*—an exploration into why the lifespan of GM's promising fuel-efficient vehicle was so short

# HOW TO LOOK FOR THIRD-PARTY CREDIBILITY

Once you have determined some causes that interest you, you may be ready to take the next step: volunteering or joining an organization. Like the wide world of blogs, the scope and diversity of the nonprofit world can be daunting. An Internet search for "environmental organizations," for example, will return just under fourteen million hits. Clear your afternoon.

## Go on Some Charity Speed Dates 🕐=3 💲=1 🏢=1

One of the best ways to wade through the organizations that best suit your interests is to ask like-minded friends about causes they support. Look for organizations with active campaigns and activities on your campus, in your community, or in parts of the world that matter to you. Pay attention to both the kind of work they are doing and what measurable results they are generating. Have they collected coats for those in need this winter? Have they prevented drilling in the Alaskan wilderness? Have they sent peacekeepers to Africa? In order to find an organization you want to support, first get a sense of what you would like to do with your time and money, and then search for organizations that match your criteria. Once you have narrowed down the possibilities, get in touch with the organizations via email, phone, or in person, and ask how you can help and/or how your money would be spent. Keep in mind that while many charities have websites that provide this information readily, there are still lots of worthwhile nonprofits that don't have the budget for a glamorous or detailed website. Don't just judge an organization by its homepage.

## Read the Charity Cliff Notes 🕐=2 💲=1 🏢=1

While you shouldn't let design be your guide when searching for the right organizations to explore, you do need to evaluate an organization before committing to it, and there are already resources in place to help you judge. For instance, once you have determined that an organization is making strides in an area where you would like to be involved, check out its credentials on **Charity Navigator**, which rates each nonprofit organization based on criteria such as organizational efficiency and capacity. Prospective volunteers, donors, and employees can also "comparison shop" for the charity of their choice: Charity Navigator has a section at the bottom of each report titled "Organizations Doing Similar Work," along with the current Charity Navigator rating for each similar organization. You can search by category or look through some of their fun top-ten lists, such as "Slam-Dunk Charities" or "Charities Overpaying Their For-Profit Fundraisers." Ouch.

For local, youth-driven campaigns and organizations, you can also check out **Future 5000**, which offers listings of community organizations around the country.

## IDEAS FOR INVESTING IN THE FUTURE

**Dare to Dream…with Your Dollars** 🕐=2 💲=3 ▦=1

If you decide to make a donation to an organization or business doing the kind of work you want to support, remember that you don't have to be a millionaire or even a thousandaire to improve the life of someone in need. In fact, according to the Social Capital Community Benchmark Survey of 2000, "Americans at the bottom of the income-distribution pyramid are the country's biggest givers per capita. The…[s]urvey shows that households with incomes below $20,000 gave a higher percentage of their earnings to charity than did any other income group."[2]

Microfinance organizations like **Kiva** make it possible for lenders to extend a small loan to an entrepreneur working to build a business in a developing country. Donors can sort by sector, region, or gender to find a venture in areas like agriculture and education. A donation in someone else's name to one of these modest businesses also makes a great gift. As a donor, you will be able to follow the progress of the business you have given money to. At the end of the loan period (usually six to twelve months), your loan is repaid, and you have the option of relending to someone else.

**Ashoka: Innovators for the Public** uses a similar model, identifying social entrepreneurs all over the world and then providing them with funding (usually for a period of about three years) to support and promote their work. Ashoka fellows work in the following six areas: civic engagement, economic development, environment, health, human rights, and learning/ education. Ashoka supporters can also volunteer with Ashoka to work with some of the existing programs and/or donate to support the work of current fellows.

## SUCCESS STORY

### Taking Down Walls from Within

Meredith Lobel has never been comfortable with the idea of being a radical activist, but she is committed to effecting change. From an early age she was guided by family members like her grandmother, who was one of the only female meteorologists in the Army at the time, and who frequently wrote letters to politicians, held brown-bag discussions on local issues, and was an active member of the Women's International League for Peace and Freedom. "I certainly got a strong streak of social activism from my grandmother, who was very vocal about what she saw as unjust or inequitable," Lobel says. "She is one of my main role models in terms of speaking up and fighting for what I believe in."

During college, Lobel interned at **Global Exchange,** working on issues surrounding social responsibility. For her senior thesis, she chose to live in Nicaragua to study agro-export models, including fair trade, to understand effective systems of commerce in developing countries. She wanted to see the tangible impact of these systems on the people who were doing the actual work, so she spent time in coffee co-ops throughout Central America. She was also an active student leader on her college campus, promoting responsibility and transparency in terms of how university endowments were being invested, especially when the investments did not align with the school's stated philosophy. She worked with several other New England universities to organize a conference at Yale about the role of universities in both promoting corporate responsibility and aligning their institutional practices with their own vision.

Lobel graduated Phi Beta Kappa with a degree in sociology and worked at a restaurant while patiently waiting to find the right job to match her interests. "I knew that I was pursuing something nontraditional and that my search would not necessarily follow any calendar cycle," she remembers. Her approach to job interviews was equally unconventional, and she saw each interview as an opportunity for a dialogue that would allow her to find the right fit. "There is a huge parallel between job hunting, house hunting, and dating," she explains. "It is important to really listen to yourself and remind yourself to do what feels right."

When Lobel interviewed at Ashoka, the international organization that pioneered social entrepreneurship, she knew she had found the right fit, as the organization was pursuing an alternative path to international development by promoting enduring local development. She initially reported directly to Ashoka's founder and CEO, Bill Drayton, and that role eventually morphed into the position of global director of the Citizen Base Initiative. It was the ideal position for her because of the autonomy and responsibility she was given, eventually traveling to over twenty countries to manage her global team and work with leading social innovators. "When I joined Ashoka, social enterprise was not really on the map. I had no idea what I was getting into, and I was fortunate to have had such an amazing experience," she says.

During Lobel's time at Ashoka, she also realized that a business education would offer her more insight into what it takes to run a successful venture, so she decided to apply to business school and received an MBA from Harvard in May 2009. During her recent summer internship, she pursued her love of entrepreneurship and environmental sustainability by working at a clean-tech start-up that turns supermarket waste into clean energy and organic fertilizer. She intends to continue to follow her instincts about what is right for her and is characteristically optimistic about her job prospects. "Everyone has a choice about whether or not they choose to engage. There is always something worthwhile to devote your time to if you are just willing to look, and if you are patient and innovative, things often happen quickly and beautifully."

## *WAYS* GUIDE TO GETTING INVOLVED RIGHT NOW

1. **Donate money and become a member.** Most nonprofit organizations rely mainly on donations and grants to operate their programs.

2. **Attend an event.** Depending on where you live, many organizations throw benefits on a regular basis. These events are great places to learn more about an organization's work and network with like-minded people.

3. **Patronize the partners.** Many nonprofit organizations have partnered with businesses: you make a purchase from one of the businesses listed on the nonprofit's website, and the organization receives a percentage of your purchase.

4. **Friend them.** From Facebook to Twitter, you can now "friend" or "follow" your favorite organizations and offer

them a little free advertising in the process. Once you have made the organization's virtual acquaintance, its logo and a link to its web page appears on your profile. It's also a great way to subtly tell your friends about your favorite causes.

5. **Get to work.** Whether you decide to donate food to a soup kitchen or spend the day cleaning up a local park, most organizations count on people like you, who are not full-time employees, to help fundraise and spread the word about their worthy causes. Find a local event, organization, or fundraiser to get involved with. For more ideas about ways to volunteer, see **page 37 in chapter 2.**

## READY TO DO MORE?

By following some of the suggestions in this chapter, I hope you have found that it is easier than you may have thought to find an organization that aligns with your values and interests. Perhaps you have learned more about an issue like global warming, poverty, or illiteracy, and you have identified some organizations that are working hard to alleviate these problems. You have taken that powerful first step toward involvement, and chances are it didn't cost you more than a few hours of research in front of your computer or a day of service spent with friends to determine that you want to do even more. **Chapter 2,** which focuses on volunteering, offers many suggestions for how to do just that.

# WAYS TO LIVE, GIVE, AND THRIVE THROUGH VOLUNTEERING

*Self-Discovery Need Not Be a Selfish Process*

I don't know what your destiny will be, but one thing I do know: the only ones among you who will be really happy are those who have sought and found how to serve.

*Albert Schweitzer*

## IN THIS CHAPTER

- **The Ripple Effect**
- **Why Volunteer?**
- **How to Find a Local Volunteer Position**
- **Take Your Show on the Road**
- ***Ways* Guide to Finding the Right Volunteer Placement**
- **Volunteer Vacations—Vital Stats**
- **Directory of Local and International Organizations That Need Your Help**
- **From Volunteer to Activist**

## THE RIPPLE EFFECT

Post-Katrina New Orleans was the emptiest city I had ever seen or was likely to. On the last day of my volunteer stint, I decided to explore some of the city to see what remained. As I headed into the Ninth Ward with my newly adopted cat in tow, I was struck by the sheer vastness of the destruction. The miles stretched on, yet the images moving past my car window remained the same. Houses with body counts painted on the outside walls, mud-covered roads, no lights, no running water, no open businesses—even the ubiquitous McDonald's lay victim, with its shattered windows and only the ghosts of employees long since driven to higher ground. The empty soundtrack of stillness transposed onto the cityscape was equally unsettling.

Despite the bleak images around me that surpassed as often as they matched anything I had seen on television, I never felt afraid as I explored New Orleans that day. Each person greeted another with a friendly wave, words of gratitude, and offers of assistance. It seems that for those who survived Katrina and stayed in New Orleans, the need for community and a sense of connection had never been more important. Certain aspects of city life, such as law and order, may indeed be fragile, but other values are more impervious to physical disasters than we may think.

Katrina survivors realized through their own tragic experiences that rebuilding their city was a process largely dependent on help from outside sources and the empathy and kindness of strangers. The overflow of water that unleashed havoc throughout the city and revealed a fundamental weakness in our national infrastructure also triggered an unprecedented outpouring of human compassion and unselfish action. The volunteers I met in New Orleans came from all over the country to help for one simple reason: in a world fraught with natural disasters, global warming, terrorist attacks, and government controversies, volunteering is one of the most immediate and tangible ways for individuals to make a positive impact on the world they live in. The national reaction to the events in New Orleans is a profound illustration that our ability to connect with other humans is one of the coolest and most underutilized talents we possess. It can neither be destroyed by nor lost in any natural disaster or terrorist attack, and as we nurture this connection to each other through volunteering, it can only grow stronger.

While I may not be able to change policies or end corruption all by myself, I realized that for the rest of my life, I could be a volunteer who brings joy and a feeling of empowerment to people by helping to build houses, teaching skills, building wells, or providing refugees with the fundamental comforts of home. Volunteering is as empowering and life altering for the volunteers as it is for the recipients of their good will.

## WHY VOLUNTEER?

Perhaps you have found some causes worthy of support, and you would like to find a way to help beyond simply mailing a check (though I am certainly not suggesting you stop sending checks). Whether you decide to go around the corner or halfway across the globe, volunteering is one of the most effective ways to change the world, and it need not cost you anything. One of the main reasons for not volunteering is often lack of time. You may not be able to put all of your obligations on hold in order to volunteer, but somewhere between that two-year gig as a Peace Corps volunteer in the mountains of Uruguay and sitting on your couch feeling bad about the state of the world lies the right volunteer opportunity for you.

If you want to make an impact in the lives of others, you must be willing to personally commit some of your time and energy to the cause. You will find that you can do amazing things by giving an hour of your time to someone else who needs your help. Perhaps this means TiVo-ing *America's Next Top Model* or foregoing that afternoon snooze once in a while, but I don't know many twentysomethings without *some* free time on their hands. Whether you are still in college or have already hit the job market, chances are you don't have the same level of responsibility (mortgage, children, you know the rest) that lies down the road. If you can find the time now, it will be that much easier to make time later.

## Join the Ranks of Volunteers 🕐=2 💲=1 🏢=2

According to Steve Rosenthal, founder of **Cross-Cultural Solutions**, whose mission is to "operate volunteer programs around the world in partnership with sustainable community initiatives," volunteering allows us all to "live in a world where people both learn about the world and are empowered to make a difference." In order to break down the walls of hopelessness, poverty, and cultural isolation, we need to foster a greater awareness of what is happening in the lives of both our local and global neighbors. And, of course, you get to meet interesting new people, learn new skills, add an incredible experience to your résumé or grad school application, and perhaps travel.

What's more, like many people featured in this chapter, you may find that a volunteer placement changes your definition of work, your specific lifestyle choices, and your characterization of success or happiness. You may even decide to devote your life to a cause you discovered while volunteering. The organization you are volunteering with could even hire you on its staff. In fact, many of the employees at the organizations I spoke with began their association with their current employers as volunteers.

Many nonprofit organizations are both understaffed and underfunded. Volunteers provide a much-needed boost of manpower, new ideas, and fresh energy. Many well-known nonprofits like **Habitat for Humanity** and the **Red Cross** have built their entire mission on the assumption that they will find volunteers willing to help build homes or respond to crises. The bottom line is that most nonprofits cannot operate without volunteers like you.

## HOW TO FIND A LOCAL VOLUNTEER POSITION

**Start the Search** 🕐=2 💲=1 🏠=1

There is really only one way to change the world through volunteering—get out there and volunteer! A note of caution, though: you may not be able to stop. One volunteer experience often leads to another, and the next thing you know, you are a serial volunteer. Many of the volunteer junkies I spoke with described volunteering as addictive, so why not start now and get hooked in your twenties? For suggestions about finding organizations to work with and evaluating their efficacy, see **page 19 in chapter 1.**

An easy way to get started is to check out the many websites and blogs devoted to volunteering opportunities. Just as the Web can now help you find a significant other, a job, an apartment, or that video of that thing you and your friends did that one time, it can just as easily help you search for the perfect volunteer opportunity. Start with a search on **VolunteerMatch** (over sixty-eight thousand nonprofit organizations use this service to find volunteers) or **Idealist.** On either website, you can enter in your zip code, the distance you are willing to travel, and the areas of focus that most interest you. There are also advanced search options such as skills needed, language needed, and appropriate age group for each volunteer project.

A quick perusal of the opportunities at either website offers encouraging results. At the time of this writing, Idealist offers over 16,000 volunteer opportunities from A to W (art and architecture to women's issues), while over at VolunteerMatch, volunteer opportunities clocked in at over 60,000. No matter what your interests, time constraints, or area(s) of expertise, you can easily find a plethora of positions that will appeal to you.

Here are a few of the thousands of opportunities I found by searching both of these databases and by doing a bit of extra surfing on the Internet:

- Be an after-school reading buddy for a second- or third-grade student in Seattle.
- Teach seniors in New York City computer skills or yoga, or check on them with a weekly phone call.
- Help build affordable duplexes in Virginia.
- Volunteer at the annual AIDS walk in San Francisco.
- Rehabilitate abandoned and abused cats and kittens at a shelter in Chicago.
- Deliver meals to the elderly and impoverished in Tennessee.
- Teach swimming to disabled youths in St. Louis.
- Restore oyster habitats in Charleston.
- Plant fruit trees and educate school kids about the importance of trees by going on a Fruit Tree Tour in California.
- Teach yoga and meditation to at-risk youth in Portland, Oregon.
- Rebuild homes or offer legal aid, social work, media/PR, or computer technology assistance in New Orleans.
- Rehabilitate rescued wolves in Colorado.

**Think Big. Start Small.** 🕐=2 💲=1 🏢=2

Almost everyone I speak to who is now volunteering abroad or who has devoted his or her life to nonprofit work started out as a volunteer at a local level. Many discovered an opportunity through a church group, school outing, or workplace initiative or at a friend's suggestion. Whether you change one life or thousands of lives, you will find that volunteering is the surest proof of your ability to change the world.

In addition to visiting volunteer databases such as those found on Idealist, it is also a good idea to go directly to the source for additional information about the organization you may be considering. See the volunteer directory at the end of this chapter for descriptions and listings of national organizations that offer volunteer placements all over the country.

## SUCCESS STORY

### Facing the Quarterlife Crisis

Like many her age, Cass Ghiorse was experiencing her quarterlife crisis. She was living in New York, working nights as a waitress, and she was vacillating about whether or not she had made the right career choice as an actress/model. She needed a change and craved a fresh perspective. "No one warns us about this time in our lives. I thought that life after college would be so much easier, but in your later twenties, you start to realize how much is at stake."

Ghiorse's solution? Volunteering. "In the midst of my confusion, I thought, 'Well, step outside of yourself and see what happens.'" She knew she wanted to work with young women, and she knew she wanted to help them to be empowered through some type of art program. Once she had taken a moment to consider both her interests and her skills, the search was easy. After a bit of research, she found the **Women's Expressive Theater's Risk Takers Film Series.** The program focuses on empowering teenage girls through the medium of film, and selected films are used as vehicles for discussing larger social issues affecting women. Volunteers encourage the girls to share their insights, emotions, and hopes in a safe environment. Ghiorse has also discovered much about herself through this experience. "I definitely want to volunteer more, and now I am clear that I have a natural ability with young people." What's next for Ghiorse? "Maybe teaching, maybe traveling, maybe volunteering—most likely all three."

## Count on the Kindness of Strangers and the Advice of Friends
🕐=2 💲=1 🏢=1

So what did we do for information before the Internet age? For most of us in our twenties and early thirties, we can't even remember those days, but we do know that word of mouth is still one of the most valuable mediums when searching for trustworthy information or advice.

In addition to searching national databases like the ones described previously, consult your pals and neighbors. Where do they volunteer? Where in the community is help most needed? What do the volunteers do? And don't forget this one—are they enjoying their experiences? Volunteering is just like any other activity; it's important to choose opportunities that are empowering, enlightening, and educational. Choose a volunteer placement that you anticipate with excitement. Choose one that leaves you feeling inspired. Choose one where you feel like you are making a difference.

## SUCCESS STORY

### Giving Back on a Day of Thanks

Christine Farnham used to go skiing with her mom every Thanksgiving. When Farnham was nineteen, a lack of snow changed their standing holiday plans, and they decided to volunteer at a local soup kitchen. "We quickly learned that volunteering was much more rewarding than skiing, and so began the tradition," she says. In the past decade, they have recruited several friends and Farnham's in-laws. Her daughter, Kelyn, has been volunteering, too—first as a baby hanging out in her mom's frontpack, then increasing her responsibilities each year. "We feel very fortunate in our lives, and I want my daughter to see at an early age how important it is to give back," Farnham explains.

Farnham says that another reward of the day is seeing the same volunteers year after year. "There is a real spirit of community in the soup kitchen, and we look forward to checking in with each other every year," she says. Meanwhile at home, her father prepares the family's meal. They all converge in the afternoon to share stories from the day and year and describe what they are grateful for. "Our holiday celebrations are so much more meaningful now," says Farnham. "We see firsthand how lucky we are and want to share this good fortune with others."

Farnham continually looks for new ways to volunteer year-round. A second-grade teacher, she enlists the help of her students to make pies for the soup kitchen as well. "I work in a high-poverty school," she says. "The pie-making adventure began as part of a unit called 'community.' Many of our students eat at the Salvation Army dinner or at least have high contact with the Salvation Army during other parts of the year, and this was a way for all forty students, regardless of their socioeconomic situation, to come together and make an offering to the larger community."

## Virtual Volunteering  🕐=2 $=1 🏠=1

Can't leave the office or home to volunteer? Confirmed couch potato or introvert? No problem. Like most everything these days, there is also a way to volunteer and make a difference from the comfort of your living room couch or office chair. Many organizations need help with administrative tasks that can be completed digitally. If you are a computer whiz and are working at a job where you are supposed to look busy even when you are not (and especially if you've already finished the day's crossword or Sudoku), "virtual volunteering" might be the way to offer your expertise or mentor someone while still holding down the fort at work. The most extensive list of virtual volunteering opportunities can be found at **VolunteerMatch**. With just a computer, phone, and/or fax, you can lend your talents to anything from advocacy and human rights to education and literacy. Tasks can range from making phone calls to helping "get out the vote" to designing a nonprofit's website. Virtual volunteering is also a great way to check out organizations that are not necessarily close to home.

## TAKE YOUR SHOW ON THE ROAD

Okay, so you dabbled with some local volunteer opportunities, and now you are officially hooked. Or perhaps you have always wanted to go abroad for something other than just sightseeing. You want to immerse yourself in another culture and at the same time offer up whatever useful skills you might have. Maybe you find that you are constantly thinking about what more you can do to help—at your job, in the shower, driving to work—and you can't stop talking to your friends about your experiences. If these scenarios sound familiar to you, then cue phase two: time to volunteer on the go.

### Go with God and/or a Group  🕐=2  💲=1  🏠=2

Let's face it. Planning your own trip and placement is not for everyone. If the idea of finding a volunteer placement as well as organizing the logistics—how you will get there, where you will stay, what the local customs are, etc.—makes you want to give up before you have even started, then consider joining a group volunteering trip. In addition, if it is your first time volunteering, you may not want to go it alone. One of the easiest ways to do this is to connect on campus. A growing trend for colleges and universities and, increasingly, businesses is to start organizing groups of volunteers to take trips locally, nationally, and even abroad.

Colleges and universities have a wide range of community service groups, environmental organizations, women's advocacy groups, and charity organizations that could all use your help. Many have chapters right on campus. If you are a college student, make it a mandatory part of the college experience (like costume parties or streaking) to participate in at least one volunteer experience. Visit your student activities center and get started.

Many church organizations also regularly organize humanitarian trips. During my time volunteering in Louisiana after Hurricane Katrina, I met several people who had taken a paid leave from a variety of jobs to volunteer their time. The Patagonia clothing company, for one, offers all employees who have been with the company for at least a year the opportunity to volunteer—*and* Patagonia pays employees their full salary while they are away.

## Change Lives: Take a Vacation  🕐=3  💲=4  🏢=3

Sometimes the best way to change the world is to take a vacation. More and more students and young professionals are bypassing Cancun "fun" for trips that help others. Service-oriented vacations are hot right now, and plenty of reputable nonprofit organizations offer affordable volunteer opportunities all over the world.

Why pay to volunteer? In addition to the logistical support involved in partnering with local organizations and finding appropriate placements, the fee for most of these programs usually covers housing, food, medical insurance, and emergency evacuation assistance (also known as "all of the stuff your parents are going to worry about"). The organizations that run volunteering trips want to ensure that participants have a safe and meaningful experience; after all, referral from previous volunteers is one of their best methods of promotion. (Fees vary greatly depending on the country you will be volunteering in. Each organization's website lists exactly what its fees cover, and it is important to know these facts before deciding on a program.)

Most of the programs will also train you before you begin working with communities, so you are bound to pick up useful life skills such as counseling procedures, public speaking, teaching, advocacy techniques, or even the basics of carpentry. Many programs also offer a chance for a full language immersion. You will be surprised how quickly you can pick up a language when you are hungry, thirsty, or need to find a bathroom. Either way, you are bound to be a richer person (at least in experience, new friends, and personality, if not in net worth) after your experience. Unexpected monetary gains could be forthcoming as well—a month abroad helping others is great material for your résumé no matter what job interests you.

So go ahead; you are only young once. You can always have that watered-down pink drink and mediocre spa treatment when you are, say, forty. Here are just a few of the thousands of opportunities available:

- Teach much-needed basic English and math skills in Romania.
- Visit patients and offer health care to those living with HIV/AIDS in Ghana.
- Assist with voluntary AIDS testing and counseling, and promote safer sex through education programs in Tanzania.
- Work on sustainable economic development initiatives in Bolivia.

- Empower marginalized women in India by working with organizations that prevent trafficking of women, teach HIV/STD prevention, promote literacy, and foster microfinance endeavors.
- Rehabilitate children in an orphanage in Vietnam, many of whom have been abandoned due to a serious illness or physical disability.
- Work on conservation efforts, both in the cloud forest and coastal regions of Guatemala.
- Build houses for some of the three hundred thousand Native Americans in Arizona and Montana currently homeless or living in dangerous conditions.

## *WAYS* GUIDE TO FINDING THE RIGHT VOLUNTEER PLACEMENT

Here is how to start planning your life's next adventure:

1.  **What do you want to do?** Jot down a paragraph or two about both the ideal community you would like to serve and the jobs you would like to do. For example, do you want to work with children, adults, or the elderly? Would you like to work on educational, health care, or clean water programs? Making a list of where your interests lie will help you narrow down the organizations you should approach and will help ensure that you find the most rewarding and meaningful experience.

2.  **Got any skills?** Make a list of skills you possess and/or languages you know. Keep in mind that many volunteer organizations require neither of the above and are willing to train those with a great attitude and desire to help.

3.  **Where do you want to go?** Choose an area (or a few areas) of the world where you would like to focus your efforts. Make a list of places you would consider volunteering. Do you

want to be around the corner, in another state, or in another country? If you answered far, far away in unfamiliar territory, would you prefer to be in an urban or rural environment?

4. **Decide how much time you have to devote to volunteering.** Do you want to work a few hours a week, do you want to take a volunteer vacation, or do you want to go abroad for several months or even a year?

5. **When can you leave?** Decide on a time line. Many of the application processes are lengthy, as they require that you are matched with the best opportunity, that medical requirements are met, and that visas/passports are secured and other travel arrangements are made.

6. **How much can you spend?** Most short-term volunteer abroad programs charge a fee, and many do not include airfare. Make a budget and decide whether or not you would be willing to fundraise to cover the cost of your trip. If you do decide to fundraise, start with family and friends, but don't be afraid to ask neighbors, businesses, and acquaintances, too! There are also scholarships and fellowships available for some volunteer placements. For more fundraising pointers, check out the fundraising tips and resource information from the **International Volunteer Programs Association (IVPA)**.

7. **How much support do you need while there?** Be sure that you know what your living arrangements will be, and strive to find a placement that matches your comfort level—i.e., can you rough it, or are you a long-lost member of the royal family? Will you need a lot of logistical support from in-country staff? Do you feel comfortable working independently, or would you rather be with a group of volunteers?

8. **You have your list; now start looking.** These questions will help you narrow your search considerably, and once you have your basic criteria you are ready to start your search. The two most comprehensive databases are at **VolunteerMatch** and **Idealist**. VolunteerMatch is best for opportunities within the United States, while Idealist has links to placements all over the world. Idealist also allows you to browse opportunities by continent.

9. **Ask the real experts.** Once you have narrowed your options down to a couple of organizations, ask for the contact information of some former volunteers. It is always wise to get a firsthand account of past volunteers' experiences. Ask them if they would volunteer with the same organization again; ask them what the best and worst parts of the experience were; ask them if they tried the *cui* in South America (pronounced "kwee" in case you want to order it, it's a guinea pig fried and eaten with the hands). Ask them anything—just make sure their exciting adventures resemble the one you want out of your volunteer vacation, and then make it happen!

## SUCCESS STORY

### From Hipster to Humanitarian

Scott Harrison was a successful party and event planner working the New York City nightclub scene. He was also miserable. "At the age of twenty-eight, I woke up on a beach in Uruguay with the 'perfect life' and realized how unhappy I was. I was the most selfish and arrogant person I knew," recalls Harrison.

He returned to the Christian faith he had been raised with and left New York City to work for the humanitarian organization **Mercy**

**Ships**, which brings medical care to people all over the world via "ship hospitals." He taught himself how to take photos and applied to be the ship's photographer. The volunteer medical staff perform major surgeries onboard the ships and also work in clinics in villages. In addition, many of the volunteers dedicate their time to community development projects like school and well construction.

His decision to volunteer aboard the ships changed his entire perspective and purpose. In Benin and then Liberia, he saw "people suffering from diseases and conditions that can be attributed both to a lack of clean water and to inadequate health care," he says. He took about fifty thousand photos and began to get many of his club friends involved with his new cause. When Harrison returned home, he put on a show in the trendy Chelsea neighborhood of New York City and raised enough money to support more surgeries as well as the building of new wells. Harrison decided to go back to Liberia and see what he could do on his own. "Eighty percent of disease is caused by lack of clean water and affects one billion people, so it was obvious to me that helping to fix this should be my first campaign."

He used the money he had raised at the fundraiser in Chelsea to return to Liberia and fund well-building projects. After his second trip abroad, he founded **charity: water**, which is dedicated to funding wells and providing clean water to people all over the world. To date, his organization has funded 1,247 water projects, served over 640,000 people, and raised more than $9 million. The rewards of Harrison's new endeavor far outweigh the glamour of his old lifestyle. "The idea of serving the poor was so opposite my old life, and I really threw myself into it. Once I saw the great need and what could be done about it, there was really no turning back."

## VOLUNTEER VACATIONS—VITAL STATS
### Ambassadors for Children
HOW LONG: One to two weeks

WHERE: Belize, El Salvador, Ethiopia, Uganda, South Africa, El Salvador, Guatemala, Colombia, India, Mexico, Jordan, New Mexico, Serbia, and Montenegro

WHAT: Variety of trip projects including beach cleanup, school and orphanage building and staffing, vocational training, and library expansion

HOW MUCH: Programs start at $1,500

### Cross-Cultural Solutions

HOW LONG: Two to twelve weeks

WHERE: Ghana, Morocco, South Africa, Tanzania, China, Thailand, India, Russia, Brazil, Peru, Guatemala, and Costa Rica

WHAT: Variety of placements with in-country partner programs including orphanages and child-care centers, schools, health clinics and hospitals, homes for the elderly, and centers for people with disabilities

HOW MUCH: Programs start at $2,588

### Earthwatch Institute

HOW LONG: One to two weeks, typically

WHERE: Global assignments

WHAT: Assist scientists with environmental research regarding issues of sustainability

HOW MUCH: Programs start around $1,500, plus transportation expenses to and from sites

### Global Service Corps

HOW LONG: Four to six weeks

WHERE: Thailand and Tanzania

WHAT: HIV/AIDS education, sustainable agriculture, community development, and orphanage care

HOW MUCH: Programs start at $2,300

## Global Volunteers

HOW LONG: One to three weeks

WHERE: Peru, Costa Rica, Thailand, Cuba, Nepal, Brazil, Cambodia, Laos, Vietnam, Jamaica, Romania, Ghana, Mexico, and China

WHAT: Variety of placements including teaching English, caring for at-risk children, painting and repairing buildings, and working with infants and toddlers

HOW MUCH: Programs start at $1,200

## Projects Abroad

HOW LONG: Two weeks to six months

WHERE: Peru, Belize, Mexico, India, and Thailand

WHAT: Community development projects such as building cleaner-burning stoves in high-Andean communities, protecting children's rights, and helping with HIV/AIDS education in Thailand

HOW MUCH: Programs start at $2,300

## Want more information?

Check out the **International Volunteer Programs Association (IVPA)**. IVPA is an association of nongovernmental organizations (NGOs) involved in international volunteer work and internship exchanges.

# SUCCESS STORY

## Crossing Cultures, Opening Minds

Lauren Brossy grew up in an upper-middle class family in New Jersey. With the encouragement of her mother, she went on her first volunteer vacation to Costa Rica at the age of twenty-one. She raised the $5,000 needed to participate in a program offered by Cross-Cultural Solutions and spent three months at an orphanage for children ranging from infants to twelve-year-olds. She offered them companionship, affection, and tutoring, and she still keeps in touch with many of them today.

The lessons Brossy learned while volunteering changed her life. She says, "My experience showed me that there is more to life than material goods and petty problems. I feel like the kids taught me more lessons than I taught them, and I am so thankful." She learned some practical skills, too: while she arrived in Costa Rica speaking no Spanish, she left fluent in the language, as she was challenged daily to communicate with the children in the orphanage as well as others in the community. Today, at the age of twenty-six, Brossy works as the senior manager of programs for Cross-Cultural Solutions, helping others to experience and prepare for the same types of fulfilling adventures that changed her life.

## Read More about It

In addition to the websites previously listed, here are some helpful books on volunteering abroad:

*Alternatives to the Peace Corps: A Guide of Global Volunteer Opportunities* by Paul Backhurst

*Green Volunteers: The World Guide to Voluntary Work in Nature Conservations* by Fabio Ausenda

*How to Live Your Dream of Volunteering Overseas* by Joseph Collins, Stefano DeZerega, Zahara Heckscher

*So You Want to Join the Peace Corps: What to Know Before You Go* by Dillon Banerjee

*Volunteer Vacations: Short-Term Adventures That Will Benefit You and Others* by Bill McMillon, Doug Cutchins, Anne Geissinger

**Toughest Job You'll Ever Love**  🕐=5  💲=1  ▦=5

Of course I would be remiss to discuss volunteering without mentioning the Peace Corps. Founded in 1961 by President Kennedy, the **Peace Corps** has received mixed reviews over the years. It is a U.S. government–run organization—as opposed to many other volunteer groups that are NGOs. In addition, while volunteers are free to leave at any time, the Peace Corps asks for a minimum two-year commitment. It is important to remember, though, that Peace Corps volunteers are doing incredible work all over the world, and if you have already traveled abroad and/or volunteered abroad and want to find a long-term placement, the Peace Corps is certainly a viable option. In addition, while many other volunteer programs charge volunteers a fee for placements, Peace Corps volunteers, once accepted and trained, receive a living stipend in their home country. Better still, upon your return there are few résumé credentials as impressive to employers as a stint in the Peace Corps, so even if you do not want a service-oriented career, your service may pay dividends down the line.

## SUCCESS STORY

### A New Perspective

Twenty-seven-year-old Jody Myrum had always wanted to be a volunteer. A trip to Mexico when she was twelve left her determined to spend her life helping others. "This trip was the first time I ever saw poverty, and it made a huge impact," she says. "I saw kids my age selling gum on the street, and it is an innate part of my being that if I see an injustice, I want to fix it." When her family moved to Switzerland, Myrum volunteered at a local refugee center for Serbians and Bosnians displaced by the war. This led to a trip to Bosnia where Myrum worked with children suffering from post-conflict woes. "These were people who couldn't farm because they had land mines in their backyard; their children were not able to run freely without being afraid of injury or worse. Even so, I saw in those people a hope in humanity that comes out in those situations and an inspiring inner strength, despite the dire circumstances."

During and after college, Myrum volunteered and was eventually hired by Even Start, which is an offshoot of the national Head Start programs. She worked with fourth- through sixth-grade girls living in an extremely poor area of Fort Collins, Colorado. With a focus on empowerment, she taught them about puberty and how to negotiate with bullies, and she even helped them with their homework. Myrum then worked at a residential treatment center for adolescent girls and boys who had been through the foster system too many times or were sex offenders. While there, she realized not only her potential to help turn young lives around but also the long-term ripple effects of her service—effects that were easy to point to, though difficult to measure.

Myrum moved on to a Peace Corps placement that focused on girls' education and women's empowerment. Specifically, she wanted to pursue international humanitarian work and knew she needed experience living in a developing country.

After a lengthy application process (typically nine months to one year) and eleven weeks of training in the United States, Myrum was sent to work in Togo in West Africa. She focused on gender-based violence and increasing access to girls' education. She also helped raise money to build a school, trained a gender-equity committee made up of community members who went on to establish committees in other villages, and taught gender-equity classes to educators, business owners, and community leaders.

As for the two-year time commitment, which is a deterrent to some, she says, "Consider that some people can easily spend two years in a job they hate, and I spent those two years transforming into the person I wanted to become."

Myrum recently completed her master's in social work at Columbia, where she interned at UNICEF in the international child-protection office. After graduation, she had a two-month fellowship with the International Center for AIDS Treatment and Care Programs in Kenya, where she evaluated hospital services for women and girls who have been sexually assaulted. Today she is a gender-based violence manager with the International Rescue Committee in Ethiopia, where she works to build capabilities among local people to respond to and prevent violence against women and girls in Somali refugee camps. Now in her dream job, Myrum knows that volunteering led to countless opportunities. "I never felt like I was making a sacrifice," she says of her two years in the Peace Corps. "I was given a stipend, the opportunity to work on domestic and sexual violence issues, and was surrounded by generous, inspiring people who gave me a whole new perspective on life."

## DIRECTORY OF LOCAL AND INTERNATIONAL ORGANIZATIONS THAT NEED YOUR HELP

Following is a sampling of the many organizations that offer volunteer opportunities (descriptions provided by the organizations themselves).

### SHORTER-TERM COMMITMENTS—NATIONAL/LOCAL SERVICE
### American Red Cross

Since its founding in 1881, the American Red Cross has been the nation's premier emergency response organization. As part of a worldwide movement that offers neutral humanitarian care to the victims of war, the Red Cross distinguishes itself by also aiding victims of devastating natural disasters. Over the years, the organization has expanded its services, always with the aim of preventing and relieving suffering.

### Big Brothers/Big Sisters

The Big Brothers/Big Sisters Mission is to help children reach their potential through professionally supported, one-to-one relationships with mentors that have a measurable impact on youth.

## Citizen Schools
Citizen Schools operates a national network of apprenticeship programs for middle-school students, connecting adult volunteers to young people in hands-on learning projects after school. At Citizen Schools, students develop the academic and leadership skills they need to do well in school, get into college, and become leaders in their careers and in their communities.

## Habitat for Humanity
Habitat for Humanity International (HFHI) is a nonprofit, ecumenical Christian housing ministry. HFHI seeks to eliminate poverty housing and homelessness around the world and to make decent shelter a matter of conscience and action. Volunteers can volunteer all over the world through over a hundred HFHI affiliates.

## Student Conservation Association
The Student Conservation Association (SCA) is a nonprofit organization that offers conservation internships and summer trail-crew opportunities to more than three thousand people each year. SCA is focused on developing conservation and community leaders while getting important work done on the land. Founded in 1957 to restore and protect the United States' public lands and preserve them for future generations, SCA remains committed to this goal today.

## LONGER-TERM COMMITMENTS—NATIONAL/LOCAL SERVICE
## AmeriCorps
AmeriCorps is a network of local, state, and national service programs that connect more than seventy thousand Americans

each year in intensive service to meet our country's critical needs in education, public safety, health, and the environment.

## City Year

City Year's mission is to build democracy through citizen service, civic engagement, and social entrepreneurship. City Year's signature program, the City Year youth corps, unites diverse young adults ages seventeen to twenty-four in a year of full-time rigorous service, during which they work in teams to address societal needs, particularly in schools and neighborhoods. These young leaders put their idealism to work as tutors and mentors to schoolchildren, reclaiming public spaces, and organizing after-school programs, school vacation camps, and civic engagement programs for elementary, middle-school, and high-school students.

## Youth Service America

Youth Service America is a resource center and premier alliance of two hundred–plus organizations committed to increasing the quantity and quality of volunteer opportunities for young Americans to serve locally, nationally, and globally. YSA's mission is to strengthen the effectiveness, sustainability, and scale of the youth-service and service-learning field. YSA envisions a powerful network of organizations committed to creating healthy communities, fostering citizenship, and making service the common experience and expectation of all young people.

## LONGER-TERM COMMITMENTS—INTERNATIONAL SERVICE
## Doctors Without Borders

Doctors Without Borders recruits medical and nonmedical personnel to provide medical care to people in crisis in more than seventy countries worldwide. If selected, you will join a group of professionals who deliver lifesaving treatment to many of the most vulnerable people in the world—victims of conflict, refugees, internally displaced persons, and people living with diseases such as HIV/AIDS and malaria. Monthly salaries start at $1,300. Minimum six-month commitment.

## Mercy Ships

Mercy Ships provides health care and community development services in developing nations free of charge to the poor and without prejudice or discrimination with regard to ethnicity, sex, age, or religion. Mercy Ships welcomes those who have the time to devote to the work of bringing hope and healing to the world's poorest peoples. Volunteers come on a short-term basis from as little as two weeks to as long as one year.

## Right to Play

Right to Play uses specially designed sport and play programs to improve health, build life skills, and foster peace for children and communities affected by war, poverty, and disease. Working in both the humanitarian and development contexts, Right to Play has projects in more than twenty countries in Africa, Asia, and the Middle East.

## WorldTeach

WorldTeach is a nonprofit NGO that provides opportunities for individuals to make a meaningful contribution to international education by living and working as volunteer teachers in developing countries. Since its inception, WorldTeach has placed thousands of volunteer educators in communities throughout Asia, Latin America, Africa, Eastern Europe, and the Pacific.

Updates to this list are available at the *Ten Ways* website.

## FROM VOLUNTEER TO ACTIVIST

By donating your time, you have nobly entered the fray to make a difference, yet much volunteer work is geared toward addressing problems on the ground. You will probably find that many of the systematic concerns you address on the local and global levels could also benefit from changes in policy. Whether you have seen the effects of inadequate health care and education or the aftermath of lax environmental regulations, all of these issues need your attention as a voter as well as a volunteer. Volunteering is one of the best ways to gain a deeper understanding of a cause, and political involvement is one of the best ways to ensure lasting change. From voting to running for office, there are many ways to take your involvement to the next level through political action. Read **chapter 3** for suggestions to make sure that your voice comes through loud and clear to those politicians whose decisions affect us all.

# Chapter 3

# WAYS TO BE THE LIFE
# OF YOUR PARTY

*Support Political Actions
That Reflect Your Values*

Today's generation of young people holds more power than any
generation before them to make a positive impact on the world.

*Bill Clinton*

## IN THIS CHAPTER

- Changing the World: The New Province of Youth

- How to Get Your Political Briefing

- Tell Your Lawmakers (and Everyone Else!) What
  You Think

- *Ways* Guide to Approaching Your Lawmakers

- Be the Change: Ideas for Joining the Campaign

- Directory of Politically Active Organizations

- Nobody Likes a Hypocrite

## CHANGING THE WORLD: THE NEW PROVINCE OF YOUTH

When I was a teacher, I was always fascinated by a phenomenon that I noticed among my students: even though they were years away from voting, they were deeply involved in the presidential campaigns. In 2004, I found myself teaching a group of seventh-grade students during the tense moments after the presidential election when the winner was still undetermined. It had been too close to call on the night of the election, and when word came that George W. Bush had defeated John Kerry, the news spread quickly around our small school. One of the students in my class began to gleefully rejoice in Bush's victory. I saw this as an opportunity for discussion (after all, they were only going to have this opportunity once every four years), so I asked her why she was so happy. This question sparked a discussion that took up our entire class as students voiced their own distinct opinions.

I remember being thirteen years old and feeling the same way during the presidential election. As the daughter of a man who had to flee Communist Czechoslovakia, I was acutely aware of my luck at being born into a country where we all have the right to debate, vote, and protest. As I listened to my students discuss the candidates that afternoon, I had one wish for all of them—that they would retain a high level of interest in politics and that when it came time for them to vote, they would.

An infusion of optimistic youth and energy combined with an ethical, educated stance on crucial issues are what is needed to tackle some of the major problems facing our country. As a young voter, you may feel disenfranchised by the current state of the political system, but you also have the greatest chance of effecting lasting change. If we can take the time to vote for the next *American Idol* or the person with the best salsa moves on *Dancing with the Stars*, we can certainly take the time to vote for the next mayor, senator, and president! The first step to taking back control from special interests and big businesses is caring enough to do something.

While we may be concerned with policies that affect us on a daily basis, such as health care, environmental regulations, and foreign policy, many of us still do not know the names of our local representatives or what they promised to do for us during their campaigns. In some cases we are not clear on what role elected officials or government bureaucrats play—am I the only one who's wondered what a comptroller is? This is an understandable but also unacceptable situation. After all, how can you weigh in on issues like public transit, recycling, or that new parking garage that's being built on your favorite park if you don't even know whom you should address your angry letters to? Whatever your political affiliation, now is the time to find an effective way to get informed and involved. According to the U.S. Census Bureau's projections, by 2015, one-third of the U.S. electorate will be made up of those born between 1978 and 2000—a demographic commonly referred to as millennials. Now that's a lot of voters, activists, lobbyists, lawyers, and concerned, vocal citizens! The world is counting on us to make responsible choices and lead the way, and it's never been easier to do so. Politicians twitter about their work for their constituents, Facebook groups organize around every issue under the sun, and the number of watchdog websites that track everything from corporate responsibility to voting records grows every day.

So how do you find a cause to keep you enthralled? Start by figuring out the issues that matter to you. Maybe a stay in the hospital (or the bill that followed!) has sparked your interest in health care reform. Perhaps you enjoy the outdoors and are concerned about the preservation of public spaces. An aging relative with Alzheimer's might raise your awareness of the issues surrounding stem cell research. Your desire to avoid seeing a friend or family member stationed in Iraq or Afghanistan might have you paying careful attention to our foreign policy. Whether or not you realize it, the decisions of elected officials already shape your life in myriad ways, and I think it's a safe bet that we'd all like a little say in the whos and hows of that process. This chapter is designed to provide you with greater access to the political machinations at every level, whether you are a seasoned political junkie or simply looking to dip your toe into the waters of the democratic process.

Thanks to the World Wide Web, it is easier than ever to become an informed, active citizen. Public policy work is all about networking, and political candidates are trying to connect with young voters on the Internet like never before. They want you to know where they stand (with a little wiggle room); so once you know the issues that matter to you, it is easy to find the elected officials who can help bring about the changes you want to see. Whether you plan on running for office someday or just want to use the principles of democracy to push your elected representatives to do the right thing, now is the time to find your political voice. This chapter will walk you through the democratic process starting with education, then progressing to direct and indirect forms of participation in the politics that matter most to you.

## HOW TO GET YOUR POLITICAL BRIEFING

The ignorance of one voter in a democracy impairs the security of all.

*John F. Kennedy*

**Just the Facts** 🕐=2 💲=1 🏛=1

The easiest and most practical step to take when deciding where you stand on local, national, and global issues is to get informed. While a wide-mouthed yawn may or may not be your first reaction to this suggestion, remember that it helps to have a solid understanding of the basic facts as you work to formulate your opinions. Somewhere out there, from the environment to the War on Terror to the thing that senator swears he didn't do, accept, or know about, there is an issue that matters to you. And if you think that *paying* attention to the news and *spending* time online educating yourself are rough, think about the *cost* of making ill-informed decisions (or worse still, leaving the ill-informed decision making to others).

## Not Sure What the Parties Stand For? Check Out Their Websites

**Constitution Party**
**Democratic Party**
**Green Party**
**Independent American Party**
**Libertarian Party**
**American Reform Party**
**Republican Party (Grand Old Party)**

Not sure how it all works? Here are five websites that describe the basics:
**GovSpot**
**The White House**
**U.S. House of Representatives**
**U.S. Senate**
**C-SPAN**
Each section contains a wealth of information about the branches of government, elected officials, pending or recent legislation, court cases, and most any other topic you can imagine. For up-to-date information about who all of your elected representatives are and how to contact them, visit **Project Vote Smart** and enter in your ZIP code.

Once you have your who's who sorted out (I finally found out what a comptroller was!), there are several ways to stay informed about current issues. Some are rather nuts-and-bolts presentations of the news, while others are clearly (or if they're good, subtly) nudging you in one direction or another. One of the easiest ways to keep abreast of political developments is to read newspapers and newsmagazines. While editorial leanings are pretty easy to discern by checking out the staff editorials, they are a generally a reliable source of what is going on each day—if not of what you should make of it. Most news organizations are also online, so if a story's in print, chances are good it was on the Web first.

## Make Friends with Your Candidates 🕐=1 💲=1 🏛=1

Even if the politicians themselves have no idea which websites are cool, they are savvy enough to hire people who do. As such, it is easier than ever to find out about candidates these days. They all have their own websites, and many now have their own MySpace and Facebook pages where you can read their blogs, bone up on their vital stats, add them as friends, and even read about their interests. For example, a quick glance through Hillary Clinton's MySpace page reveals that she "is a lousy cook, but can make pretty good soft-scrambled eggs"; her favorite reality TV show is *American Idol*; and her favorite fitness activity is speed walking (which, a quick search of YouTube will illustrate, is still faster than her husband jogging). Once you get a sense of the candidates' personas as "real" people, you can also read about their stances on issues such as climate change, health care, and the conflicts in Iraq and Afghanistan. While a Facebook page certainly doesn't guarantee the quality of a candidate, it is a good indication that the candidates are at least reaching out to young voters. It is important to give your valuable vote to someone who truly deserves it. After all, we don't even go on dates these days without looking someone up on Google or Facebook first.

Dip into the Issues on the Internet 🕐=2 💲=1 🏠=1

## Reliable Political Weblogs

**FiveThirtyEight**
**The Huffington Post**
**Politico**
**Daily Kos**

## Websites with the Millennial in Mind

**Future Majority**
**Rock the Vote**
**Bother Voting**

Websites and blogs have become another powerful way to spread political messages and to engage in important debates. Consequently, the cybersphere has gained new respect as a potent political tool. In fact, some blogs are so influential that political staffers monitor blog clearinghouses like **Technorati** on a daily basis to see which stories are garnering the most attention. From the **Daily Dish** to **Daily Kos**, there are political blogs for every affiliation. When reading them, be sure to keep their particular slants in mind. Some of these biases are obvious by the name, such as **The Democratic Daily**, while others, like **Little Green Footballs**, take a little digging to uncover. Blogs also allow you a low-stress forum in which you can begin to share and debate your ideas with the world at large.

## TELL YOUR LAWMAKERS (AND EVERYONE ELSE!) WHAT YOU THINK

**Enter the Blogosphere** ⏰=3 $=1 ▦=2

Once you have established a strong viewpoint on a political issue, find the appropriate blog to disseminate your message. Blogging is a good way to make an immediate impact. At the very least, you can send a link to your friends and guilt them into reading it, and if they find your opinions and ideas engaging, encourage them to pass the blog along. An engaging blog will get people talking about issues, and respectful discourse (a good rule of thumb: no cursing or threats of bodily harm) is the first step toward finding solutions. You can start writing your own blog, or you can write for one of the many political blogs that are open to public contributions. One of the best resources for beginning bloggers can be found at **Blogtrepreneur**, where the post "101 Essential Blogging Resources" is regularly updated. Many of these open-forum blogs find their new editors and contributing writers from the pool of blogs posted to their site. If you are good enough at blogging, your habit could even land you a job!

### Open-Forum Political Blogs to Check Out

**Daily Kos**

**MyDD**

**Open Left**

**Pam's House Blend**

**TPM Café**

# SUCCESS STORY

## Blog Star

Markos Moulitsas Zúnigais was just thirty when he started **Daily Kos** in 2002. Daily Kos was one of the main blogs credited with launching the web campaign that made Howard Dean a presidential front-runner (at least until the "yeehaw" heard 'round the globe). With two to four million visitors a day, the Daily Kos blog attracts a wide spectrum of viewpoints. The convention that grew from its community, the Netroots Nation Convention, which anyone can attend, is now a gathering of the entire progressive blogosphere.

## Make a Political Fashion Statement 🕐=1 💲=2 ▦=1

Want to give your cause or candidate a little free advertising and raise awareness and electability at the same time? If wearing your allegiance appeals to you—think getting a tattoo but less permanent—you can make your political statement on everything from bumper stickers to thong underwear. However, if you are not the tattoo type, consider carefully before affixing that bumper sticker to the back of your car. It will probably last much longer than the campaign itself, and you may not want to be known as the guy who's backed every loser since Walter Mondale (look him up) each time you head out to pick up some milk. Shirts, on the other hand, are always fun; political wear one day can become vintage couture the next. In fact, I think my "Howard Dean for America" tank is even more fun to wear now that it has been rendered obsolete.

**Get In on the Vote**  🕐=2  💲=1  🏢=2

Anyone still looking for proof of the power and influence of youth-voter turnout need only look to the 2008 presidential election. According to the Center for Information and Research on Civic Learning and Engagement (CIRCLE), voter turnout in the under-thirty age bracket had been declining since 1972. Poor showings, indeed; however, in the 2004 presidential election, 51.6 percent of voters in this demographic participated in the election, up nearly 10 percent from the 2000 election.[3] The 2008 election, driven by large youth turnout, had the highest rate in forty years (just over 62 percent). Turnout topped 70 percent in Iowa, Maine, and New Hampshire; and Minnesota neared 80 percent. If you ever doubt the importance of your vote, Al Franken became senator of Minnesota in 2008 by a margin of just over three hundred votes—out of the 2.8 million cast! There are several organizations that make it easy for young voters to participate. Two of the most helpful websites are **Vote411.org**, maintained by the League of Women Voters, and **Declare Yourself**. Declare Yourself is a primer of sorts for young voters, offering facts about voting as well as descriptions of primaries, candidates, absentee voting (important for college students, especially), and voter registration. You can sign up to receive text message alerts about important dates, and you can also link to UWire for student-created campaign coverage. Vote411.org offers similar information, as well as a polling-place locator and a state-by-state guide with links to local resources. Remember, if you don't vote, people like you-know-who end up getting reelected. Also, forget about complaining. Those who whine about the state of the country and the world without doing anything to fix it are just, well, whiners. Of course, in order to join or continue to stand behind this growing trend, you need to be registered to vote. There are several easy ways to do this:

- Pick up a voter registration form at the post office, fill it out, and mail it in. In most states, the postage is free!
- Register when you renew or change your driver's license. (Note: In order to vote in local elections, you need to be registered in your city or town of residence.)
- Register online at **Rock the Vote, Declare Yourself, Bother Voting,** or **Vote411.org.**
- Go to your local party headquarters to register and to get information about candidates.

## Want the Unbiased Info on Issues and Candidates?

Check out **Resources for the Future, FactCheck,** and **Project Vote Smart.** Resources for the Future is a nonprofit and nonpartisan organization devoted to researching environmental issues and our dependence on natural resources. RFF was one of the first organizations to use economic tools to develop environmental and energy policy recommendations. FactCheck, which is funded mainly by the Annenberg Foundation and is also nonprofit and nonpartisan, monitors the statements of key U.S. political figures to ensure their accuracy. Project Vote Smart offers access to representatives' biographical information, voting records, positions on key issues, public statements, interest group ratings, and campaign finances. Visitors can also follow key votes at the national and state level.

### Get Involved in State and Local Elections, Too  🕐=2 💲=1 🏢=2

While local elections may not get as much coverage or seem as glamorous as presidential and congressional votes, they are just as important. Local elections also offer a good opportunity to see the political process firsthand: cities and towns always need poll workers or election judges to assist voters and ensure that the process goes smoothly. General elections take place on the first Tuesday of every November, primary elections generally take place early in the year, and special referendums and votes on community issues occur throughout the year. National politicians get their start locally, so it is important to get them working for you early on! Even if your local politicians hold no presidential aspirations, local decisions such as school budgets, open-space acts, emissions restrictions, property development, and traffic laws all affect your quality of life on a daily basis. On top of that, many laws and regulations about abortion and same-sex marriage are decided at the state level. As a result, legal precedents set by one state can impact the rest of the nation—finally, a reason to pay attention to North Dakota!

## Become a Laptop Lobbyist  🕐=2 💲=1 🏛=2

Okay, you are voting in all of the elections, but you still don't think your politicians are getting the message. What to do?

Thanks to the efforts of nonprofit and partisan organizations, there are easy ways to join forces and add your voice to others in order to get your point across to your representatives. While most politicians will take the time to consider and respond to all of their constituents, they are much more likely to pay attention to an issue when they receive similar messages en masse. Many of these organizations have websites with titles like "Get Involved," "Politics and Issues," or "Take Action Now." Once you click on these sites, the process of reaching your politicians could not be simpler. It works like this:

1. You receive an email about a ban on same-sex marriage or an administration push to clear-cut more old-growth forest.
2. Outrage ensues.
3. You sign the prewritten email or edit the message.

4. When satisfied that you agree with the message, you sign your name to the bottom of the letter and press send.

5. Once you have sent your message, you have the option of sending out an email to friends (prewritten or personalized), asking them to get involved, too.

Many organizations also offer a more creative suggestion for contacting your politicians, such as making a video or attending a rally. Couch-potato alert: occasionally, you may be asked to lobby the old-fashioned way and call your senator or representative directly. The best part about these action alerts is that these organizations make it their job to keep you up to date with what is going on in the legislature and beyond. You can stay informed on any issue that matters to you simply by checking your email. See **pages 75–81** at the end of this chapter for a sampling of the many organizations that help take your opinions to your politicians.

## SUCCESS STORY

### Shooting Stuff to Help the Environment

Twenty-one-year-old Nigel Fellman Greene, a conservation biology major at St. Lawrence University in Canton, New York, had always been environmentally conscious, but he had never been motivated to take action until he spent a semester studying in the Adirondacks. This academic program, along with the experience of meeting Bill McKibben, one of the founders of Step It Up and one of the authors of *Fight Global Warming Now,* demonstrated that "it is really obvious that humans are having a huge impact on the planet," Greene says. "I felt a sense of urgency and personal responsibility." During the summer of 2007, Greene read about the **League of Conservation Voters** Hot Spot contest, which challenges young voters to make a video telling candidates why climate change should be a priority in their 2008 campaigns. Greene entered the contest and won an all-expense-paid trip to the 2007 Live Earth Concert in New Jersey. Now a senior, Greene remains active both on campus and off. He was recently the campus PR organizer for Step It Up, and he plans to pursue a career in the wind-power industry. For more information about Step It Up and similar environmental organizations, check out **chapter 5.**

## Send Your Own Message 🕐=3 $=1 ▦=2

If you decide that you would like to craft your own message, choose your favorite mode of communication. If you love to write, send a letter. If you are a budding Ken Burns, send a video. If you are impossible to refuse on the phone, give your representative a call. Remember that your representatives get hundreds, sometimes thousands, of letters and calls a week from their constituents. If you are going to take the time to compose a message, you want to send something that is going to have an impact, and with a little careful preparation, it will. If you decide that your chosen cause could benefit from additional support, gather signatures from friends and write a letter that you all can sign. Your politicians will pay attention to a well-crafted, personal message. A twentysomething friend of mine used to work for a congresswoman, and according to him, she read every single letter that came in. Remember, the more specific and concise you can be, the more likely your reps are to take notice; an articulate, persuasive voter is one that politicians want on their side.

## *WAYS* GUIDE TO APPROACHING YOUR LAWMAKERS

1. Be creative—but remember to maintain a bit of decorum.
2. Educate yourself about all sides of the issue.

3. Outline your talking points and stay focused on those: What is the problem? Why should it be fixed? How would you recommend the issue be solved? What specific action(s) do you want your lawmaker to take?
4. Include your profession, city, and state of residence.
5. Enlist the help of friends to be in your video, to sign a petition, or even just to proofread for any rants that might land you on an FBI watch list.

## Here Is How You Do It

When Andrew Frishman and Leigh Needleman moved to California, they were appalled at the overuse of air-conditioning, especially when used as a tactic in outdoor malls to draw people into stores. Given the current energy crisis, it seemed a senseless marketing ploy to be blowing money out the door on a hot summer day. Needleman explains, "I feel that using air-conditioning to pull people into their shops is a slap in the face of those of us who do all we can to use the least amount of energy possible." Frishman and Needleman were angry enough to write a letter to both their California state assemblywoman and senator. They received a response from their senator stating that he shared their concern for energy-saving measures, and today they continue to push their elected officials for action on energy efficiency. Frishman and Needleman also recommend sending copies of letters to local newspapers to help bring more attention to an issue. Here is their letter; it is a great example of the strategies outlined earlier:

*September 4, 2007*
*Dear Assemblywoman Lois Wolk and Senator Michael Machado:*

*California continues to struggle with a severe energy crisis.*

*One afternoon early this July, with sustained temperatures over 100 degrees for a week, we were walking through an outdoor Sacramento mall. Even more appalling than the relentless heat were the periodic blasts of ice-cold air-conditioning. Recoiling in horror, we realized that the doors of the majority of the stores had been propped wide open. This is not a problem unique to any one particular retail establishment. All over the state of California, when temperatures rise, stores needlessly waste significant electricity in a desperate effort to compete for customers.*

*It seems ironic that while the California state legislature meets to discuss energy-conservation legislation in the capitol—a building under strict self-imposed energy-saving measures—only a few blocks away, electricity in the form of air-conditioning is forcibly expelled from a profusion of local retailers and national chain stores.*

*We ask that you introduce a bill on our behalf. We would like to prohibit the propping open of doors by retail businesses when their air-conditioning is on. We believe that this legislation would provide a simple and elegant mechanism to actively encourage energy conservation by retail businesses across the state. We understand that stores should be allowed flexibility in the way in which they conduct business; however, when they engage in practices that are indirectly harmful to public interest, it is the responsibility of lawmakers to intercede.*

*At this time, we do not have a detailed recommendation for the enforcement of such a law. However, we believe that it could be a potentially important revenue stream for environmental/energy-saving initiatives in the state of California. Subsequent offenses might lead to increased fines: $100, $1,000, etc.?*

*Similar to the views that so many California lawmakers*

*have expressed, we are excited about decreasing power consumption in California. Please let us know if there is any way in which we can be helpful in the process of creating this legislation. We would be delighted to talk with you further.*

*Most sincerely,*

*Andrew Frishman and Leigh A. Needleman*

## Not Getting a Response? Storm the Capitol 🕐=4 💲=2 🏢=2

Okay, don't *actually* storm the capitol, but do try to schedule a meeting. Most of your state representatives and even your senators and representatives in Congress will be willing to schedule meetings with you to hear your concerns and suggestions. And remember two things:

1. They like young voters, or at least they must pretend to: they know that if you went to this much trouble, you probably vote in every election and plan on doing so for a long time to come.
2. They work for you!

You can initiate contact with a letter like the one previously mentioned, detailing the issues you would like to address. You should receive a response within a few weeks. If the response is not sufficient or you feel like you could make a stronger case in person, call their office and request a meeting. You can also join forces with other concerned citizens and attend one of the hundreds of rallies that take place in Washington, D.C., and in state capitals every year.

Lastly, don't be shy. Sometimes opportunities simply present themselves, so make sure you seize the moment! Lindsey Franklin, a staffer at Step It Up, ran into Senator John Kerry at a World Series baseball game. Lucky for her, they both seemed to be rooting for the same team. Supporters of Step It Up had been inviting presidential candidates and members of Congress to a national day of action to raise awareness about climate change, and Franklin was able to extend an invitation to Kerry in person. "As we reached our seats, I practically bumped into the senator himself, out to enjoy the phenomenon that was the 2007 Red Sox, taking pictures and chatting with fans. I seized the opportunity (call me opportunistic) and invited him out to an event," she says. After a few logistical emails, Kerry arranged to attend an event in Massachusetts, which reinforces Franklin's opinion that "our politicians are people, like us, who are ready to listen and ultimately follow our lead."

# SUCCESS STORY

## Power Shift

**Power Shift** '07 and '09 were gatherings of college students and young people in November 2007 and March 2009. Their aim was to influence climate change legislation by taking the message of the need for scientifically based solutions to the climate crisis directly to congressional leaders in Washington, D.C. The Power Shift team enlisted the help of volunteer campus coordinators all over the country to achieve their three main goals:

1. Make the U.S. presidential candidates and Congress take global warming seriously.
2. Empower a truly diverse network of young leaders.
3. Achieve broad geographic diversity.

Leaders and participants of the conference shared ideas, made connections, and sent a united message about the need for immediate environmental action in Congress. According to May Boeve, a participant at Power Shift '07, "Political change is afoot. For months on end, popular support for U.S. government action to address climate change has grown. It has been documented all over the Web, in major papers, and even on TV shows. But now, finally, winds of change are sweeping through the halls of Congress. At the Power Shift conference, winds of change were unleashed by 2,500 students who lobbied Congress in the largest such event in history."

## BE THE CHANGE: IDEAS FOR JOINING THE CAMPAIGN

Ancient Greeks defined idiots as citizens who are so concerned with their private lives and preferences that they fail to attend to, or even comprehend, the common good.

*Walter Parker*

### Party with Your Party 🕐=2 💲=2 ⌂=2

One of the best ways to find activists and organizations to work with is to start attending social events where you might meet a few. These gatherings are also great places to mingle with like-minded singles. Back to business, though, and specifically the business of drinking. **Drinking Liberally**, whose motto is "Promoting democracy one pint at a time," has chapters all over the country where members can gather in informal settings (like a bar!) and talk politics. Many political organizations have mixers and conventions where people can share ideas, network, and yes, if the mood strikes them, have a beverage. While this may not fly a few years from now with your beloved—"Sorry, honey, I can't mow the lawn today. I have to go drink with some right-wing drunks and liberal lushes"—you can still get away with at least a few more years of bar-sponsored political activity.

# SUCCESS STORY

## Net Gain

When Nolan Treadway was twenty-six, he was living in San Francisco and was interested in becoming involved in the political scene. He was first spurred to take action after the 2004 election, but he wasn't sure how to best direct his efforts. He started attending political meetings to see what opportunities were available but failed to find an exact outlet for his interests. When he heard that Daily Kos was looking for people to help organize its 2006 YearlyKos convention, he thought he had found a match. "What I do every day is book conventions," Treadway says. "So I was excited that I had finally found a need where I had expertise and could contribute immediately in a tangible way."

Treadway's work with YearlyKos showed him that it is possible to effect change through political and governmental work, especially when you can find a fit for your talent. Treadway tells those interested in becoming a part of the political scene to "just get out there and do it. Put yourself outside of your comfort zone. Find an issue or organization that you can get behind and start volunteering." He also warns young activists against falling into the trap of thinking that they will not be able to make a difference unless they devote their whole life to it. Treadway says, "This is a dangerous way of thinking, because people can dedicate themselves part-time and still really make a difference." Following his own advice, Treadway, now the logistics director for what is now known as Netroots Nation, has been one of the primary organizers of the annual convention ever since. In that time, he has also earned a master's degree in public policy from American University.

## Hit the Campaign Trail 🕐=4 💲=1 ▦=2

Once you have found a political cause worthy of your time and support, get in touch with local headquarters and offer to volunteer. Many political campaigns have a section on their website where you can sign up and list your specific talents as a potential volunteer. If you are interested in finding out more about the political scene, campaign work is not only a great place to learn about the issues but also to connect with others in the political arena. And, again, they love young voters and politicos. You have the energy (read: long days and nights of work subsisting on pizza and Tootsie Pops), enthusiasm (feel free to hug the candidates and constituents—you will know when the mood is right), and long-term voting stock that the candidates and their managers love.

College and high-school students also may be able to find work through their State House page program or by volunteering to intern for state and federal representatives and senators.

## SUCCESS STORY

### A Shared Gene for Activism

Identical twins Allison and Christine Letts have been politically active since the fifth grade, when they handed out information at their local polling station during the 2000 Bush/Gore election. They both voted for the first time in the 2006 election and were ecstatic about the opportunity. Says Christine, "Voting is important because it is difficult to tell people that an issue like funding for education, abortion laws, or same-sex marriage matters unless you vote. Otherwise, you are a hypocrite."

Allison adds, "We see the issues as so important, and voting is a way of showing it; you can't effect change unless you vote."

After their volunteer initiation during the 2000 presidential election, the twins were hooked. They worked on the Kerry campaign in 2004. They followed up by volunteering for both congressional and gubernatorial campaigns in 2006 and then the Obama presidential campaign in 2008. Christine was also the communications director for a state representative campaign. She says, "I think one of the most important things to realize is that people are excited when young people care about the world. When we go out canvassing, so many people say to us, 'Your candidate is so lucky to have you working on their campaign.' As teenagers we get positive responses all the time."

They also both have high hopes for the future, especially if more young people get involved with the political process. "We still have a ton of idealism, and we don't have the limitations that you have once you have been in the system for too long. We volunteer because we are trying to make the world a better place," says Christine.

Allison concurs, "We don't see that one person individually can change the world, but as a group we can."

### Go to Camp 🕐=4 💲=1 🏠=3

Perhaps you have already volunteered on a political campaign, written letters to your representatives, or attended a rally, and you still are hungry for more. Time spent in the trenches of a campaign is not only an incredible learning experience, but your efforts to inform and promote can have both immediate and long-term effects on the policies and personnel in our government.

In 2008, **MoveOn**, a political action organization, launched a fellowship program and began encouraging budding activists to apply for positions. Those that are accepted work in five-month paid positions alongside organizers and campaigners. Fellows work with a mentor on issues like ending the war in Iraq and the climate crisis. At the end of the fellowship, MoveOn assists the fellows with finding a similar job. The **Human Rights Campaign** has initiated two similar programs: Campaign College and Camp Equality. Participants attend an intensive weeklong training session about gay, lesbian, bisexual, and transgender (GLBT) equality and then are placed on twelve-week campaigns throughout the country. **Green Corps** also offers advocacy training for those interested in organizing environmental campaigns. All of these types of opportunities give aspiring politicians and activists the chance to work on current campaigns.

## Make It Your Job ⏱=5 💲=4 🏢=5

If you are interested in an internship or job with a public interest group, **Idealist** is a good place to start your search. Peruse the website to get a sense of the opportunities and necessary qualifications. If you are considering law school, **Equal Justice Works** publishes *The Equal Justice Works Guide to Law Schools*. For more ideas about how to turn your passion into promise, **see chapter 10.**

You can also change the laws yourself by running for office. Really. While the stereotypical view of politicians is that they are old, white, male, and not always in the habit of listening to their constituents, there is plenty of room for youthful politicians in today's political climate. For proof, one need only look at the twenty-nine-year-old mayor of Pittsburgh, Pennsylvania, Luke Ravenstahl, or the thirty-five-year-old Iraq War veteran and current Pennsylvania congressman, Patrick J. Murphy. Some higher political offices do have specific age and experience requirements, but it is possible to run for local offices such as town councilmember or state representative with limited experience.

Running for office will take a bit of money and the know-how to file the necessary paperwork, but you can easily navigate the necessary steps by visiting your city hall or state capitol. Here are the basic steps:

- Make sure you are registered to vote in the city and state where you are running.
- File an intent to run for office.
- Gather the requisite number of signatures to get on the ballot.
- Establish your platform: What party do you belong to? What is your stance on the issues?
- Get the word out—start going door to door, pass out flyers, call the local media, launch a website, enlist the help of friends and volunteers, etc.

## SUCCESS STORY

### A Real-Life Maverick

David Segal has always paid attention to politics, although he never saw himself as a politician. After graduating from Columbia in 2001, he moved to Providence, Rhode Island, and taught math part-time. Less than two years later, at the age of twenty-three, he was sworn in as the youngest member ever of the Providence City Council. He ran as a Green Party candidate in a district with many college students and based his campaign on a pledge to represent the needs of his constituents. He went door to door with his message and enlisted the help of friends to raise awareness about his campaign. Once elected, Segal kept his word by supporting a living wage, environmental sustainability, ethical government, and energy efficiency.

In 2006, Segal became a state representative for his district, and he is currently working on such issues as education, civil rights, election reform, and prison reform. He offers this advice for those considering a run for office: "Take stock of where you live and what is going on in that area in order to decide where you can do the most good. Don't be intimidated by the process."

Whatever steps you decide to take toward becoming more active in the political process, remember that you have the power to initiate change with your discussions, letters, votes, and career. Be the life of your party, and make sure your voice is heard!

## DIRECTORY OF POLITICALLY ACTIVE ORGANIZATIONS

Following is a sampling of the many organizations (descriptions provided by the organizations themselves) and the issues they are bringing to the attention of your politicians:

### POLITICAL ACTION
#### Center for American Progress Action Fund

Its mission is to transform progressive ideas into policy through rapid-response communications, legislative action, grassroots organizing and advocacy, and partnerships with other progressive leaders throughout the country and the world.

#### Citizens for Responsibility and Ethics in Washington (CREW)

Citizens for Responsibility and Ethics in Washington is a nonprofit 501(c)(3) organization dedicated to promoting ethics and accountability in government and public life by targeting government officials—regardless of party affiliation—who sacrifice the common good to special interests. CREW advances its mission using a combination of research, litigation, and media outreach. CREW employs the law as a tool to force officials to act ethically and lawfully and to bring unethical conduct to the public's attention.

#### Common Cause

Common Cause is a nonpartisan, nonprofit advocacy organization founded in 1970 as a vehicle for citizens to make their voices heard in the political process and to hold their elected leaders accountable to the public interest. Now with nearly three hundred thousand members and supporters and thirty-six state organizations, Common Cause remains committed to honest, open, and accountable government, as well as to encouraging citizen participation in democracy.

## Democracy 21

Democracy 21 is a nonprofit, nonpartisan organization dedicated to making democracy work for all Americans. Democracy 21 and its education arm, Democracy 21 Education Fund, work to eliminate the undue influence of big money in U.S. politics and to ensure the integrity and fairness of government decisions and elections. The organization promotes campaign finance reform and other political reforms to accomplish these goals.

## Generation Engage

Generation Engage is a nonpartisan initiative that engages young Americans—particularly those outside the boundaries of university campuses—in the evolving political debate to provide the knowledge, the organization, and the voice needed to shape the future they will inherit.

## MoveOn

The MoveOn family of organizations works to bring real Americans back into the political process. With over 3.3 million members across the United States—from carpenters to stay-at-home moms to business leaders—they work together to realize the progressive promise of our country. MoveOn is a service, a way for busy but concerned citizens to find their political voice in a system dominated by big money and big media.

## CONSTITUTIONAL RIGHTS
### Center for Constitutional Rights

The Center for Constitutional Rights is dedicated to advancing and protecting the rights guaranteed by the U.S. Constitution and the Universal Declaration of Human Rights. Founded in 1966 by attorneys who represented civil rights movements in the South, CCR is a nonprofit legal and educational organization committed to the creative use of law as a positive force for social change.

## VOTING RIGHTS
### FairVote

FairVote is acting to transform elections to achieve universal access to participation—a full spectrum of meaningful ballot choices and majority rule with fair representation for all. As a catalyst for change, it builds support for innovative strategies to win a constitutionally protected right to vote, universal voter registration, a national popular vote for president, instant runoff voting, and proportional representation.

## YOUTH EDUCATION AND ACTION
### Advocates for Youth

Advocates for Youth is dedicated to creating programs and advocating for policies that help young people make informed and responsible decisions about their reproductive and sexual health. Advocates provides information, training, and strategic assistance to youth-serving organizations, policy makers, youth activists, and the media in the United States and the developing world.

### YouthActionNet

YouthActionNet invests in the power and promise of young social entrepreneurs around the globe. Launched in 2001 by the International Youth Foundation, YouthActionNet strengthens, supports, and celebrates the role of young people in leading positive change in their communities.

### Youth In Focus

The guiding vision of Youth In Focus is of a world in which youth and adults share knowledge and power to create a more just, sustainable, and democratic society. Since 1990 YIF has pursued this vision by providing training, consulting, and coaching support in youth-led action research, evaluation, and planning (Youth REP) to underrepresented youth and adult allies working for positive change. Young people play lead roles in designing, doing, and following up on research or evaluation projects that serve to change or initiate a program, organization, community initiative, organizing campaign, or policy that affects them and their peers.

## ENVIRONMENTAL ACTION
### 1Sky
1Sky is dedicated to aggregating a massive nationwide movement by communicating a positive vision and a coherent set of national policies that rise to the scale of the climate challenge. It has been borne from the collective urgency and determination of leaders throughout the country.

### 350.org
350 is the "red line" for human beings, the most important number on the planet. The most recent science tells us that unless we can reduce the amount of carbon dioxide in the atmosphere to 350 parts per million, we will cause huge and irreversible damage to the earth. But solutions exist: all around the world, a movement is building to take on the climate crisis, to get humanity out of the danger zone and below 350.

### Energy Action Coalition
Energy Action united a diversity of organizations in an alliance that supports and strengthens the youth climate and energy movement.

### Environmental Working Group
The mission of the Environmental Working Group (EWG) is to use the power of public information to protect public health and the environment. EWG specializes in providing useful

resources (like *Skin Deep* and the *Shoppers' Guide to Pesticides in Produce*) to consumers while simultaneously pushing for national policy change.

## League of Conservation Voters

The mission of the League of Conservation Voters (LCV) is to advocate for sound environmental policies and to elect pro-environmental candidates who will adopt and implement such policies. Through its National Environmental Scorecard and Presidential Report Card, LCV informs the public about the most important environmental legislation of the past congressional session and shows people how their own and other representatives voted.

## Natural Resources Defense Council

The Natural Resources Defense Council (NRDC) is an environmental action group whose mission is to safeguard the earth: its people, its plants and animals, and the natural systems on which all life depends.

## Sierra Club

Since 1892, the Sierra Club has been working to protect communities, wild places, and the planet itself. It is the oldest, largest grassroots environmental organization in the United States.

## GAY RIGHTS
## Human Rights Campaign

The Human Rights Campaign is the country's largest civil rights organization working to achieve gay, lesbian, bisexual, and transgender equality. HRC strives to end discrimination against GLBT citizens and realize a nation that achieves fundamental fairness and equality for all. HRC seeks to improve the lives of GLBT Americans by advocating for equal rights and benefits in the workplace, ensuring families are treated equally under the law, and increasing public support among all Americans through innovative advocacy, education, and outreach programs.

## National Gay and Lesbian Task Force

The mission of the National Gay and Lesbian Task Force is to build the grassroots power of the GLBT community. It does this by training activists, equipping state and local organizations with the skills needed to organize broad-based campaigns to defeat anti-GLBT referenda and advance pro-GLBT legislation, and building the organizational capacity of its movement.

## HUMANITARIAN ACTION
## Genocide Intervention Network

The Genocide Intervention Network envisions a world in which the global community is willing and able to protect civilians from genocide and mass atrocities. Its mission is to empower individuals and communities with the tools to prevent and stop genocide.

## One

One is a campaign of over 2.4 million from all fifty states and over one hundred of the country's best-known and respected nonprofit, advocacy, and humanitarian organizations. The campaign is asking our leaders to do more to fight the emergency of global AIDS and extreme poverty and believes that allocating more of the U.S. budget toward providing basic needs like health, education, clean water, and food would transform the futures and hopes of an entire generation in the world's poorest countries.

## Witness

Witness uses video and online technologies to open the eyes of the world to human rights violations. It empowers people to transform personal stories of abuse into powerful tools for justice, promoting public engagement and policy change.

Updates to the preceding list will be available at the ***Ten Ways*** website.

## NOBODY LIKES A HYPOCRITE

Once you are done scrutinizing the activities of your local elected officials, it is time to make sure that you are practicing what you preach. There are many facets to explore when discussing how your consumption, transportation, and overall lifestyle choices affect not only our local communities but also the world at large. The next three chapters are devoted to the preservation of resources, the reduction of pollution, and using the power of your dollar to influence corporate consciousness. The best place to start exploring environmentally and ethically sound lifestyle choices is at home, so that is where we will begin.

# Chapter 4

# WAYS TO BE A GREEN GIANT

*Practical Ideas for Leading
an Eco-active Lifestyle*

When one tugs at a single thing in nature, he finds it attached
to the rest of the world.

*John Muir*

## IN THIS CHAPTER

- Sign of the Times: Caution!
- Restore, Reuse, and Recycle...But What? And How?
- Renew and Repurpose: Good for Your Wallet and the Earth's Finite Resources
- Embrace and Encourage Eco-friendly Habits
- Support Sound Environmental Policy
- *Ways* Guide to Leading the Green Charge
- Directory of Organizations Dedicated to the Environment
- Two Rs Down...

## SIGN OF THE TIMES: CAUTION!

We are living in unprecedented ecological times affecting humans and habitat alike. From violent tropical storms to disappearing polar bear populations, it is difficult to ignore the disturbing stories of loss and havoc being wrought all over the world. Struggles to control rapidly diminishing natural resources lead to displacement, poverty, illness, and violence—often for those already living on the margins. Crises like these are enormous in scope and complex in understanding and can be overwhelming, confusing, and scary. It's easy to feel disempowered, as though one person cannot single-handedly stop the inevitable. If you are feeling scared about the state of the planet, you are certainly justified; however, there is also plenty you can do today to be more environmentally responsible and ecologically minded. In many cases, little more than a commitment to changing a few of your everyday behaviors is required to make a difference.

When we enter into a conversation about the state of the environment and the implications of climate change, it is important to start locally and take stock of how our daily choices can be modified to be less taxing on the earth's resources. We can lead lifestyles that strive to reuse, renew, and recycle resources whenever possible, and this chapter offers suggestions for how to do just that. In addition, you will find information about environmental organizations that are doing work at local, national, and international levels. By joining forces with them, you can keep abreast of current environmental movements and lend your voice to the growing chorus calling for more stringent environmental legislation and corporate responsibility.

## RESTORE, REUSE, AND RECYCLE...BUT WHAT? AND HOW?

**Think Outside the Bin**  🕐=2  💲=1  🏠=2

We all know what to do with glass, paper, and plastic (see the plastic recycling guide on **page 90** to make sure you are getting it right), but recycling gets a little trickier as soon as we stray from the usual suspects. Before you relegate your cell phones or packing peanuts to the dump (where they too will leach toxins into the environment as they stubbornly resist decomposition), see if a little extra effort can't save them from an eternity in the landfill.

I use three main resources to aid me in my quest to throw away as little as possible. The first is **Earth 911's** recycling locator, which allows you to find places to recycle anything from fluorescent light bulbs (which contain mercury and can be recycled at most Ikea and Home Depot stores) to old phone books, just by entering in your ZIP code. It is one of the most comprehensive databases out there. The second resource is a blog by **Green America** titled "21 Things You Didn't Know You Can Recycle" with links to recycling agencies for everything from CD jewel cases to appliances. The third resource is *Real Simple's* "How to Recycle Anything" article, which is also available online from the magazine's website. Keep in mind that many of the following listed items contain such dangerous materials as mercury, lead, and chromium—all of which are toxins that should be kept out of landfills, whether your municipality mandates it yet or not.

Here are a few tough-to-recycle items that can be recycled using suggestions from the previous lists (and a little creative thinking, too!):

- **Appliances:** If your old appliances (air conditioners, microwaves, televisions) are not Energy Star rated, it is probably better to recycle them instead of donating them. Usually the store where you buy your new appliances will accept your old ones for recycling, especially since recycled steel is a valuable commodity. Otherwise, use Earth 911's recycling locator or find a reclamation center through the **Steel Recycling Institute.**

- **Athletic sneakers:** When you are a size 12 (yes, dainty me), your castoffs can add up quickly when calculating cubic feet in the landfill! Luckily, Nike will take back all old athletic sneakers regardless of brand at any of their over three hundred worldwide collection sites and will recycle them into Nike Grind, which is used to make playgrounds and other sports surfaces.

- **Beanie Babies (or any other random, not overly used novelty item):** No idea where ours came from. I know they are not mine, and my husband is also pleading ignorance. No matter: **eBay**, which is especially good for collectibles, is a good place to sell your unburied treasures. **Craig's List** is also a reliable place to post items for sale. As an added benefit, you are not only recycling, you are also earning some extra cash.

- **Broken video-game consoles, stereos, and speakers:** Use Earth 911's recycling locator to find a place to recycle these. Some electronics stores like Best Buy have recycling "events," which are days when all kinds of e-waste will be accepted for recycling.

- **CDs:** Look for a CD store that buys and sells used CDs. You can list and swap the rejects—a little hasty on that Hanson purchase, in retrospect, weren't you?—at **SwapaCD**. You can do the same with DVDs at **SwapaDVD**.

- **Printer cartridges/rechargeable batteries/computer hardware:** Many companies that make printer cartridges offer free recycling programs. Printer cartridges can be refilled and reused, so when you purchase your new cartridge, look for a postage-paid envelope in the new package. For example, Hewlett Packard's Planet Partners offers a recycling program for rechargeable batteries (the kind found in your laptops, phones, cameras, and printers), HP ink jet or laser printer cartridges, and all brands of computer and printing hardware. **Recycleplace** will pay for ink jet, laser, and toner cartridges as well as cell phones. Staples also offers rebates in exchange for cartridges.

- **Technotrash:** This includes CD jewel cases, various chargers, music and VHS tapes, and an old cell phone (cell phones are both useful and incredibly easy to recycle). **CollectiveGood** refurbishes cell phones and sells them for use in developing countries. **Call to Protect** gives cell phones to victims of domestic violence. Finally, for a fee of $30, **Greendisk** will send you a box that you can fill with up to seventy pounds of technotrash and mail back to them for processing.

- **Televisions:** With the switch to digital, there are a lot of people interested in (read: forced into) upgrading their sets. Tube televisions can contain up to eight pounds of lead, and some municipalities have already banned them from landfills. Start with Earth 911's recycling locator, or get in touch with your local Office Depot; many of them accept TVs for recycling.

- **The rest of it:** If you still find that you have items to dispose of, post your goodies where people looking for freebies go to look—**Freecycle** and **Craig's List**—or bring them to a local **Goodwill** or other thrift store.

## Put Away the Plastics  🕐=2 💲=2 🏠=3

Ah, the ubiquitous plastic—from bags to television sets and computers to automobiles, plastic is everywhere. The best thing and worst thing about conventional plastic is that this petrochemical product lasts forever—or close enough to it to outlast humans. Plastic, while often durable and sometimes recyclable, usually downcycles (becomes less and less functional with each cycle) until it finally settles into the landfill. In addition, certain plastics have been shown to leach chemicals into the environment. In a depressing double whammy, two of the biggest names in toxicity, polyvinyl chloride (PVC, which is found in food containers, toys, and pipes) and polycarbonate (the hard plastic used in computers and some reusable drinking bottles), are not generally recyclable, so they almost always go straight to the landfill.

Most every plastic product is marked with a numbered stamp according to its makeup. While you are probably familiar with the easy-to-recycle number one and two items, numbers three and seven (polycarbonate and PVC, respectively) seem to be everywhere—take a look at your containers if you don't believe me. However, as more and more companies offer similar products made from alternative ingredients, many products made with number three and seven plastics can easily be avoided. For a guide to the different types of plastics, see the following list.

Plastic may be necessary and unavoidable in certain instances (ever try using a wooden phone?), but certainly the less we use each day, the better off we'll all be. In order to curb your plastic consumption, start by eliminating your use of bottled water and plastic bags, both of which are produced by the billions. Also pay attention to the types of plastic that are used as packaging for products as varied as a new television to a container of yogurt. If you must buy a product swaddled in plastic, do your best to get the ones that are packaged in the types of plastic that can be recycled.

Of course now that you have decided to reduce your plastic usage, you will be left with a new problem: what to do with the plastic you already have? As I began to investigate how to safely dispose of my plastic, I realized two important facts:

1. **Not all plastics are created equal.** After a series of research studies suggested that number seven polycarbonates leached BPA (a toxic chemical) into our bodies, I decided to ditch my number seven Nalgene water bottles.[4] However, it was not that simple. Most curbside recycling programs don't take them, which made me realize that those puppies were headed to the landfill for a few thousand years, and this led to my second realization...

2. **Plastic is confusing!** I didn't know enough about plastic products, their potential health hazards, or how to recycle all the different types properly. I imagine many people, staring blankly at the numbered codes on the bottom of, say, their peanut butter jars, have felt this same frustration.

To further add to the confusion, rules for plastic collection vary depending on where you live. To quickly and easily get the information you need, check your town or city's recycling website to see which codes are accepted in your area. When you see just how much of your plastic is actually garbage-in-waiting, it will probably serve as even more motivation to begin reducing your consumption. While at first all of these numbers and acronyms may sound more complicated than the U.S. tax code, trust me, they're not. With a little legwork, you can learn the recycling rules in your area and avoid throwing away anything that could be reborn as a new product.

## Decoding Plastics

Here is a quick, easy guide to what each of those numbers actually means. Steer clear of those in bold, since they are potentially hazardous to your health.

- Numbers one and two: Most water, soda, juice, milk, and shampoo and soap bottles are made with PET or HDPE plastics. They are widely recyclable and safe as long as they are not reused, since they have been shown to leach chemicals after repeated washing or heating.

- **Number three: Includes vinyl or PVC—potentially hazardous because they can leach plasticizers and lead. They are also not recyclable.**

- Numbers four and five: Safe and recyclable—many food-storage containers and plastic wraps are made from these two types of plastic. Buy and use sparingly, though, as not all municipalities recycle, and they are often downcycled.

- **Number six: Polystyrene—more commonly known by the brand name, Styrofoam—is technically recyclable, but it is difficult to recycle due to its light weight. Many curbside recycling programs do not accept it. Polystyrene is also potentially hazardous to the environment, since it can leach styrene, a known carcinogen, as it breaks down.**

- **Number seven: PC/PA, number seven is the catchall for the types of plastic that do not fall into the previous six categories. Products in this category range from polycarbonate (PC), which is nonbiodegradable and potentially hazardous, to the safe and compostable polylactide (PA), which is made from**

plant materials like corn and used to produce products like
plates, bags, and bottles.

## Be a Bag Lady or Lad  🕐=1 💲=2 🏠=1

Several cities in the United States have banned or are moving
to ban the use of plastic bags, including Boston, Chicago,
San Francisco, and Seattle. Other countries such as Australia,
Bangladesh, Canada, China, France, India, and Ireland have
instituted bans or fees on plastic bags. Take a moment and
check out your plastic bag stash. You will probably find they
have accumulated everywhere—under the cabinet, in the
bottom of the closet, stuffed in a drawer, or even ironically
packed in a cloth bag that was specially designed to hold plastic
bags. No matter where you store your plastic bags, you will be
hard-pressed to get to the bottom of the heap unless you make
a concerted effort to stop accepting any more.

Fortunately, the solution to the bag quandary is easy: bring
your own!

**Reusable Bags** and **Envirosax** sell many varieties of shopping
and produce bags. Some fold into an ultra-compact pouch, while
many companies now put out bags that multitask as political
messages, charitable gifts, or fashion statements. Take the FEED
bags, for example, produced by twentysomething Lauren Bush.
The profits from the sale of these natural cotton and burlap
totes go toward reducing child hunger. And for those bags you
just have to dump—I'm thinking of the ones that hold my cat's
litter treats here—**BioBag** makes 100 percent biodegradable
and compostable plastic bags designed for more "delicate"
nonrenewable uses.

## Still Clinging to Your Plastics? Consider These Facts

- Plastic does not biodegrade. Instead, it photodegrades from exposure to sunlight (not present in landfills, by the way) and simply becomes smaller and smaller pieces of plastic, which linger indefinitely in the ecosystem.
- Disturbing amounts of plastic are now being found in the ocean. The section of the Pacific known as the Eastern Garbage Patch is a U.S.–sized floating continent of plastic that now outweighs the surface zooplankton there six to one.[5]
- Annual consumption of plastic bags in the United States is in the hundreds of billions.
- According to the Container Recycling Institute, Americans buy more than thirty-four billion bottles of water each year, yet only one-third are actually recycled. The other twenty-five billion or so? Landfilled, dumped, or incinerated.[6]

### Break the Bottled-Water Habit  🕐=1  $=1  🏭=2

Your one-dollar bottle of water may seem easily affordable, but get your calculators out, because the environmental price tag of those bottles is steep. It's not just water we are guzzling out of those single-use bottles; according to the Earth Policy Institute, the main ingredient in water bottles is oil—seventeen million barrels of crude oil each year, to be exact.[7] What's more, producing the bottle requires nearly seven times the amount of water that actually fills it, and the manufacturing and transportation process of *one bottle* of water—especially when it comes from exotic lands such as Fiji or France—can use up to a quarter gallon of fossil fuel and emit 1.2 pounds of greenhouse gases (times thirty-four billion, remember). The United States alone could fuel a hundred thousand cars a year from the oil it currently uses to produce water bottles. All this for a product that begins as tap water nearly 25 percent of the time and is essentially free, if you're willing to procure a reusable vessel.[8] So the next time you are tempted to pay for a plastic bottle of water, consider taking these steps instead:

- If you live in a place where tap water can be consumed safely (and most people in the United States do), then you are paying between 250 and 10,000 times the cost of tap water each time you purchase a bottle. What's more, if you're drinking purified water like Aquafina or Dasani, your bottle probably comes from municipal sources anyway. Sucker.
- If you don't like the taste of your tap water, use an inexpensive water-filtration system—such as Pur or Brita. See if you need a filtration system, and weigh your options over at **Water Filter Comparisons** or the **Green Guide**.
- Carry a reusable water container for water on the go. I love the stainless steel water bottles from **Klean Kanteen, Earthlust,** and **EcoUsable.** EcoUsable even has a line of stainless steel bottles with a built-in filter.
- While you're at it, carry a reusable mug for hot beverages like coffee and tea as well as reusable lunch containers. As an added bonus, many shops and cafes have begun offering discounts to patrons who provide their own containers.

## SUCCESS STORY

### Reducing the World's Forkprint

Plastic silverware and most plastic containers are difficult or impossible to recycle, as well as just a poor alternative to real silverware—have you ever had a stainless steel fork break midbite or tried to cut anything with a plastic knife? Stephanie Bernstein never meant to start a company, but she was so appalled during college by the emerging trend of giving out to-go containers at her local ice cream shop—even when patrons wanted to eat *in*—that she began to search for alternatives. Her rationale was simple: "We were carrying around our coffee mugs, so why weren't we just carrying around everything we needed to eat a to-go meal?"

Based on her experience working for several purveyors of natural products and as a yoga instructor and raw food chef, Bernstein started to sell her own line of reusable silverware in 2004 at the age of twenty-eight. At first, **To-Go Ware** was a company of one, and Bernstein sourced and sold all of her bamboo silverware while still working a full-time job as a sales manager for **World of Good**. In 2007, she hired her first employees and began to oversee her rapidly expanding business full-time. Today the company continues to expand and now sells stainless-steel food carriers, bags, and flatware wraps made from recycled plastic bags and bottles, in addition to reusable flatware. Bernstein is both pragmatic and excited about her fledgling foray into sustainable business. "There were times when I resisted being a business because I wasn't sure that I knew how to run one, but if you really believe in your product, there are resources for women entrepreneurs and socially responsible companies."

### Complete the Cycle with Compost 🕐=2 💲=2 🏢=2

According to the Environmental Protection Agency (EPA), Americans send nearly fifty billion tons of food waste to landfills, at a cost of one billion dollars, every year. That's nearly a quarter of the food we prepare.[9] Aside from being a terrible waste, especially given the numbers of hungry and poor in this country, this practice also squanders food's potential for good (in the form of compost). Instead, these leftovers turn into methane (a global warming gas) in the lightless, airless environment of the landfill. Double waste. With a little help from a compost pile, though, you can turn much of your rotten stuff into the sweetest of soils. Consider that after putting all your recyclables in the appropriate bins, your remaining garbage will mostly be compostable matter such as eggshells, vegetable trimmings, coffee grounds, and other food scraps. By composting, you mimic nature's method of closing the loop, as organic matter breaks down into nutrient-rich supersoil. If those billions of tons of food waste could be effectively composted, just imagine how many farms could forego toxic chemical fertilizers in favor of this naturally superior alternative. I'll give you a hint: lots.

Depending on where you live and the weather conditions in your region, certain compost bins and systems may be better than others. For tips on starting your own outdoor compost, visit the **Environmental Protection Agency (EPA)** website, and use the search terms "create your own compost pile." You can also check out *Let It Rot! The Gardener's Guide to Composting* by Stu Campbell, *Composting: An Easy Household Guide* by Nicky Scott, or *Basic Composting: All the Skills and Tools You Need to Get Started* edited by Eric Ebeling.

If you live in a city or apartment where the typical compost pile would not likely be welcome (with regard to either square footage or smell), you can buy an indoor composter. For example, the **NatureMill** can handle up to 120 pounds a month of organic waste—vegetables, coffee grounds, dairy, meat, or fish. The upper tray provides the necessary environment for composting—cultures that consume the waste products, heat, moisture, and air flow—and the lower tray holds the completed product. Every two weeks or so, a light goes on in the lower tray to let you know that your new compost is ready to add to your grateful garden or house plants, and all without the smell of rotting food! If you find that you need even more natural fertilizer, many coffee shops now give away leftover grounds that are ready to use in your garden.

# SUCCESS STORY

## The Accidental Recycler

As a psychology major, Jeff Simeon swore that he would avoid marketing, a common career path for those with his degree. However, when he realized he could use his talents to encourage people to recycle and compost, his plans changed. Simeon, now a program specialist for the Santa Barbara County Public Works Department Resource Recovery and Waste Management Division (an acronym in need of some vowels, if ever there was one), had not planned on working with recycling programs at all. His plan after college was to work at high-paying service jobs, save a bunch of money, and start his own organic farm—but an environmental studies class in his junior year of college changed all that. His interest in growing food and his discovery of how the energy it takes to produce food impacts our health and the environment spurred him to study more about the relationship between the environment and food; he was even able to squeeze in an environmental studies minor by the time he graduated.

After graduating, he worked for the Santa Barbara Sailing Center, all the while keeping an eye out for jobs that would allow him to help people learn about diverting resources from the landfill. The way materials are dumped indiscriminately into landfills is a lot of the reason Simeon is so concerned. He says, "We have a choice about how we interact with the earth's resources. Of course we have basic needs such as food, nutrients, and shelter, so there is always going to be a level of take. However, there are also ways to manage these extractions, so it is not just a one-way ticket to the landfill."

In a county that diverts 69 percent of its waste from the landfill and was recently awarded the Solid Waste Association of North America's (SWANA) gold award, Simeon's responsibilities are varied and innovative. He is in charge of the county's backyard composting program, school recycling programs, and education programs, and he manages large outreach events such as the county's participation in Earth Day and Coastal Cleanup Day. While Simeon knows he is changing attitudes and raising awareness about waste reduction, he acknowledges there is still more work to be done. "Just because we [Santa Barbara County] are in the landfill business now doesn't mean we always want to be," he says. Sounds like a good goal for us all.

## Encourage Friends and Municipalities to Join You in the Fun
🕐=3 💲=1 🏠=3

Some municipalities charge residents to dispose of garbage, but yard trimmings, food waste, and recyclables are all collected for free—so find out if your town or county is recycling everything it can. If it isn't, contact your local elected officials and ask for more extensive recycling policies. With enough effort on the part of local communities, it is possible to dispose of almost nothing. A friend of mine who spent a year living in Sweden threw away *one* item during her entire stay—a broken wine glass. How does Sweden do it? According to the website of the Bubbetorp transfer station in the town of Karlskrona, the Swedish system operates under the simple principle that "the better we sort, the fewer dumps we need." Hard to argue with that. Make sure that everyone you know is following the recycling rules, too. In the end, you'll be saving everyone money and resources. You can also find additional local recycling facilities at **Recycling Centers**. If you live on a college campus, start with your campus environmental club, and see if you can team up with them to get a campus-wide composting/recycling program going. Chances are there is a garden growing somewhere on campus that will be very grateful for your organic matter. Lastly, don't forget to spread the message by impressing your friends with your new and catchy composting puns. Worms can't describe how easy it is.

## RENEW AND REPURPOSE: GOOD FOR YOUR WALLET AND THE EARTH'S FINITE RESOURCES

One of the best things about being in your twenties is that chances are good you will find yourself with the need to be creative about how to survive on limited resources. Given the fact that we live in uncertain environmental and economic times, it is nice to know that reusing is a great way to save money while going easy on the planet.

### Swap Your Books (and CDs, DVDs, and Video Games)
🕐=2 💲=2 ⛁=1

One excellent option that has sprung up for reuse in the last few years is Internet swapping clubs for books, CDs, and DVDs. The services are generally free or available for a nominal fee. Among these clubs are **Paperback Swap** (books, CDs, DVDs), **Bookins** (books and DVDs), and **Swaptree** (books, CDs, DVDs, and video games). For college or grad students, these services are also a great way to acquire some of those superexpensive academic books for the price of postage. I am a member over at Paperback Swap, and the swapping works like this:

1. I establish an account and a swapping nickname (such as Ladynerd Johnson).
2. I list the ISBN numbers of the books I have to swap (this minimizes confusion about editions, correct titles, etc.).
3. I have to send a book before I can get credit to order a book, so I wait for a request, usually while going about other business.
4. I get an excited communication from Paperback Swap that a book has been requested.
5. I take a breather from my giddiness in order to print a label, wrap the book, and mail it—media rate of course. This little bit of work is definitely the low point in my book swapping.

6. I create a wish list of titles I would like, and the kindly and wise algorithm on the PB Swap sight keeps an eye out for me.

7. I wait.

8. OH, HAPPY DAY! I get an email saying that a book I had placed on my wish list is now available!

9. I put in a request for the book, which takes approximately two seconds. A couple of days later, I get an email telling me that my book is on its way—it's full of exclamation points again.

10. I wait, again.

11. WHEEEE!!! I receive a book in the mail. I am overjoyed. Step five was worth it. I have a new-to-me book in hand.

## Yard Sale 🕐=3 💲=1 ▦=1

Before you deem your unwanted possessions junk or bound for the recycling bin, see if they are treasures for anyone else. A yard sale (note: you don't actually need a yard to have one of these) is a great way to meet some fun people, make some extra cash, and lighten your load. If you don't like talking to people, then perhaps you have a curmudgeonly grandparent who can work the table for you. Everyone knows grandparents drive the hardest bargains anyway. Here are a few tips for a successful yard sale:

- **Plan a date when you know people will be out and about.** Choose a summer weekend or one that coincides with another event already occurring in your neighborhood or apartment building. Consider joining forces with a few friends as well and hold a neighborhood yard sale. It is a nice way to build community, and you won't have to advertise all by yourself!

- **Advertise!** Send out an email to your friends, those in your community, and/or place a free posting on **Craig's List.**

- **Put up signs.** Even if the yard sale has been well publicized, a little nudge from a sign on the day of the sale may be just what people need to check it out.

- **Display everything in an attractive and neat manner.** You are less likely to buy items in a store when everything is in a heap—the same goes for a yard sale.

- **Be prepared to haggle...but not too much.** Of course, there are always those looking for a deal—hold your ground with prices only if something has significant value. Otherwise, the point of a sale like this is to rid yourself of excess possessions, so let them go!

## EMBRACE AND ENCOURAGE ECO-FRIENDLY HABITS

My favorite characters in the much-acclaimed *Lord of the Rings* trilogy were not the fuzzy-toed hobbits or the gallant Aragorn. Rather, my heart belonged to those bit players, the Ents, who are featured prominently in the second of the three books/ movies when they rise to the defense of the forests (and also the protagonists, as luck would have it) and defeat the evil wizard, Saruman. Written largely during World War II by J. R. R. Tolkien, it has been argued that much of this complex story was an allegory about the dangers of industrialism, discrimination, and might over right—all problems that face our society today. It was impossible not to cheer for these gentle giants, who rose up to protect those who were fighting for the cause of Middle Earth. Sadly, here on regular, unmagical earth, massive deforestation, pollution, and degradation of habitat are major problems: trees, oceans, and other fragile ecosystems are not able to protect themselves. By changing our everyday habits with regard to the use of natural resources and encouraging others to do the same, we can make a big dent in our overall environmental impact on the planet.

## Become a Tree Hugger  🕐=2 $=1 🏠=1

Trees are not just crucial parts of habitats, they are also a crucial part of maintaining global temperatures and air quality. When trees are cut down en masse, it is a threefold tragedy: first, their ability to gather carbon from the atmosphere is lost; second, the carbon stored in the tree is released as the tree is used; and third, entire ecosystems that depended on the trees for existence are destroyed.[10] According to the **Intergovernmental Panel on Climate Change**, almost 20 percent of greenhouse gases released into the atmosphere are produced from cutting down trees.[11] This is second only to the greenhouse gases emitted from fossil fuel emissions. With temperatures rising, trees have never been more in need of your voice than they are now. So short of living in a tree for 738 days, as Julie Butterfly Hill so famously did, what can you do?

First, get to know the issues and areas most in jeopardy by visiting the websites of the **Global Canopy Programme** and the **Amazon Conservation Team**, both of which are dedicated to conservation and education. Often those who are cutting down trees are doing so because it is their only way to make a living, so a holistic approach to the problem of deforestation is crucial. For more ideas about ways to get involved with sustainable development efforts, check out the environmental organizations listed at the end of this chapter. You can also advocate for preservation of natural habitats and forests by donating, volunteering, and working with many of the environmental organizations listed in the appendix.

## Be a Paperwise Post-consumer  🕐=2 $=2 🏠=1

We won't see an end to paper use in our lifetime, and as an author, I suppose this is good news, but it is crucial that we keep in mind that until alternative forms of paper production are developed on a large scale, all paper originates as forest. What's more, virgin-paper production is both water and chlorine intensive. Whether you're printing or blowing your nose, the bottom line with paper is that you should strive to buy and use as few paper products as possible. Here are more tips to help you green your paper use:

- **Go retro.** What did we do before disposable paper products? Yes, some products would be difficult to eschew completely (ahem, toilet paper); others not so much. Napkins, paper towels, and facial tissues, for example, can all be replaced with their cloth originators. After all, handkerchiefs were used to blow noses long before they became a fashion accessory.

- **Use sparingly and recycle.** From paper towels to computer paper, use only what you need. Always print paper double-sided, and use old envelopes and excess printed paper for scrap. Never throw recyclable paper away. Those branches buried in the landfill are lost forever.

- **Eighty or above is passing.** Buy paper products made from the highest amount of post-consumer recycled paper you can find. Seventh Generation and 365 (Whole Foods), whose products range from toilet paper to facial tissue, have some of the highest overall content. Besides, it's not like your butt knows the difference between virgin and recycled toilet paper. According to the Natural Resources Defense Council (NRDC), "If every household in the United States replaced just one roll of virgin fiber toilet paper (500 squares) with 100 percent recycled ones, we could save 423,900 trees."

- **Don't squeeze the Charmin.** Boycott brands and send emails to the companies that needlessly cut down trees for these types of products. It is crucial that you know where your paper comes from. Never use products made from timber logged from old-growth forests. As of this writing, some of the most well-known names—Kleenex facial tissues, Bounty paper towels, and Charmin toilet paper, to name a few—are made with 0 percent recycled paper content.[12] Look for the Forest Stewardship Council (FSC) seal of approval on the paper products you buy.

- **Just say no to chlorine.** Buy paper products that have been made without chlorine bleach, which ends up in the water supply and is toxic to people and fish. Furthermore, dioxins are also released during the manufacturing process of chlorine-bleached paper.[13] Look for the TCF (totally chlorine-free) or PCF (processed chlorine-free) labels.

- **Take it to work.** If you work at a company that doesn't use recycled paper, urge them to do so. The extra cost of recycled paper can be justified by using less paper overall—something that can be easily achieved through increased efforts to print on both sides and eliminate superfluous print jobs.

See the complete list of napkins, paper towels, facial tissues, and bathroom tissues to purchase and avoid on the **NRDC's Shopper's Guide to Home Tissue Products.**

### Invest in Ocean Stocks  🕐=2  💲=1  ▦=2

Our oceans are another crucial part of the earth's ecosystem, and they too are showing alarming signs of ill health, such as a decreasing number of fish, an increase of "dead zones" (areas of no or low oxygen that are unable to support marine life), and warmer, more acidic conditions. Much of the deterioration of the earth's oceans is due to three main factors: pollution (often in the form of runoff), destructive fishing practices, and rising temperatures. In short, people are to blame. One of the reasons we have begun to rethink what we throw away is that it turns out "away" isn't as far as we thought. Remember that the mercury we now eat with our tuna was once thrown "away" by some company, and you will begin to appreciate the importance of using products that biodegrade and are not composed of chemicals that can leave behind dangerous residues. There are several easy ways to help take care of the world's oceans. Marah Hardt, a research fellow at the **Blue Ocean Institute**, offers ten tips to help heal our oceans.

## Ways to Keep Our Oceans (and Our Menus) Well Stocked

1. **Make educated choices when purchasing seafood in restaurants or grocery stores.** Visit the Blue Ocean Institute website for a guide to healthy, sustainable seafood and for information about the institute's text messaging service that offers on-the-go information. It also offers a wallet-sized sushi chart to keep on hand.

2. **Tell your local representatives that you support expansion of marine reserves to protect valuable and threatened marine species and habitats.** To learn more about marine reserves and take action visit the websites of the **Partnership for Interdisciplinary Studies of Coastal Oceans (PISCO)** and the **National Marine Sanctuaries.**

3. **Visit the National Oceanic and Atmospheric Administration (NOAA) website to learn about management of marine areas in your neck of the woods.** Click on the link to your local fisheries management council. This will provide information about upcoming council meetings and other events in your area.

4. **Help reduce climate change.** Take steps to curb your own carbon footprint, and encourage action by your local community and schools. Support urgent action to reduce greenhouse gas emissions by writing to your representatives in Congress. Several bills regarding ocean legislation and climate change are currently in Congress; you can make a difference by voicing support for measures that protect the seas and the people who depend on them, which is ultimately all of us. Visit the **OceanConservancy** website to sign up for legislative action alerts.

5. **Limit your use of plastic.** Not only does new plastic require use of fossil fuels, but every year tens of thousands of seabirds, sea turtles, and marine mammals drown or starve due to entanglement in marine debris, over half of which is from plastic. Once in the ocean, it is hard to clean up plastic waste, so it is best to stop it at the source. Demand less, and less will be produced.

6. **Participate in beach cleanups.** These events are a good way to get to know your community and help keep garbage out of the sea or prevent it from reentering the sea. This is also a great way to introduce kids to the concept that "all drains lead to the ocean" and that the ocean is not endless; it is just a big, salty pool, and what goes in eventually washes back—literally and symbolically.

7. **Reduce lawn fertilizers, stop washing your car on the street, and don't litter.** Again, all drains lead to the sea. Preventing chemicals and pollutants from going in is much easier than trying to get them back out

8. **Support organic farming and local farming practices that produce grass-fed, free-range meats and that do not**

**use massive amounts of fertilizer.** The latter contains tons of nitrogen, which washes into the ocean and contributes to massive "dead zones," like the one in the Gulf of Mexico.

9. **Buy seafood that is locally raised/caught whenever possible.** This ensures that you know where the fish comes from and how it was caught. Of course, you'll want to make sure that this information leads you to conclude that it was caught sustainably! Choosing local fish also reduces the carbon footprint of shipping and packaging, which means that your fish will be fresher and tastier, too.

10. **Experience it.** This is the best way to gain the inspiration that will ultimately fuel your actions to help protect the oceans. Go on—slip into that watery realm. Grab a mask and just float for a while. Or if swimming isn't your thing, take a boat ride on a small boat—the kind where you can feel the spray of the waves. Or walk along the seashore, collect some shells, skip some rocks, and watch the moon pull the tide. If you don't live near the water, check out the BBC documentary *Blue Planet*, an incredible look beneath the waves in those places most of us will never quite get to. Get to know this largest living space on the planet. It is a world of inspiration, vitality, mystery, remarkable beauty, and untold promise. Learn what is there, and let yourself be inspired.

## More Organizations Devoted to Oceans

**Heal the Bay**
**Monterey Bay Aquarium**
**OceanConservancy**
**Waterkeeper Alliance**

## Do It in the Dorm   🕐=3  💲=1  🏢=3

While environmental stewardship might not be the only kind of green you experiment with in those formative college years (I *ree*fer, of course, to summer jobs), this particular dalliance has the potential to change the world. Many college students are already making efforts to increase sustainability around campus. **The Sierra Club** puts together an annual list of the greenest colleges called the "Cool Schools." What makes a school cool? Initiatives range from recycling and composting to energy and water conservation. The list is updated annually, and descriptions of schools and programs are available on the Sierra Club's website. Visit the site to get ideas for your school and to draw attention to eco-projects that have already been implemented.[14] Even if your university hasn't been ranked as a cool school yet, visit the website for the **American College and University Presidents Climate Commitment,** and be sure that your college or university president has signed the commitment. The Presidents Climate Commitment signatories pledge to "exercise leadership in their communities and throughout society by modeling ways to minimize global warming emissions, and by providing the knowledge and the educated graduates to achieve climate neutrality." You can read the full commitment and also download the complete list of schools on the website.

## SUCCESS STORY

### An Unusual Kid

May Boeve went to Middlebury College expecting to receive a good education, but she never realized that by the time she graduated, she'd have co-founded a national environmental movement and co-authored a book, *Fight Global Warming Now.*

As I listened to Boeve describe accomplishment after accomplishment while at school, I began to wonder if she went to college for seven years. She did take a semester off, but she and her friends spent those three months touring the country in a biodiesel-powered bus, visiting sixty-five high schools, and working to get students engaged in issues of the environment.

Back at school, she began to study global climate change, and along with her classmates, formed a student group that quickly became the largest of its kind in the country. "Everyone was working toward common, achievable goals, such as lowering the thermostat by 2 degrees or instituting a fee for parking on campus. One after another we would win these little battles, and we even got the board of trustees to commit to being carbon neutral by 2016," she explains. Through her involvement with this group, Boeve also was able to attend the 2005 UN Climate Conference in Montreal.

The group eventually joined up with Bill McKibben, one of the preeminent writers on climate change issues and a scholar in residence at Middlebury College. McKibben asked Boeve and other members of her climate change group to help with a five-day march in Vermont to call on leaders to cut carbon emissions 80 percent by the year 2050. The march was the largest global warming rally in history, and the group decided to go national—and just like that, the Step It Up movement was born.

With 1,400 events in every state, the Spring 2007 Step It Up campaign was a hugely successful grassroots collaboration of many environmental groups. The goals were simple: get politicians to commit to cutting carbon emissions 80 percent by 2050, and get the general public educated and empowered about ways to demand change. Many high-profile politicians including Barack Obama and Hillary Clinton signed the pledge. Boeve says, "It was about building a national grassroots movement that would have political power. We felt like we were doing something important and that we were on the vanguard of this initiative."

Boeve got her degree a few months before the first Step It Up event, but the thought of getting a "real job" had never crossed her mind. "I was never one of those people that goes to career fairs. I have always considered myself an activist, and my parents were very supportive. They always knew they had a bit of an unusual kid on their hands, so it didn't come as a wild shock to them that I didn't want to get a normal job."

After another event later that fall, the entire Step It Up team went to the International Climate Conference in Bali and tried to figure out the next steps toward an international day of climate-change action. Boeve and friends came back with an updated mission, and **350.org** was born. 350.org is working to inform the public about the current science of climate change and encouraging all political leaders to adopt an international carbon reduction agreement…quickly.

Boeve is currently based in the 350.org offices in San Francisco, working to communicate the importance of the organization's mission to people all over the world. For those who are interested in getting involved in environmental initiatives, Boeve says that while she knows many millennials may feel overwhelmed, the most important thing to do is to start participating, and trust that you will eventually find the right fit. "You can't always work on the perfect campaign right off the bat," she says. "Just look for the job that will have the most impact in a field you care a lot about. Then you are guaranteed to engage people on the issues, influence others, influence politics, and ultimately make a difference."

## Bring Your Eco-friendly Ideas to Work Day 🕐=2 💲=1 ▦=3

Most of us spend more time in the office than we do at home, so it makes sense that we should try to bring our green practices with us to our places of business. More likely than not, your co-workers and bosses will be receptive to gentle suggestions about such simple energy-saving (read: money-saving) ideas as recycling and emissions reductions. As an added bonus, the more money you save your company, the more they'll have lying around for raises and office parties (environmentally friendly ones, of course). Regardless of your personal reward, though, everyone benefits when companies embrace more sustainable practices, so don't leave your values at home.

Encourage the same types of environmentally savvy ventures at work that you have initiated at home. Recommend that your company use CFL light bulbs, turn off equipment at night, buy paper products with a high level of post-consumer recycled material, and conserve water. In addition, encourage your employer to join the **EPA's Green Power Partnership**, which works with companies and organizations to find and utilize available green power in the region. Check into the possibility of telecommuting a few days a week as well. You know you wouldn't mind wearing pajamas all day, watching *Judge Judy*, and eating cereal for lunch. For more tips on dialing down your commute, see **page 233 in chapter 9.**

All of your excitement about saving your company energy and money might even be parlayed into a new job for you. Many companies are so eager to launch environmental initiatives that they have begun to create positions to oversee implementation and outreach of these types of programs. According to David Beschen, former manager of corporate communications at Microsoft and founder of Greendisk, an electronics recycling company, "In order to attract young, talented employees who are also likely to be interested in the environment, corporations must have sustainable programs in place."

## SUCCESS STORY

### *Respektingivande:* Swedish for "Awesome"

Twenty-eight-year-old Anne DeMelle always knew that she wanted to align her career with her values, so the nonprofit world was a logical place to start. "The work atmosphere is so much fun; everyone is there for the same reason, and they are all passionate about what they are doing," she says. After graduating from the College of William and Mary with a bachelor's degree in philosophy, DeMelle quickly found a job working as a development associate at the **Environmental Working Group (EWG)**. Her determination to work for a variety of nonprofits and to immerse herself in the field spurred her on to work in various roles with several environmental and social justice nonprofits. While she enjoyed the challenge of each subsequent job's additional responsibilities, she realized that she wanted to be involved more directly with the projects she was writing grants about. So, in an unusual move, DeMelle decided to make the jump from the public sector to the private one; she applied and was accepted into a program for a master's in strategic leadership toward sustainability at the Blekinge Institute of Technology in Karlskrona, Sweden.

The program is based on a whole-systems perspective and trains graduates to work with businesses, communities, and organizations to become more sustainable. This degree helped to hone skills DeMelle now uses to help companies make strategic plans and implement sustainable business practices.

After completing the program in Sweden, DeMelle worked as a sustainability analyst for a multimillion-dollar outdoor retailer, and when an opportunity came to work for a sustainability business-consulting firm in her home state of Washington, she jumped at the chance. Now her days are spent working with companies ranging from renewable energy start-ups to multinationals to government agencies developing and implementing plans for systemic, sustainable changes. "I usually start by assessing a company's carbon footprint and making suggestions about what they can do to reduce it and save money," she says. "When they see the results, they are excited to do more. Our goal is to give businesses a better understanding of sustainability and how it actually benefits their bottom line. When you ground sustainability in business terms and financial analysis, they're very receptive to making changes." Once companies have implemented DeMelle's suggestions, she and her company work themselves out of the equation and move on to the next business in need of an environmental overhaul.

**Tell Them about It** 🕐=3 💲=1 🏢=1

Once you have established your own personal environmental initiatives, why not gently encourage others to do the same? Many people are not conserving energy or recycling, simply because they don't have the information or infrastructure necessary to do it. By acting as a catalyst to bring some of these issues to the forefront of a discussion with your larger community (work, school, and friends), you will help advance the widespread environmental changes you wish to see enacted. At the very least, you'll have something interesting to twitter about or edit your current Facebook status with.

## SUPPORT SOUND ENVIRONMENTAL POLICY

No matter what your political affiliations, it is critical for the health of the environment that we reach some common energy-efficiency goals. These objectives should include a reduction of nonrenewable energy use (i.e., fossil fuels), the development of regenerative energy solutions (i.e., wind, solar, tidal), and the creation of more jobs based on these widely implemented technologies. Be sure that you stay educated about environmental issues by reading the news, following the latest legislative matters, and subscribing to email announcements from the organizations you support.

Armed with this knowledge, be willing to discuss these issues with friends and to vote for the candidates that most align with your beliefs. Check out your candidates' environmental voting records at the League of Conservation Voters and at the **Sierra Club,** which updates candidates' positions on its website and puts out a voting guide for each election. To see what you can do to support a greener economy, check out **Green for All.** For more ideas about how to get more politically involved on behalf of the environment (or any other cause), see **chapter 3.**

## Hire Mother Earth a Good Lawyer  🕐=2 💲=2 🏢=1

There are several organizations that are devoted to fighting (in court, if necessary) to protect the earth's natural resources. The scientists, lawyers, and environmental specialists who work for these nonprofit organizations take direct action to protect wildlife against such injustices as pollution, overfishing, and overgrazing. These types of organizations include **Earthjustice, Natural Resources Defense Council (NRDC),** and **Defenders of Wildlife.** All of these organizations keep members updated about campaigns they are working on, which can range from preventing more drilling in the Arctic to holding the line on rules and regulations governing the Endangered Species Act. In addition to donating money and becoming a member to support the work of these groups, you can also volunteer, intern, or find a career with these organizations. For more ideas about ways to turn your passion into your career, see chapter 10.

## Work with Your Favorite Environmental Organization
🕐=3 💲=1 🏢=2

From sending emails on behalf of the environmental cause you are most passionate about to taking part in a full-on rally or protest in order to get the attention of a pollution-causing corporation, there are many ways to get involved directly with the environmental movement. For more ideas on writing effective letters about policies, see **page 64 in chapter 3**, and for volunteer resources and ideas, check out **chapter 2**. No matter what actions you decide to take, getting involved with an environmental organization is a good way to learn more about issues, meet like-minded people, and join forces with others who are trying to implement world-changing ideas.

**Launch Your Own Campaign** 🕐=4 💲=3 🏢=4

There are many ways to turn your personal passion into a national movement. Perhaps you want to encourage all of your friends to send a petition to local lawmakers, or maybe you want to draw attention to a local company's less-than-stellar environmental practices. Whether you choose a letter writing drive or a rally at town hall, the following are a few tips for running an effective environmental campaign.

## *WAYS* GUIDE TO LEADING THE GREEN CHARGE

1. **Do your research.** From cleaning the ocean to saving the rainforest, be sure to have all of your facts in order about the problem you're addressing and how your campaign can help, and be ready to explain succinctly why the issue is important and deserves attention.

2. **Think short and sweet.** Remember that you want to appeal to the largest number of people from the broadest demographic, so be sure your message is clear and answers these three questions: What's the problem? Why should people care? What can people do to help? Both **350.org** and **Green Jobs Now** are good examples of focused, effective campaigns, so check out their websites for further inspiration.

3. **Form partnerships.** In order to launch a large-scale campaign or movement, it will be necessary to reach

beyond your immediate circle of friends. Research other organizations with similar goals and approach them about sponsorship, partnership, or the possibility of sharing ideas and mailing lists.

4. **Congrats! You ARE the communications director.** Depending on the scale and length of your campaign, you may want to start your own website and/or blog. Be sure to ask any partner organizations to post information about your campaign on their websites, and if they have regular email communications with members, ask them to include information about your cause.

5. **Have an affair...with the media.** If you are going to hold an event, utilize the free publicity media and social-networking sites offer. Start a campaign and ask your Facebook friends and Twitter followers to become fans and ask their friends to do the same. Write a compelling press release, post it on your Facebook page, and send it out to local newspapers and television and radio stations. Follow up with a phone call inquiring if these news outlets have any questions or would like any additional information. News outlets are often looking for stories to fill a time slot or partial page, so a well-written press release is often welcome in the newsroom. Sometimes a well-placed story is all your campaign needs to turn a good idea with limited resources into a large-scale, effective event.

6. **Get a little help from celebs.** If you know that your cause is one that would benefit from a little star power, be sure to invite local politicians and other high-profile people whose presence may ensure that your event is well attended and well publicized.

# DIRECTORY OF ORGANIZATIONS DEDICATED TO THE ENVIRONMENT

In addition to the environmental organizations already mentioned in this chapter, here is a sample of the many environmental organizations (descriptions provided by organizations) doing great work to help heal and protect the environment. For more organizations and updates to this list, visit the *Ten Ways* website.

## The Campus Climate Challenge

The Campus Climate Challenge is a project of more than thirty leading youth organizations throughout the United States and Canada. The Challenge leverages the power of young people to organize on college campuses and high schools across Canada and the United States to win 100% Clean Energy policies at their schools.

## The Climate Project

The Climate Project (TCP) is an international nonprofit founded by Nobel laureate and former vice president Al Gore with a mission to increase public awareness of the climate crisis at a grassroots level worldwide. TCP consists of a professional staff and more than 2,600 dedicated volunteers throughout the United States, Australia, Canada, India, Spain, the UK, and Indonesia, all personally trained by Al Gore to present a version of the slide show featured in the Academy Award–winning film *An Inconvenient Truth*.

## Defenders of Wildlife

Dedicated to the protection of all native wild animals and plants in their natural communities, Defenders of Wildlife focuses its programs on what scientists consider two of the most serious environmental threats to the planet: (1) the accelerating rate of extinction of species and the associated loss of biological diversity, and (2) habitat alteration and destruction.

## Earth Action Network

The Earth Action Network is a nonprofit, environmental/social justice organization dedicated to promoting the healing of our society and our planet.

## Earth Share

Founded by its member charities in 1988, EarthShare is an opportunity for environmentally conscious employees and workplaces to support hundreds of environmental groups through workplace payroll contribution campaigns. EarthShare participates in campaigns at hundreds of public- and private-sector workplaces.

## Environmental Defense Fund

Guided by science, the Environmental Defense Fund evaluates environmental problems and works to create and advocate solutions that win lasting political, economic, and social support, because they are nonpartisan, cost-efficient, and fair.

## Greenpeace

Greenpeace is the leading independent campaigning organization that uses peaceful, direct action and creative communication to expose global environmental problems and to promote solutions that are essential to a green and peaceful future.

## The Rainforest Alliance

The Rainforest Alliance works to conserve biodiversity and ensure sustainable livelihoods by transforming land-use practices, business practices, and consumer behavior.

## The Sierra Club

The Sierra Club's members are more than 1.3 million of your friends and neighbors. Inspired by nature, they work together to protect our communities and the planet. The Club is the nation's oldest, largest, and most influential grassroots environmental organization.

### The World Wildlife Fund

The World Wildlife Fund leads international efforts to protect endangered species and their habitats. Now in its fifth decade, WWF works in more than a hundred countries around the globe to conserve the diversity of life on earth.

## TWO RS DOWN...

Changing your everyday environmental habits and encouraging others to do the same can often be achieved quickly and without much impact on your daily dealings. However, the most important of the Rs, reduction, often involves more long-term lifestyle changes. When thinking about your overall environmental impact, reduction is the most crucial way to slow down your consumption and waste production and to reduce your personal contribution to the emissions that are a main cause of global warming. Read **chapter 5** to learn how to conserve such precious, finite resources as water and fuel, how to adapt your home for energy efficiency, and how all of these changes will save you money! A commitment to consuming less need not be a burden, but rather a pledge to leading a simplified, eco-friendly life.

# Chapter 5

# WAYS TO LOSE
# WASTE FAST

*Reduce Your Footprint and Simplify Your Life*

Computer models of the earth's climate suggest that a critical
threshold is approaching. Crossing over it will be easy, crossing back quite likely impossible.

*Elizabeth Kolbert,* Field Notes from a Catastrophe

## IN THIS CHAPTER

- It's Getting Hot in Here: Global Climate Change Primer

- What You Can Do to Keep Us Cool

- Become an Efficiency Expert

- What's Your Waterprint?

- Reduce Your Overall Consumption

- *Ways* Guide to Consuming Less

- The Student Shall Become the Master

## IT'S GETTING HOT IN HERE: GLOBAL CLIMATE CHANGE PRIMER

Here is a brief list compiled by the **United States Global Change Research Program** of reasons why global warming should matter to you:

- **Global warming is unequivocal and primarily human induced:** Global temperature has increased over the past 50 years. This observed increase is due primarily to human-induced emissions of heat-trapping gases.
- **Climate changes are underway in the United States and are projected to grow:** Climate-related changes are already observed in the United States and its coastal waters. These include increases in heavy downpours, rising temperature and sea level, rapidly retreating glaciers, thawing permafrost, lengthening growing seasons, lengthening ice-free seasons in the ocean and on lakes and rivers, earlier snowmelt, and alterations in river flows.
- **Widespread climate-related impacts are occurring now and are expected to increase:** Climate changes are already affecting water, energy, transportation, agriculture, ecosystems, and health.
- **Threats to human health will increase:** Health impacts of climate change are related to heat stress, waterborne diseases, poor air quality, extreme weather events, and diseases transmitted by insects and rodents.
- **Climate change will interact with many social and environmental stresses:** Climate change will combine

with pollution, population growth, overuse of resources, urbanization, and other social, economic, and environmental stresses to create larger impacts than from any of these factors alone.

- **Thresholds will be crossed, leading to large changes in climate and ecosystems:** There are a variety of thresholds in the climate system and ecosystems. These thresholds determine, for example, the presence of sea ice and permafrost, and the survival of species, from fish to insect pests, with implications for society.[15]

## WHAT YOU CAN DO TO KEEP US COOL

So what exactly is the connection between consumption, carbon emissions, and global warming, and why is it so important to reduce yours? As the ever-decreasing number of naysayers may still be asking, what is the big deal if the earth heats up a few degrees? Most scientists believe that even a two-degree rise in temperatures from preindustrial levels could have serious, long-lasting environmental consequences. This includes more violent and unpredictable swings in weather patterns, greater numbers of and more intense storms, droughts, and the spread of disease, economic hardship, and regional conflict as food and water sources shrink.[16]

Many major scientists agree that the world is at a crucial point with regard to global warming. Some of the latest research from scientists at NASA says that while the earth's current carbon dioxide amount is clocking in at 390 parts per million, it must be reduced to no more than 350 parts per million. This is the safe upper limit with regard to slowing down and reversing the effects of global warming. In fact, if we don't start decreasing this number, we are on track for "runaway climate change."[17]

What's more, much of the responsibility for these emissions lies with the more developed countries. Consider these statistics from *Low Carbon Diet—A 30 Day Program to Lose 5000 Pounds* by David Gershon: "Taken collectively, U.S. households directly produce about 8 percent of the planet's carbon dioxide emissions, and through our purchases we are indirectly responsible for another 17 percent."[18] But there are many ways that you can reduce your carbon output right now and encourage your friends to do the same. It is possible to live simple, fulfilling lives with the limited resources we have, and there are many ways to make easy, tangible changes today that could have a huge impact on the earth's future.

Reduction is the royal R of the Three R Triumvirate (reduce, reuse, recycle) because it lowers our dependence on limited resources and provides us with a simplified life, which is good for not only the planet but also our wallets. Reducing the number of products you buy, and by extension the waste you generate— recyclable or otherwise—is the best way to make a difference. After all, what product uses less energy and fewer resources than one that is never made? Read on for sensible ways to consume less, reuse more, and dispose of as little as possible.

## Join a Club Dedicated to Helping the Earth Chill Out
🕐=1 💲=1 🏠=1

No matter where you stand on other issues, the concern about global warming and the environment extends far beyond political or religious affiliation. Don't believe me? Consider that in early 2008 Pat Robertson and Al Sharpton joined forces, as part of the **We Can Solve It** campaign (a campaign with which Al Gore is closely associated) to promote unity and action around issues of global warming. If Al, Al, and Pat can put aside their many, many differences to encourage people of all walks of life to reduce their carbon emissions, clearly it is time for us to follow suit.

So what to do if you are not a former vice president or prominent religious leader? Here are five websites to visit and actions to take in order to jump-start your own emissions diet.

1. **Take a stand with We Can Solve It.** We Can Solve It is an organization that offers ideas for action and solutions to help end the climate crisis. One of the main goals of the campaign is to convert all of the electricity in the United States to clean power within the next ten years. After you have joined, take some of the actions suggested on the website, and encourage your friends to do the same. After all, they're going to be in the same mess as everyone else if things don't improve.

2. **Join forces with 350.org.** Author and activist Bill McKibben has teamed up with several young people straight out of college and fresh from other successful environmental campaigns to raise awareness about the need for immediate and international action to reduce the amount of carbon dioxide present in the atmosphere. Why 350? In terms of the health of the planet, the number 350 is crucial: McKibben explains that "the most recent science tells us that unless we can reduce the amount of carbon dioxide in the atmosphere to 350 parts per million, we will cause huge and irreversible damage to the earth."

3. **Visit Nature and Climate Central. Nature** is one of the leading scientific websites, and as an added bonus, it is easily understood by a layperson. The website's section on climate change includes the latest news, analysis, and research on our warming planet. Two worlds collide at **Climate Central**: science and media. The goal of this site is to provide up-to-date climate-change information that can be easily understood, conveyed, and ingested in the form of web content and videos.

4. **Start marching.** Join over a million other people on the virtual **Stop Global Warming March**. The website offers action

items for reducing carbon emissions, supporting good energy policy, and encouraging others to get involved. It is also a good source for the latest global warming headlines.

**Know Your Number** 🕐=2 💲=1 🏢=1

Now that you have made a commitment to reduce your emissions, you need a way to track your shrinking carbon footprint. The first step is to get an accurate picture of your carbon output right now. There are carbon footprint calculators galore on the Internet. I recommend perusing a few before settling on the one that you are going to establish a longer-term relationship with. Think of it as Internet dating, only without the fear of rejection or need to brush your teeth. Most of the calculators will start by asking a series of questions about lifestyle, means of transportation, and household expenses. Your answers are used to calculate your little slice of the greenhouse-induced-humanity-ending-catastrophe pie.

My favorite of the many online calculators is the one over at **EarthLab**. Here are a few reasons why I recommend you use it:

- **It requires very little patience.** As the website claims, it really does take only three minutes to calculate individual carbon usage.

- **It covers all the bases.** The calculator evaluates the six major facets of how we live: home, energy, commute, travel, work, and overall lifestyle.

- **Your score means something.** Once you are done (let's say during minute four), you get a score from 150–900 (150 means you are a carbon-saving rock star, while 900 suggests that death from shame may not be inappropriate after all), and you can compare your score to other people in your city, state, and country.

- **It provides tangible ways to reduce.** No matter what your number, there are specific pledges you can take to further reduce your carbon emissions. For example, in the energy section, you can pledge to air dry your dishes, start composting, or turn off lights whenever you leave a room.

- **You can track your progress.** Think of it as an alternative to Facebook when looking for a way to procrastinate at work. You can visit your account at EarthLab regularly to report your progress, update your score, and make new pledges.

## Carbon Calculators

For those who love calculators or crave a second opinion, here are some other calculators to try:

**Carbon Footprint**

**Carbonfund.org**

**Climate Crisis** (from the folks who brought you *An Inconvenient Truth*)

**The Conservation Fund**

**Environmental Protection Agency (EPA)**

**Redefining Progress**

**Stop Global Warming** (users can calculate carbon and cash savings)

## BECOME AN EFFICIENCY EXPERT

Wasting Money and Hurting the Planet Go Hand in Hand
*David Bach,* Go Green, Live Rich

**Know Your Other Number** 🕐=2 💲=1 ⊞=1

The one on the energy bill, that is. Unless you are getting 100 percent of your power from renewable sources such as hydropower, wind, or solar, then the energy you use is created by burning fossil fuels, which in turn increases greenhouse gas emissions. While the total on the bill is a good indication of how much energy you are using, you can get even more detailed information about times of peak use and specific ways to save energy by getting an audit—yes, there is actually a type of audit that has the potential to save you money. An auditor will look over your past bills, go through all aspects of energy use in your home, and then provide you with a list of suggestions for improving your energy efficiency. Contact your power company to see if it offers energy auditing as a free service.

So now what to do about your carbon-consumption habits? As an individual, it turns out that there is plenty to do, *and* most of it is pretty easy. From light bulbs to solar panels, there is a host of changes you can make, whether you live in a house, apartment, or dorm room. If you follow these simple steps, you can reduce your yearly carbon emissions by hundreds, even thousands of pounds, all while exhaling as much as you want! Once you leave your house, you can lose even more weight. For tips on reducing your $CO_2$ output when traveling, see **page 233 in chapter 9**.

> We have the technology.
>
> *Six Million Dollar Man*

## How Many Politicians Does It Take to Get Us to Change Our Light Bulbs? ⏰=3 💲=1 🏢=2

In *An Inconvenient Truth*, Al Gore recommended that we all install energy-efficient light bulbs. Just in case you don't want to take Gore's advice, consider that Congress has voted to ban incandescent bulbs by 2012. Congress has also passed a mandate to make all bulbs 70 percent more efficient by 2020, which will phase out halogen bulbs, too—the staple of any poorly decorated dorm room. But while companies have years to act, you can start saving money right now.

In a moment, you should stop reading this book and start walking around your home. Report back when you have answered these three questions:

1. How many light bulbs do you have in your home/apartment?
2. How many lights are on right now?
3. How many of these lights are compact fluorescent bulbs (CFLs)?

Magnified by the millions of homes across the nation, the results add up to tremendous energy waste. No matter what your answers to this highly scientific assessment, these two tips are guaranteed to further reduce your energy use and your bills:

- **Only turn on lights (and air conditioners, ceiling fans, etc.) in rooms that you are actually occupying.** Yes, the very tip your parents have nagged you about for years. Turns out that throwing money away is less fun when it's *your* electric bill. When you are in a room, try to set a tone of relaxation, as opposed to interrogation.

- **Recycle those incandescents immediately!** In order to ensure that your lighting is as efficient as it can be, your bulbs need to match your mission. CFL light bulbs use about 75 percent less energy than their incandescent cousins, *and* they last about seven times longer. Keep in mind that CFL bulbs contain a teensy bit of mercury that can really add up, so make sure that they are recycled properly. Check out **Earth 911** to find a CFL recycling center near you. Find more tips on tough to recycle items in **chapter 4**.

Keep a lookout for even better lighting technology, which is on the horizon. The ESL (electron-stimulated luminescence) bulb is in development at **VU1**. This bulb will be as efficient as a CFL bulb minus the mercury, and all of the parts will be fully recyclable or safe to be disposed of at home.

### Unplugged Is Not Just for MTV Anymore 🕐=1 💲=2 🏠=1

Your lights are not the only drain on your home energy use. Appliances and electronics can be a big drag on the old grid, too. As much as 15 percent of our monthly energy bills—up to $125 per year—comes from appliances that are not being used.[19] This is because many electric devices that are plugged in (even if they are in standby mode) still draw power. Use a power strip for such devices, and turn the whole strip off when they're not in use. Some of the worst offenders of absentee energy users are the ones we employ the most, such as chargers for our cell phones and iPods.

### Get Out the Gadgets 🕐=1 💲=3 🏠=2

If you don't have the attention span to keep track of your electronics (and in this age of IMing and YouTube surfing, who does?), there are now a few handy gadgets to aid you in your quest for efficiency. The Smart Strip turns off your computer, TV, and other household electronics automatically. The Kill a Watt EZ Electricity Meter doesn't turn anything off, but it will measure how much electricity each device and appliance is actually using, as well as how much money they are costing you. It's sort of like buying a nagging parent. Solio makes a host of solar chargers that power both music players and cell phones. And while you're at it, don't forget to pick up a few rechargeable AA batteries. All of these products as well as ideas for reducing your electricity use are available from **TerraPass**.

### Use a Clirty Hook 🕐=1 💲=1 🏠=2

What's kind of clean but not totally dirty? Well, if you have ever lived in a place sans the benefit of a conveniently located washer and dryer, I suspect you know exactly what "clirty" is. For the pristine among you, clirty refers to clothes (with the strict exception of undies and socks) that can be worn more than once, especially if given the opportunity to air out on a hook in between time spent with you. Every load of laundry uses water and electricity, so a clirty hook can add up to big savings on both bills.

## Hang Them Out to Dry ⏱=3 $=1 🏠=2

When clothes graduate from clirty to really, truly dirty, wash them in a full load of cold water and hang them out to dry. There is no need to use warm or hot water unless clothes are really soiled, and the majority of washing machines' energy costs come from heating the water. According to Project Laundry List, "Electric dryers use 5 to 10 percent of residential electricity in the United States."[20] Yikes—so save that money and electricity by hanging your clothes on an outdoor line or an indoor drying rack. This might be a more seasonal practice for those of you living in more temperate areas, but why pay for dryer sheets to make your clothes smell summer fresh when hanging them out accomplishes a better fragrance for free? Find more tips on hanging out clothes, as well as links to purchasing every accoutrement you will ever need to dry your clothes indoors and out, at **Project Laundry List**.

## Deal with a Dual Climate ⏱=1 $=2 🏠=2

The climate choices you make inside also affect the global temperature. But it would be ridiculous to ask people in Arizona to never turn on the AC or those living in Maine to never turn on the heat. No matter where you live, a change of seasons, or at least a variance in temperature, is inevitable. But rather than pouring energy into AC units or blasting the heat, try implementing these tips to keep you comfortable and efficient no matter what the temperature:

- **Dress for it**. If it's cold outside, it will probably be cooler inside, too. Wear a sweater and some wool socks, and keep the thermostat down a few degrees. And in the summer? Less is more—think shorts, skirts, and tank tops.

- **Control the temp**. Use a programmable temperature control for easy maintenance of daytime and nighttime temps—no higher than 68 degrees during the day in the winter and 60 at night. Don't forget the warm blanket, cat, and sleeping partner (stay safe, kids!) to make those cool nights even cozier.

- **Encourage the flow**. A few well-placed fans can keep the air circulating; they are good year-round for utilizing heat and keeping cool.

- **Keep the good stuff in.** A well-insulated home or apartment will keep the heat inside and the cold air out, with the opposite true in warmer months. Also, remember the rules of sun and shade apply to buildings just as they do to cars or parks, and use your blinds accordingly.

- **Use only what you need.** If you find that you *have* to use an air conditioner, be sure it is Energy Star rated and only as powerful as you need for the space you are trying to cool.

## Avoid Appliance Apathy   🕐=3   💲=1   ▦=2

Whether you own or rent, it is in the best interest of your wallet and the planet that your appliances operate as efficiently as possible. An improperly sealed refrigerator or a poorly insulated hot-water heater will quietly leak energy. Also, be sure that your fridge is set to the highest temp necessary to keep frozen stuff frozen and cold stuff cold. Most refrigerators have an adjustable thermostat that you can tinker with. If your ice cream is getting soft, it's too warm, and if your milk is freezing, it's too cold. Somewhere near the middle of the dial is usually ideal.

## Power Your Home with the Green Stuff 🕐=1 💲=2 🏠=1

Utility companies are also worried about where they are going to get all of the power they need, and many have started programs that allow customers to request that a percentage of their power (or even all of it!) be supplied by renewable resources (i.e., not fossil fuels). This "green power" encompasses many different types including wind, solar, geothermal, and hydroelectric. Do your homework about your green power options at **Green-e**, which offers an independent third-party certification of green energy. The website also offers a search engine for renewable energy by region and type of energy, as well as a detailed explanation about how energy becomes Green-e certified. Check with your local utility to see if it offers green power. Further resources can be found at the **Department of Energy** website, which maintains a list of green power availability and cost.

At this point, green power is often slightly more expensive than conventional power. However, as technology shifts in favor of green power, the cost is sure to go down. Until then, there are federal and state tax incentives for those who green their power. Check out what is available to you at the **Database of State Incentives for Renewables and Efficiencies**.

## Be Truly Energy Independent 🕐=2 💲=3 🏠=3

With all this talk of energy independence, fossil fuel shortages, peak oil (the point at which we've exhausted half of the world's oil supplies), and the weak economy in general, it is hard not to feel a bit panicked. After all, what does "energy independence" even mean, and how do we achieve it? Many organizations, politicians, and regular people are advocating for clean, renewable energy and the development of green jobs, and both are worthy causes. See the list of environmental organizations **on page 116 in chapter 4** for organizations that are advocating for a greener economy and changes in energy policy.

While you may not be able to immediately change policies, you can become an energy supersaver in your own home. Look around and see how many of your appliances have the Energy Star sticker. If you are not at 100 percent, then you have a little bit of work to do. Energy Star appliances are certified by the Environmental Protection Agency (EPA) and Department of Energy as energy efficient and can save you as much as 30 percent on your monthly electricity bills. Granted, renters, homeowners, and college students have different degrees of control over the types of appliances in their dwellings. Still, no matter where you fall on this continuum, if you have any say in such decisions, be sure that Energy Star appliances are purchased (unless you don't need that extra savings, in which case you can send a check to my publisher). If you have to make a decision about where to start, might I recommend the biggest energy gulper of them all, the fridge? A complete list of approved appliances can be found at **Energy Star**.

Again, depending on where you live, homeowners should also consider installing solar panels, which will allow you to put energy into the power grid rather than being a drain on it. While the initial cash outlay may seem prohibitive, tax incentives and credit from the power companies make this one investment that can pay for itself in just a few years (sooner in Arizona, maybe later in Seattle). After all, what's more reliable, the stock market or the sun? My money is on the sun, for the next ten million years or so at least.

Water, water everywhere, / Nor any drop to drink.

*Samuel Taylor Coleridge,*
*"The Rime of the Ancient Mariner"*

## WHAT'S YOUR WATERPRINT?

There are currently an estimated 1.1 billion people in the world who lack clean water.[21] Why is this? Is there a shortage of water or just a shortage of wells and a lack of infrastructure for transporting safe, clean water? The answer is both. Only .03 percent of the water on earth is potable, and according to Peter H. Gleick, president of the Pacific Institute, "As many as 76 million people—mainly children—will die annually from preventable water-related diseases by 2020, even if current United Nations goals are reached."[22]

### So What Can We Do?

You can help solve the water crisis both directly and indirectly. By donating to organizations like **charity: water** or **UNICEF**, which work to make clean drinking water available to everyone, you can contribute to a crucial cause with just a click of your mouse. For more ways to bring medicine, water, and food to those in need, check out **chapter 2**. You can also help conserve the precious drinking water we have left by reducing the water you use every day.

### Calculate Your Thirst 🕐=1 💲=1 🏠=1

Go to **H₂O Conserve** or **Waterfootprint** to tally your water footprint. Personally, I'm a sucker for the cartoon characters over at H₂O Conserve. You will be asked questions about where you live, how much of your power comes from solar or wind energy, whether or not you have low-flow devices on your showers, toilets, and faucets, how much laundry you do per week, etc.

While it may turn out that you are indeed a water glutton, you will also find suggestions for reducing your use in each question the survey asks.

In addition to the typical questions about water use, you will find others that concern your "virtual" water footprint—part of the big picture when calculating your water use. In his article "Everything You Know about Water Conservation Is Wrong," Thomas Kostigen writes, "Virtual water is a calculation of the water needed for the production of any product from start to finish."[23] Just as you might factor in the carbon costs of producing, packaging, and shipping that Kobe steak from Japan, you can do the same with water costs.

Of course, it is important to turn off the water while brushing your teeth and to take shorter showers, but it is crucial to be mindful of your virtual water consumption. Almost everything takes water to produce, so it is useful to consider the water that is consumed in the production and shipment of the food and commercial goods we throw away so casually. According to the Water Footprint Network, "The virtual water footprint of a cup of coffee is 37 gallons; an apple, 19 gallons; a banana, 27; a slice of bread, 10; a sheet of paper, 3; and a pair of leather shoes, 4,400 gallons." As is the case with energy, the United States uses much more than its proportion of water. Our average annual use of 656,012 gallons per person is more than double the world average.[24]

Adding to our water woes is the widely held belief that there really is "water, water everywhere." While it is true that water is plentiful in much of the United States, this attitude is a bit like saying disappearing rainforests are not a problem because we have trees in our backyards. Water shortages affect us all, either directly or indirectly, through increased poverty, which leads to conflict and instability, as well as through more expensive goods. For example, drought conditions in Spain and California, two of the main agricultural producers in their respective regions, have led to increased food prices for consumers. In addition to checking for the obvious water wasters like leaky faucets and pipes, which you should repair immediately, here are a few more simple ways to keep from drowning in water and energy waste.

## Shorter Showers under the Low Flow ⏱=1 💲=2 🏠=2

How efficient and powerful is the flow of your shower? One of the best ways to reduce both water and energy use is by taking shorter showers under a low-flow showerhead. Regular showerheads use five to seven gallons a minute, but the inexpensive low-flow upgrades only use an average of 2.5 gallons per minute. If every millennial switched to a low-flow showerhead, the annual water savings would be on the order of billions of gallons (assuming most of you shower every day).

We all have those days when we need a nice, hot soak in the shower, but taking into account length of hair, shaving needs, the "clirtiness" of your butt, etc., most of us can generally get everything accomplished in five to seven minutes. Try cutting off a few minutes at a time, perhaps by turning the water off when lathering and shaving; for a few bucks you can also install a soaping valve that will let you do just that without changing temperature. After the initial blast, these types of tasks don't need water, and shaving five minutes off your daily showers (even with a low-flow head) and limiting the number of baths you take (which use up to twice as much water) can save you thousands of gallons a year. The same water-preservation methods go for brushing your teeth.

## Be a Discriminating Flusher ⏱=2 💲=1 🏠=2

Not yet "letting it mellow"? Might be time to consider new flushing policies in the household! Along the same lines, consider installing a water-saving dual-flush toilet. If you live in a dorm or apartment, you can do it yourself by removing the lid on your tank and inserting a full half-gallon jug of water, thus saving a half-gallon with each flush. While you are inspecting the throne, also be sure that the toilet isn't running continuously. Leaks in toilets, showers, and sinks can waste as much as twenty thousand gallons of water each year and are usually easy and inexpensive to remedy. [25] Your local hardware store can probably walk you through the process, and you can take your plumbing know-how with you no matter how many times you move.

## Do Fewer Dishes 🕐=2 💲=1 ▦=2

Just to be clear, I am not advocating for reuse of a plate covered with dried egg yolk or tomato sauce, but there are certain dishes like a water glass or a coffee mug that even the most obsessive-compulsive germaphobe (like me) can easily use all day long. Also, while it's okay to get off the big chunks of food (for composting, of course, which you can read all about on **page 94 in chapter 4**), prewashing dishes is a big waste of water. When it is time to do the dishes, run the dishwasher only when it is full, set it to the lowest temperature possible, use a biodegradable dishwashing soap, and air dry when done. For the life of me, I've never understood the need to dry dishes with a heater. Who needs that kind of turnaround? If you don't have a dishwasher, hand wash your dishes with similar attention to water use. Don't leave the water running, and fill two tubs—one for washing and one for rinsing.

## Don't Throw Good Water down the Drain 🕐=1 💲=1 ▦=2

The same goes for other sink tasks, too: rinsing vegetables and filling reusable water bottles should be done as efficiently as possible—never leave the water running. Another water-saving trick is to rinse vegetables in a bowl and then use the leftover water for your thirsty plants. Lastly, be sure all of your sinks have aerators installed. These inexpensive attachments reduce water flow by about 25 percent, and they make the water nice and bubbly, too.

Garbage should worry us. It should prod us. We don't need better ways to get rid of things. We need to not get rid of things, either by keeping them cycling through the system or not designing and desiring them in the first place.

*Elizabeth Royte,* Garbage Land

## REDUCE YOUR OVERALL CONSUMPTION
### Are We a Disposable Society?

Now that you have lowered your use of fuel and water, it is time to tackle the next phase of the royal R: reducing your overall need for material goods. For better and worse, consumption and convenience are hallmarks of the twentieth and twenty-first centuries. Unfortunately, this means that so is waste. But delve a little more deeply, and you will find that many people's consumption habits could easily be curbed. Most of us want to produce as little waste as possible, and if we can find a recycling bin, we will use it. But with a little more effort and education, we can do a much better job of not creating unnecessary material in the first place. According to the Environmental Protection Agency (EPA), in 2006 the average American dumped an average of 4.6 pounds per day. While this is almost a half-pound *less* than the average in 2000, it is two pounds *more* than the national average back in 1960. And all this trash adds up—to 251.3 million tons in 2006, actually—nearly three times the 1960 total.[26] These numbers are just a fraction of the garbage created in the manufacturing, packaging, and transportation infrastructure necessary to get all of these new goods to the consumer. The sad fact of the matter is that regardless of when our trash gets deposited in the dump, the vast majority of it will remain there long after we are gone.

### Keep a Dump Diary 🕐=3 💲=1 🏢=2

No, this isn't a journal you keep next to the toilet paper dispenser. It's a way for you to get an accurate idea of your garbage production. Spend a week keeping a list of *everything* you throw out, and then spend the next week doing a bit of research (with this book close at hand) to see if any of that waste could have been recycled, reused, or avoided altogether. While recycling is obviously a better option than throwing your waste away, most items are downcycled, which means that the recovered materials will be used to make a lower-quality product. For example, much of the glass that is collected for recycling is ground up and added to landfills to separate layers of garbage, and paper only has about seven cycles in it before it is no longer useful. So it's really more like one-cycling. Furthermore, all recycling processes require energy as well as the processing of chemicals and sometimes water, so the total savings of resources is less than you might first imagine.

## Ditch the Dump   🕐=2 💲=1 🏠=3

Besides concerns over ever-decreasing landfill space, there are also the greenhouse gas emissions generated by garbage festering in an environment without air and various persistent toxic chemicals leaching from landfills into the groundwater and soil. In fact, nearly 35 percent of methane-gas emissions (one of the gases that causes global warming) comes directly from the landfill, easily the biggest source of human-related methane release. And landfills across the country have the potential to leach heavy metals and chemicals like lead, mercury, PCBs (polychlorinated biphenyls), and PBDEs (polybrominated diphenyl ethers) long after they have been thrown away. Many of these substances do not biodegrade and they bioaccumulate, meaning they pass from species to species; hence, the reason why certain types of fish contain mercury that will pass into our systems if we eat them.

Of course, the need for new, or at least new-to-you items, is inevitable. When buying new items or figuring out how to recycle old ones, here are a few tips to help you be a clean, green consumer:

- **Use your imagination, and reuse as many materials as possible.** Glass jars and wine bottles can be transformed into vases, drinking glasses, and candleholders. A friend of mine with an extensive workshop keeps all tools, nails, and screws organized in old food containers, and a similar organizing principle could be put into place at your desk or craft area.

- **Reduce the size of your garbage.** One of the best ways I have found to lessen my waste is by reducing the size of my garbage. A small garbage container makes me even more aware of how much I throw out. I keep one garbage can in my kitchen and one in my bathroom, and they are both a compact 4.5 liters.

- **Compost food waste.** When I lived in my apartment in New York, I always lamented the fact that most of my garbage was compostable food waste. After a bit of research, I realized that an indoor composter was a great option for an urban dweller like me. If you have a bit of yard space, you can also set up an outdoor composting system. See **page 94 in chapter 4** for suggestions on setting up your own compost.

- **Make every effort to buy products that can be reused, and recycle anything that can not.** No matter where you live, with a little extra effort you can recycle much more than you ever thought possible. If an item is truly impossible to recycle, try to find an eco-friendly alternative. For a little recycling inspiration, see **page 85 in chapter 4** for a list of recycling resources as well as a list of recyclable items that you may be mistaking for trash.

# SUCCESS STORY

## Making Magic Out of Mushrooms

When twenty-three year-old Eben Bayer and Gavin McIntyre were earning dual bachelor's degrees from Rensselaer Polytechnic Institute (RPI) in mechanical engineering and product design and innovation, it is clear they were staying awake in class. Upon graduation, they founded **Ecovative Design**, which produces compostable alternatives to polystyrene packing materials and foam insulation.

The main resource in the production process? Waste. Ecovative uses agricultural by-products such as cotton burrs and rice husks. First, the seed husks are wet and combined with mushroom roots, which act as a binding agent. With a conventional product like polystyrene, petroleum is used as the binder. The husks serve as "food" for the mushroom and self-assembly begins. According to Bayer, "the factory is the organism" in this highly efficient process. What's more, mushrooms like the dark, so no light or energy is needed until the end of the process, when the material is dried out and shaped into packaging material for everything from televisions to medicine or "greensulate" installation.

Thanks to grants from such heavy hitters as the EPA and the USDA and a recent 500,000 euro grand prize for their business plan from the Picnic Green Challenge, Ecovative is working with a growing team of scientists and entrepreneurs to expand their national and global ventures.

For those budding entrepreneurs with their own eco-innovative idea, Bayer recommends three things: persistence, hard work, and the advice of those who have been there before. Bayer says, "If you are working on something that you think is not only a great business opportunity, but also great for the world, keep your eyes on other unorthodox ways of funding your business.

Almost every state has some sort of grant program for emerging green technologies, especially energy, but also other products that may create social change or solve problems around inefficiency and waste." He also recommends looking into business plan competitions from both the government and private organizations, as well as obtaining letters of endorsement from potential customers. Most of all, Bayer encourages those pursuing sustainable business ideas to reach out to potential mentors and to stay positive. "If you are working on something promising and meaningful, you are pretty much guaranteed to have an off day, week, or month," he explains. "It's part of the game, and just the act of persevering through the hard times (and finding solutions along the way) will give you the stamina and motivation to really execute when you get to the good times."

## Go Digital  🕐=1 💲=1 🏢=1

Our personal paper reduction can really add up. According to mail-reduction service **41pounds.org** (a title that refers to the weight of junk mail sent to Americans each year), "To produce and process 4 million tons of junk mail a year, 100 million trees are destroyed and 28 billion gallons of water are wasted. Also, global warming gases equivalent to 9 million cars are produced."[27] After all of this, 44 percent of this mail is thrown away unopened.

It is easy for you to opt out of the mailing lists maintained by credit-reporting agencies and sold to credit card and insurance companies for mass solicitation. Just call the agencies' opt out number at 888-5-OPTOUT. Easy! You can also remove your name from mailing lists through the **Direct Marketing Association** website. If you have the stamina, you can also call the sender each time a piece of junk mail arrives and ask to be permanently removed from the mailing list.

## Services to Help You Make the Switch to Paperless

In addition, there are several companies ready to help you get rid of 90 to 95 percent of your junk mail both easily and inexpensively:

**MailStopper (formerly GreenDimes)**

MailStopper is a service that costs $20; however, the company plants five trees when you initially sign up, plus one additional tree for each catalog you opt out of receiving.

**41pounds.org**

41pounds.org is run by a nonprofit organization that gives one-third of the $41 junk-mail-reduction fee to a charity of your choice.

**Stop the Junk Mail**

Stop the Junk Mail allows you to opt out of receiving catalogs, magazines, book clubs, and nonprofit fliers for $19.95 a year.

**Catalog Choice**

A project of the **Ecology Center**, Catalog Choice allows you to opt out of receiving many major catalogs for free!

**Eco-Cycle**

Eco-Cycle offers many more suggestion on how to stop the junk-mail flow for free.

Don't forget that most of your bank statements, investment reports, and bills can be received and paid online. Contact your companies and ask for paperless statements. Let's be frank—the only mail we want to find in our box is a new movie to watch, a check, or a letter from a friend, so make it happen and save some precious resources at the same time!

You can even ask that your yellow-page directory go virtual, too; sign up at **Yellowpagesgoesgreen.org** to avoid unwanted yellow page delivery. Remember to read as many newspapers and magazines as possible online, too.

## Buy Less Stuff 🕐=1 💲=1 🏢=3

One benefit of your twenties, though you might not see it as such, is the fact that you are likely living on a tight budget and must make decisions about where and how you spend your money. Instead of viewing your income as a hardship, look at it as an opportunity to learn responsible habits that can last a lifetime. The last thing I want to do is nag, but seriously, credit cards are a recipe for disaster, especially for the uninitiated. And even if you don't have to live on a budget, the key to solving many of our problems is to understand that money is not a justification for reckless consumerism. From that morning coffee steaming in a disposable Styrofoam cup (which *never* biodegrades) to that new shirt you need for your latest date (which required land for growing cotton, pesticides—unless it's organic—fuel to manufacture and ship, and packaging to keep it pristine), every new product we buy has an environmental price tag.

Of course, you can always renounce all worldly possessions, but the life of an ascetic is not for everyone—especially if you've already been exposed to iPhones and *The Hills*. But don't fret; you can be trendsetting and planet loving at the same time. Start by mapping out and sticking to a budget and living within your means. Together we can start a millennial tradition for the twenty-first century: avoiding the purchase of cheap crap that we don't really need. Burying ourselves in possessions and debt is not really the American way, no matter what the marketers try to tell us.

## *WAYS* GUIDE TO CONSUMING LESS

1. Keep a list of everything you are spending money on for at least a week.

2. **Whittle it down.** What is on that list that you can do without? Can you pack your own lunch, bring a reusable water bottle,

or make your coffee at home? Can you forgo the eyebrow wax or new pair of shoes?

3. **Go through your cabinets, desk, bathroom, and closets, and take stock of what you already have.** Unearth possessions that may have been lost in the clutter. Often, rediscovering cool stuff saves you from making unnecessary purchases and satisfies the urge to buy something new.

4. **Before adding to your purchase list, evaluate whether or not you can make do.** Can you borrow a sewing machine from a crafty friend for that wardrobe enhancement project, or can you MacGyver that Ikea dresser instead of buying a new one?

5. **Buy products that will last.** From rechargeable batteries to quality clothing, items with a longer lifecycle are better for all. And even if you decide not to keep an item forever, there are many avenues for reuse, such as a clothing swap (see **page 221 in chapter 8** for tips on organizing one), a yard sale, the infamous practice of regifting, and donating goods to a local thrift store.

### Start New Trends with Thrift  ⏰=2 💲=2 🏢=2

Of course, sometimes there are necessities that must be purchased. Shopping at thrift or secondhand stores allows you to strike a balance between acquisition and consumption, which results in big savings at the same time. Reuse is the ultimate way to decrease unnecessary demand for limited resources. In addition to shopping at secondhand and vintage stores, you can also troll the ubiquitous **Craig's List** for anything from a couch to a chandelier. We often hear about the trendiness of vintage, but it is also an environmentally sound and inexpensive way to shop.

Consider new clothing, for example. The textile industry is one of the most water- and chemical-intensive industries in the world. Over two thousand chemicals are used in the production of clothing and fabrics, many of which contaminate the wastewater generated by these processes.[28] One of the trendiest and cheapest ways to reduce your clothing consumption and find fabulous new clothes is to spend some quality time at your favorite thrift stores. In order to find the best ones near you, ask some fashionable friends that don't seem to spend a lot of time at the mall, or do an Internet search with the name of your town and "thrift," "secondhand," or "consignment" shops. There are also Salvation Army and Goodwill stores in most areas of the country. With a gentle wash, many barely used and well-made designer-clothing finds are better quality than the bargain clothes you buy new.

And, of course, you're likely to find a one-of-a kind trendsetting outfit. According to Alexis Steinman, a film and television costumer (and the most fashionable gal I know), "As with other art forms, like music, cinema, or paintings, fashion is constantly inspired by the past. Last year, we were bombarded with eighties' gems such as skinny jeans and metallic fabrics. This year, we're bringing back the seventies with high-waisted, wide-leg trousers and the feminine frocks of the forties with slim pencil skirts and silky blouses.

"Sadly, these trends have become so oversaturated in stores that whether you are in the Gap or Bloomingdales, everything looks the same. Thankfully, there is an answer to these fashion frustrations: thrift stores. The benefits of shopping secondhand are numerous. First, there's the pricing. A corduroy blazer that fetches $150 in a mall can be had for a mere $20 in vintage. Unless one is shopping for vintage haute couture, there are always major bargains to be had at thrift stores. Second, the selection is unbeatable compared to new clothing stores. Rather than focus on the 'decade of the moment,' thrift stores provide a variety of inspiration from all eras of fashion."

According to Steinman, it has also been her experience that the older a garment is, the more well made it tends to be. Couple this with the fact that buying secondhand uses none of the labor, materials, and packaging of new clothes, and it is easy to see why thrift stores are a fashionable and eco-friendly place to update (or backdate) your wardrobe. Secondhand shops are also great places to find funky furnishings for your apartment and assorted miscellany like rare CDs from 1995 or Disney-themed soap dispensers. So while you're trying to consume less overall, obviously everyone needs to shop once in a while. These stores hit the perfect balance, allowing you to buy new stuff but recycle at the same time.

## THE STUDENT SHALL BECOME THE MASTER

Perhaps you have used some of the tips in this chapter to reduce your overall waste, and you have happily committed to buying less and buying differently. There will come a day, likely this week, when you will need to buy something, and as a master of self-discipline, remember to wield your consumer power. Sellers of goods are nothing without your money, and as long as you withhold it, they will respond to your demands. With little more than your dollar and your voice, you can compel companies to make products in an ethically and environmentally responsible way. **Chapter 6** will show you how to speak up and let companies know how you feel about their products as well as how to monitor and encourage corporate social responsibility and stewardship. Marketers and producers ultimately work for you, so be a good boss, and let them know exactly what you want them to do.

# WAYS TO MAKE YOUR MONEY TALK AND COMPANIES LISTEN

*Harness the Power of Your Dollar by Supporting Ethically and Environmentally Sound Businesses*

What if humans designed products and systems that celebrate an abundance of human creativity, culture, and productivity? That are so intelligent and safe, our species leaves an ecological footprint to delight in, not lament?

*William McDonough and Michael Braungart,* Cradle to Cradle

## IN THIS CHAPTER

- Why Your Purchases Matter
- Know Before You Go
- Putting the Bang in Your Bucks
- Ways to Support a Green Economy
- Flex Your Purchasing Muscle
- Directory of Ethically and Environmentally Sound Alternatives
- *Ways* Guide to Giving Generously
- Toward Conscious Comestible Consumption

## WHY YOUR PURCHASES MATTER

Go into many stores these days, and you will be greeted by a barrage of "responsible" shopping possibilities—from "fair trade" to "shade grown" to "local" to "sweatshop free," a consumer has to navigate through a maze of claims in order to determine which products are the most ethically and environmentally sound choices. Most of the goods you purchase have probably passed through a complex chain of people and production beginning with raw materials and ending with that tempting product on the store shelf. As the consumer, where and what you purchase matters, because you dictate what will be produced.

The equation for suppliers and stores is simple: the more product that disappears from the shelf, the more additional product they order. For those of you who didn't take basic economics or who made the mistake of taking it as an 8 a.m. class (guilty), don't panic; this is as complicated as it gets. All you have to understand is this basic principle of supply and demand. Businesses supply what consumers demand; therefore, consumers have a ton of power to shape the market according to their priorities. If the forty-plus million millennials harness this power by purchasing only products that are produced responsibly, their individual buying power will quickly magnify to superhero proportions. Even the mega-retailers will listen. After consumers raised concerns about water bottles containing the chemical bisphenol-A (BPA), Wal-Mart decided to remove all baby bottles with BPA from its stores in the United States by early 2009.[29]

It also helps if you rank companies and try to adhere to certain absolutes; for some people, this means avoiding all products made by companies that test on animals or products made with environmental pollutants or products manufactured by employees who are paid less than a living wage (a wage that allows employees to live decently in the region where they are employed). Of course, I recommend paying attention to all of these aspects when making purchasing decisions, but I also know that you are much more likely to adhere to your new shopping rules if you choose your parameters based on the issues that matter most to you.

## KNOW BEFORE YOU GO

### Learn the Lingo   🕐=2  💲=1  🏢=1

Before wading out into the marketing madness, familiarize yourself with a few widely used terms and labels such as "fair trade," "bird friendly," and "biodegradable." Regulations on claims made by products vary greatly between industries, but generally you can trust these third-party verifications: **Fair Trade Certified** for products such as coffee or chocolate, **Green Seal** for remodeling and cleaning products, and the **Forest Stewardship Council** for lumber and paper products. These organizations offer detailed explanations of the standards that products must meet to earn a certification seal. In order to be certified fair trade, for instance, producers must adhere to several principles including fair labor conditions, commitment to community development, and environmental sustainability. For a list of environmentally and socially responsible verification organizations, visit the *Ten Ways* website.

### Look for the Triple Bottom Line   🕐=2  💲=1  🏢=2

As Patrick Cescau, CEO of Unilever, says in the book *Sustainable Value* by Chris Laszlo, "There can be few people in business today who could doubt that social and environmental sustainability will be the defining business drivers for multinational corporations in the first part of the twenty-first century."[30] What our polysyllabic friend is getting at is that in today's economy, green, ethical policies equal greenbacks, and now that you are armed with a basic knowledge of sustainability vernacular, take stock of the products you already buy, and see how you can use your purchasing power to support the move toward a greener economy.

Many businesses have begun to embrace the corporate social responsibility (CSR) model. According to the news service **CSRwire,** "CSR is defined as the integration of business operations and values, whereby the interests of all stakeholders including investors, customers, employees, the community and the environment are reflected in the company's policies and actions." That's a tall order, and while many companies are moving in this direction, many still have a long way to go. CSRwire regularly updates corporate sustainability reports submitted by corporations and maintains a database of independent corporate research and ratings.[31] You can also download *Green America's Guide to Researching Corporations* from the **Green America** website for more tips on finding out the business practices of your favorite companies.

Whether your priority is fair labor practices, animal-free testing, or environmental policy, it is your right to know what exactly your money is paying for. Finding out the business practices of companies you patronize may take a little work, but try to look at your research as giving you the ability to make a choice for change rather a dreaded Internet chore. Keep in mind that once you have done the initial legwork of creating a list of businesses you deem ethical, you won't have to conduct research every time you go to the store. Another benefit of shopping locally is that you can often ask the producer for CSR information directly. For a list of some of the companies I like, see **"A Few of My Favorite Things"** on page 172.

In order to make your own list, compile the names of a few companies you are curious about or whose products you already use on a regular basis, and visit their websites. If these companies are already making efforts to be environmentally sustainable, socially responsible, or even regenerative, you can bet they will be shouting their efforts from the rooftops. Look for companies that are focused on the long-term triple bottom line: people, planet, *and* profit.

## Research, Rank, and Reward Companies  🕐=3 💲=2 🏠=2

If you are still not sure where to shop or what to buy, delve a bit more deeply into companies' records and third-party reports on their ethical and environmental practices. Take into account labor conditions, environmental practices, and overall commitment to communities. According to Carol Sanford, CEO of InterOctave Development, a "regenerative" consulting firm working with corporations, nonprofits, and government agencies, there are five levels of sustainability achievable within a business or organization. For companies to be truly regenerative, they must strive to create manufacturing and retail cycles that utilize and create renewable systems of production and consumption. "Even trying to be carbon neutral and recycling is not enough. We need to encourage companies to make products that are 'regenerative'; the product, process, and producer need to be healthier at the end of each production cycle," Sanford says.

### Five Levels of Corporate Sustainability[32]

1. **Heavy greenwashing:** Green is decidedly the new black, and many companies have hitched their public relations wagons to these tree-hugging trains with little else besides an excellent PR campaign to support claims of social and/or environmental responsibility. These companies tend to support high-profile

environmental causes in the hope that they will appear sustainable by association. These are companies to avoid. Some warning signs of this type of "greenwashing" include high visibility at green events and donations to environmental organizations without the real commitment to changing how products are produced; i.e., companies that are using hazardous chemicals to make their products, those that test on animals, and those that have abysmal health care, wage, or pollution records.

2.  **Elemental:** These are companies that have also latched onto the green trend and have changed a portion of the company but are still doing the majority of business with products that have the potential to be detrimental to the environment. An example of this type of company is Clorox, which has now launched the line of Greenworks cleaners and has made other environmental gestures, such as being a member of the EPA's Waste Wise program and the Sustainable Packaging Coalition.[33] However, Clorox is still producing products like bleach, testing on animals, and was listed as one of the "Dangerous Dozen" by the U.S. PIRGs (Public Interest Research Groups) due to the public health risks posed by its production facilities.

3.  **Heart in the right place:** As awareness and demand grows, more and more companies are falling into this category, and this is the rung on the ladder where you should start to consider making purchases. While these companies have good intentions and are trying to do less harm, they can still do more to systematically change the way their products are made. Keep in mind that since so many companies fall into this category, there are many colors in this category's rainbow. From Wal-Mart at the very low end (trying to sell more organic and environmentally responsible products) to Patagonia at the very high end (tracking the environmental footprints of its products and recycling some of its clothing), companies in this

category might just need a little more encouragement from the consumer to push them to the next level of responsibility.

4. **Almost all systems are go:** Very few companies have reached this level of change. These companies are working within the natural systems of nature and are actually increasing the health of the planet through the manufacture and use of their products. TerraCycle (profiled on page 162) is a company that uses recycled plastics bottles to package its biodegradable cleaners and vermacompost (worm poop) fertilizer and is an example of a company that is moving beyond recycling to regeneration.

5. **Nirvana:** These are companies or producers that leave communities and environments significantly better than when they found them. They are creating products that bring life rather than creating a consumption pattern. To date, the only example of a producer that is doing this is a farmer—one who creates better soil, a healthier product, and a healthier farm during each successive year. As Carol Sanford of InterOctave puts it, "I like the idea that companies will ultimately see their product from 'earth to earth' rather than from 'cradle to grave' or even 'cradle to cradle.'" Companies can make this shift, and it is up to us as consumers to use our green to demand this level of regeneration from the companies and producers with whom we choose to do business.

## Resources for Responsible Shoppers

### GENERAL OVERVIEW OF COMPANIES AND PRACTICES
#### Green America
Green America produces the *National Green Pages*, a directory of socially and environmentally responsible businesses. The organization also sends members email updates about actions

consumers can take to influence both policy and production standards. All of the businesses listed in the *National Green Pages* must pass a screening process and sign the following pledge:

"As a member of Coop America Business Network, my company conducts business according to standards that reach beyond contemporary practices in addressing the needs of consumers, employees, the community, and the environment. I certify and can demonstrate that we strive to operate in a socially just and environmentally sustainable manner."

The Green America website is a good place to start when researching any product, from green gifts to fair trade. The "Responsible Shopper" section is particularly helpful when researching companies within an industry.

## FOOD AND PERSONAL-CARE PRODUCTS
### Environmental Working Group

In addition to maintaining a frequently updated archive of information about chemicals and toxins found in everything from cosmetics to food and providing suggestions for alternatives, the Environmental Working Group (EWG) also maintains **Skin Deep**, the cosmetic safety database. Once there, you can search a frequently updated database of personal-care products in order to find out *exactly* what potentially harmful additives are in your toothpaste, deodorant, or shower gel. You can search by product, ingredient, or company, and each product is ranked from 0 to 10 (0 being completely free of taint from either toxins or animal testing, and 10? Well, 10 is a good indication that it might be time to find a new favorite shampoo or mascara.

## ENVIRONMENTAL ISSUES
### Climate Counts

This nonprofit organization is a joint project of Stonyfield Farm, Inc., and Clean Air-Cool Planet. Together, they have created a consumer scorecard that is updated yearly based on company transparency, policy stance, and carbon-reduction efforts.

## Consumer Reports

Still not sure if you are being greenwashed? *Consumer Reports* maintains a website called **Greener Choices**, where you can search by label or product category (household cleaners, food, personal hygiene, wood/paper to name a few). It's a great way to see detailed descriptions of what terms such as "biodegradable" and "antibacterial" really mean, how these labels are regulated, and where you can find products that match your search criteria.

## Global 100

Since 2005, this list of "the 100 most sustainable corporations in the world" has ranked companies based on their social, environmental, and fiscal performances.

## ANIMAL TESTING
### Caring Consumer

This website, run by People for the Ethical Treatment of Animals (PETA), offers a list of all the companies that test on animals as well as those that don't. The list is updated frequently, and all information is in a convenient A to Z directory. Along the same lines, PETA also maintains a "Shopping Guide to Compassionate Clothing."

## LABOR CONDITIONS
### Business and Human Rights Resource Center

This organization is committed to "tracking the positive and negative impacts of over four thousand companies worldwide." The Resource Center is a nonprofit that updates its reports daily, and visitors can browse by companies, issues, and countries.

**Commit to Being a Compassionate Consumer** 🕐=2 💲=2 🏢=2

Once you have done your research, start purchasing products from companies that match your personal ethics. If you do choose to patronize companies that don't align with your beliefs, remember that your dollar is directly supporting these practices.

---

## Seven to Follow When Shopping

Diane MacEachern, author of *The Big Green Purse,* recommends following these principles[34]:

1. Buy less.
2. Read the label.
3. Support sustainable standards.
4. Look for third-party verification.
5. Choose fewer ingredients.
6. Pick less packaging.
7. Buy local.

---

## PUTTING THE BANG IN YOUR BUCKS

**Put Your Money Where Your Heart Is** 🕐=2 💲=3 🏢=2

While living in your twenties often consists of trying to make ends meet, living month to month, or living hand to mouth (choose the cliché that best applies to you), the prudent thing to do in any scenario is to start putting some money away (even a teensy, tiny bit) for that faraway point in time called retirement. After all, investing is not just for old folks. In fact, the more you think about investing now, the less you will have to worry about it as a geezer. According to many financial experts, an account started at age twenty can end up with over a million dollars more in it than one started at age thirty.[35] Crazy, but true. If your employer has a 401(k), participate and investigate. Encourage your company to work with firms that offer socially responsible investment portfolios. If you are still in college and your school has a large endowment, investigate where its money (and yours—remember tuition?) is going. In fact, under pressure from their student bodies, many colleges have divested their sizable endowments from companies with tainted environmental and/or ethical practices.

Look at investment prospectuses online to see where your money is going. If you have questions or concerns about a particular company, do a bit of research on your own, and then contact your investment company directly to see if it has sustainable and/or environmentally responsible portfolio alternatives. As sustainability becomes less of an alternative and more of a key to economic viability, many "mainstream" investment firms are offering socially and environmentally responsible funds, so be sure to ask. You can also check out a socially responsible fund's rating at **Morningstar,** or read about its performance and allocation of money at **Social Funds**.

Try to choose bank and credit card companies with good social and environmental practices as well. In these fragile financial and environmental times, it is crucial to know that the money we invest is used wisely and compassionately. Credit unions and community development banks are good alternatives to multinational banks. For more information about banks and credit cards that put your money toward causes you believe in, visit **Green America's Community Investing Resource Center**.[36]

## Places to Find Principled Investments

**Calvert Investments**
**Domini Social Investments**
**Pax World Mutual Funds**
**Winslow Management Company**

## Become a Shareholder 🕐=2 💲=3 🏢=2

For very little money, you can often buy stock in a publicly held company, which gives you the right to attend shareholder meetings. Think about it: angry protestor on the street versus invested shareholder—you guess who will have more say. Even if there isn't a decimal small enough to represent your share, you are still entitled to your right to advocate for more socially and environmentally responsible business practices within the company. Bring ideas with you to the meeting, and help companies take the next step. Encourage businesses to expand and save money simultaneously by creating a smaller footprint.

## Write a Letter 🕐=2 💲=1 🏢=1

Whether or not you buy stock in a company, you can always send a letter, an email, or place a quick call to customer service to let the businesses whose products you buy know how you feel about their practices. Smaller companies will be especially receptive to your suggestions, and it will probably be easier for you to reach someone who has direct access to those who make the decisions. However you choose to communicate, be sure to remain positive. Start off by telling the company what they are doing right. Emphasize the positive, because that will keep the recipient of your message from feeling defensive and make them much more likely to be receptive to your suggestions. Carol Sanford of InterOctave recommends, "Start by saying something like, 'I really like what you are doing, *and* here is something you can do to continue to sustain my loyalty.'" If you don't get a response or you get one that is unsatisfactory, follow up with a phone call and/or email. If you still are not satisfied, rethink whether or not this is an establishment you want to continue doing business with.

## Start a Boycott  🕐=4  💲=1  🏫=5

Which brings us to the moment when you have to decide which companies to avoid. Letters, phone calls, and emails have gone unreturned or yielded an unsatisfactory response; and so in these cases, you may come to the conclusion that sometimes *not* spending anything is the most effective way to send a message. Perhaps you have discovered that ExxonMobil is reluctant to acknowledge its role in climate change,[37] or that Kimberly-Clark is cutting down old-growth trees in boreal forests to make toilet paper,[38] or that your favorite brand of athletic gear may be produced using exploited child labor in a developing country. Now you have decided that it may be necessary to take your discontent to the next level by actively boycotting products and encouraging friends and co-workers to do the same. Be sure to also let the company know via email, letter, or phone call why you are no longer buying its products. For more tips on starting or joining a boycott, visit the **Green America** website.

## WAYS TO SUPPORT A GREEN ECONOMY

Sustainable Business Consulting, an environmental consulting firm based in Seattle, offers these ten suggestions for supporting a sustainable economy:

1.  **Bring your values to work.** Even if your employer doesn't totally "get it," you can still have a big impact by making small changes at work like using recycled products and saving electricity.

2.  **Vote with your dollar.** Supporting local businesses can translate to a lower environmental impact *and* keep your dollars in your community.

3. **Educate yourself.** Rankings such as the Global 100[39] and Climate Counts Company Scorecard[40] can shed some light on which companies are worthy of your hard-earned money.

4. **Eat real food.** The average U.S. household devotes 10 percent of its budget to food[41]. By eating sustainably grown food you can help reform the global agriculture system.

5. **Emphasize quality over quantity.** Opt out of the "stuff" economy, and send a market signal that you value things that are built to last.

6. **Extend the life of useful items.** Help reduce demand for new products by donating those that still have some life left in them. If something is broken, check to see if the manufacturer will take it back. If not, ask the company to reconsider its policy.

7. **Speak up.** Ask companies what they're doing on issues you care about. If you like what you see—or think they could do something better—tell them! Direct and personal feedback really does make a difference.

8. **Make the business case.** Challenge the popular perception that "green" is more expensive. There is a mountain of evidence out there affirming that sustainability is better for the bottom line.

9. **Spread the word.** Amplify the impact of your own actions by talking to your friends and family.

10. **Vote.** Market signals are often sent from government. Electing green-minded candidates can be an effective way to influence corporate priorities.

> ### Resources for a Green Economy
> **Responsible Shopper**
> **Global 100**
> **Climate Counts**
> **Natural Resources Defense Council (NRDC)**

## FLEX YOUR PURCHASING MUSCLE

### Have the Big Boxes Do Your Bidding  🕐=2 $=1 ▥=1

If you do find yourself shopping at large chains like Wal-Mart, Costco, or Target, make a commitment to buy the products in these stores that support environmental and social responsibility, such as energy-efficient light bulbs or organic clothing and linens made by people being paid a fair wage. Because of the tremendous buying power of big-box stores, these companies heavily influence how the goods they sell are produced and packaged. Wal-Mart's decision to stop carrying products with the chemical BPA, for example, did not come from the FDA (whose report proclaiming it to be safe was found to have ignored important research[42]); rather, it was a response to consumer demands—thousands and thousands of consumer demands. What better way to magnify your voice than to have one of these industry titans speak for you?

### Save Packaging, Money, and, Oh Yeah, the Planet
🕐=1 $=1 ▥=2

What don't you need? In this age of consumerism, this is often a tough question to answer, but as general rule, I try to buy in bulk, avoid single-serving containers, and bring reusable mugs for drinks like coffee and water. While I realize that "need" is, of course, a relative term, here are two examples of how following these simple guidelines can add up to big savings for both you and the environment.

- **Bottled water:** Bottled water can cost more per gallon than gasoline, is rarely higher quality than tap water, uses more water in the production of its bottles than those bottles will ever hold, and is recycled only about 10 percent of the time in the United States. Let's just say bottled water is problematic.[43]

- **That morning and/or afternoon cup of Joe:** Americans use almost a third of their drinking water to make coffee. Another thirty-nine gallons of water is necessary to actually get a cup's worth of coffee from seed to store. By foregoing an extra cup of coffee each day, or simply by making sure not to waste a cup by brewing too much, Americans could save over two billion gallons of water each year.[44] Besides, you know you hate caffeine headaches, so maybe this is a great time to cut back. For more energy- and money-savings ideas, check out **chapter 5.**

## SUCCESS STORY

### No Such Thing as Garbage

Who says dropping out of Princeton is a foolhardy move? Not Tom Szaky, who in 2001, along with co-founder Jon Beyer, had a vision for a new kind of product created completely from waste. In fact, their moment of inspiration came while visiting friends who were successfully using worm poop to grow thriving plants (I'll let you guess which types of plants they were trying to grow; hint, they were boys…in college).

After this "visionary" moment in 2002 (guessed which plant they were growing yet?), Szaky and Beyer founded TerraCycle, and the "eco-capitalist" company has grown exponentially since its humble beginnings in a Princeton dorm room.

## How It Works
- TerraCycle partners with corporations and accepts their "waste."
- By signing up on the TerraCycle site, you can receive an envelope to mail in waste, like cookie wrappers and wine corks.
- TerraCycle pays for each waste product (two cents per energy-bar wrapper, for example) as well as for shipping costs, and each collection location raises money for a cause or charity.
- The wrappers, plastic containers, plastic bags, and corks are used as packaging or raw material for such products as plant food, reusable shopping bags, kites, shower curtains, and messenger bags.

Szaky wants to redefine the idea of garbage. He says that it is "a commodity people are willing to pay to get rid of." To date, the company has repurposed over three million of Target's used plastic bags and collected seventy-four million Capri Sun drink pouches. Packaging that was once destined for the landfill has been reborn as backpacks, reusable bags, totes, and pencil cases.

As awareness grows about pollution and limited landfill space, TerraCycle's innovative model has been well received by many companies looking to reduce their waste. Szaky says, "Everyone is interested in eco-friendly solutions, and this is why all of these sponsors want to work with us." TerraCycle continues to grow with plans to expand into the international market in the near future, launching in Brazil in the summer of 2009. Sales are doubling every year as the company expands its product offerings into different categories and continues to take in high profile waste items. Holiday products, more bags, more office products, and a more extensive line of cleaners and laundry detergent have recently been brought to market.

Szaky operates with the firm belief that there really isn't garbage. "Garbage is a product that we haven't come up with a solution for yet. It doesn't exist in nature. If you look at any commodity creatively enough, you can eliminate the idea of garbage."

**Time to Buy!** 🕐=2 💲=3 🏢=3

Now that you have become a more educated consumer and know how powerful your purchases can be, we can get to the fun part— shopping! First, a word of caution: before you decide to dump the entire contents of your closet or your bathroom drawer in favor of an eco-friendlier version, remember that throwing things away is not socially or environmentally savvy at all. Consider the people power and resources that were necessary to make these goods in the first place. If you decide that something should be discarded, first get organized and safely dispose of anything you are concerned about due to potentially hazardous content, and then decide if you need anything new. If so, read on; if not, check back when your deodorant runs out.

## DIRECTORY OF ETHICALLY AND ENVIRONMENTALLY SOUND ALTERNATIVES

Where applicable, this directory also offers suggestions for making your own products (it doesn't get more local than that!) or purchasing reused items. For more on the joys of secondhand shopping, see **page 144 in chapter 5**. Keep in mind while browsing through this section that it is not meant to encourage a shopping spree. After all, the less we buy, the fewer resources are consumed. As a general rule, try to buy quality products made locally or by a company that you know is paying its employees a living wage. Also look for products with the lowest synthetic chemical content and ones that are made with the highest-quality materials to ensure that they will (a) release no toxins into the environment either while you are using them or after you dispose of them, and (b) last a long time. I have chosen to focus on the "necessities" in this section: clothing, home décor, cleaning products, and health and beauty products. Here is a sampling of some of the best options available to the ethical shopper. Updates to this list will be available at the *Ten Ways* website.

## Wear Eco-chic Clothing on Any Budget  🕐=2 $=2 🏠=2

I'm starting with a category that is near and dear to my heart: clothing. I'm a sucker for a new dress, a pair of shoes, or a sweater. Once in a while, I like to engage in a bit of retail therapy, and I am happy to report that it is easy to make this particular indulgence an entirely sustainable one. Also, since the average American family spends around two grand on clothing every year,[45] your fashion choices represent significant buying power.

Eco-fashion is taking hold because consumers, who have long since integrated responsible buying practices into other facets of their consumption habits, are demanding the same from their clothing makers. They want products that are produced without pesticides, made using recycled materials. Take cotton, for instance—that lovable, puffy, soft crop from which our towels, T-shirts, and linens are made. It turns out that conventional cotton farming accounts for 25 percent of all insecticide and 10 percent of pesticide use (in fact, production of just one T-shirt requires about five ounces of pesticides and fertilizers), and the runoff from these toxins flows and blows into neighboring communities.[46] Armed with that knowledge and a check card, who wouldn't look for the organic alternative? Fortunately, the more we look for these products, the more we will find them, and the cheaper—make that more affordable—they will become. For more information about cotton, check out **The Sustainable Cotton Project**.

From innovative clothes and accessories made from bamboo and recycled juice boxes to livable wages for textile workers, eco-fashion is one of the next major movements on the environmental consumerism front. For those trendsetters eager to green your wardrobes, you will be happy to discover that there is a plethora of cutting-edge possibilities.

## Jump-Start Your Eco-fabulosity by Following These Five Steps

1. **Decide if you really need it.** The most sustainable textile purchase is no textile purchase at all. Look closely through your closet next time you feel the urge to shop for the next perfect piece. Can you modify something you already have or borrow from a friend? After all, "new to you" is usually plenty new enough.

2. **Before buying new, check out vintage and gently used clothing shops.** Everything old is new again, and fashion is constantly hearkening to decades past for the latest trend. Why not get ahead of the curve at your local thrift and vintage clothing stores?

3. **Buy clothes made from sustainable textiles.** Look for materials such as bamboo and hemp (fast growing) or organic cotton (grown without the use of pesticides) or sustainably produced wool or cashmere.

4. **Be sure every textile purchase, from men's undies to bath towels, is produced without the labor of those working in sweatshops.** Look for "sweatshop free" on the label, visit the clothing company's website, or call the corporate offices to find out how and where your textiles have been produced. You can also find a list of "sweat-free" products at the **Green America** website. Remember, if you don't want to support sweatshops, it's up to you not to buy clothes that are made there.

5. **Stick to your style.** While the idea of organic clothing may conjure up images of overalls, flowing patchwork skirts, and

flowered peasant-girl shirts, organic fashion has become so much more than that (of course, it can be that, too).

# Fabulous Fashion Favorites

From the creations seen on the catwalk during New York Fashion Week to clothes made by environmental stalwart Patagonia, there is a style and price point for every palate and budget.

## Edun

Fashion designer Rogan Gregory teamed up with Bono and Bono's wife, Ali Hewson, to create Edun, a fashion line that works to support causes in Africa, South America, and India not only by manufacturing clothes there but also by contributing a portion of the proceeds to humanitarian causes on those continents.

## ParkVogel

Organic, cozy, casual, and sensual shirts, dresses, and sweaters for women, ParkVogel clothing is manufactured at a textile mill that recycles and uses methods that reduce carbon emissions created during the manufacturing process.

## Patagonia

In addition to its recycled and organic outdoor-clothing lines, Patagonia's eco-initiatives include a land trust and founding membership in 1% For The Planet.

## Stewart and Brown

Stewart and Brown was founded by a husband-and-wife team (last names Stewart and, you guessed it, Brown), who launched their first eco-chic line in 2002. Stewart and Brown's infinitely wearable designs are made using organic cotton, Mongolian cashmere, and renewable pesticide-free materials like hemp, linen, and factory surplus materials.

## Make Your Home a Green Haven 🕐=2 $=4 ▦=3

Now that you look eco-fabulous, be sure your home looks the same. When it comes time to repair, replace, or remodel your pad, be sure that you make environmentally responsible choices. If your inner designer does not exist, and the idea of unpacking, much less redecorating, gives you anxiety, find a friend whose apartment or home you admire and ask for his or her help (after your friend reads this section, of course!).

### Green Décor Galore

Whether you are repainting a chair or remodeling a house, here are some tips for ensuring that your home improvement projects are as environmentally responsible as possible:

- **Don't attempt to change everything at once.** It will be expensive, overwhelming, and probably discouraging. Choose a room, preferably one that you already want to revamp, and make a commitment to fill it only with products that are environmentally responsible and energy efficient.

- **Always consider alternatives.** Is it possible to install solar panels if replacing or repairing a roof? Can reclaimed materials be used instead of virgin wood? What about nontoxic insulation made with 85 percent post-consumer paper made by **GreenFiber**? Ask your contractor/landlord/building supervisor about what green alternatives are available, and do a web search for stores that may sell reclaimed building materials in your area. Even if you don't own a home, suggesting these renovations to your current landlord can help improve energy efficiency, reduce maintenance costs, and possibly even slow the rise in rent prices. As an added bonus, your landlord may even be eligible for a tax break for making some of these types of improvements, so make sure a bit of that savings gets passed on to you!

- **Buy quality products.** They last longer and will save you money over the long haul. Many building materials are still very difficult to recycle. The longer they stay serviceable and in your home, the longer they stay out of the landfill.

- **Use eco-friendly materials.** This includes nontoxic paint and carpet made of natural or recycled fiber. Sadly, that "new" smell from recently remodeled rooms is actually the off-gassing of volatile organic compounds (VOCs) from carpet, paint, and other finishes. This is a needless health hazard because all of these conventional products can be replaced with less-toxic alternatives.

- **Ask that the carpet and other materials that you are replacing be recycled or reused.** You can also visit the **Carpet America Recovery Effort (CARE)** website to find a recycling center for your old carpet. Keep in mind that most industrial recycling is not regulated by municipalities like curbside recycling is, so it is up to the consumer to ask that tough-to-recycle materials are not thrown in a dumpster. Some carpeting companies, like **Shaw Floors**, have begun to implement recycling programs as well.

- **For new appliances, be sure to buy ones with an Energy Star rating.** Check out the most efficient models at the **Energy Star** website. For more energy-savings tips, see **page 131 in chapter 5**.

- **Start your search for new furniture by looking for items made with recycled or repurposed materials.** Start at a local Goodwill or other thrift store, and if you can't find what you are looking for in a secondhand setting or you insist on matching pieces or Mom and Dad are pitching in to your new-furniture fund, check out **Branch, Eco-Green Living, Equita, Greener Lifestyles, modernlink**, and **VivaTerra**.

- **Add the final touch.** For everything from sheets and towels to curtains, look for products made with organic cotton or low-impact, fast-growing textile materials such as hemp or bamboo. Be sure your mattress is made with nontoxic materials, too. Some of my favorite places to find these soft goodies are **Branch, Green Sleep, Gaiam, Anna Sova, Loop Organic,** and **VivaTerra.**

### Keep It Clean and Green ●=2 $=2 ⊞=1

Okay, you have the ethically made and fabulous wardrobe and the responsible but lush décor, but how to keep everything looking shiny and new? Chemical cleaners? Only if you like the smell of noxious gases. In fact, when it comes to the cleaning arena, many of us are well meaning but brutishly uneducated. We have been trained to think that the smell of bleach or the odor of artificial pine is pristine proof positive rather than what it really is: noxious fumes filling our homes. Volatile organic compounds (VOCs) are not limited to paint and carpet; they are also released into the air when we use cleaning products derived from petrochemicals. One of the best ways to find nontoxic cleaners is to read the label. Our choice of cleaning products affects both our air and water—as we breathe in fumes and as chemical waste is washed down the drain. As always, a little education will go a long way toward helping you make the most responsible decisions. Be sure to read the label, and avoid using toxic chemicals such as those listed here.

### Some Cleaning Ingredients to Avoid

**Chlorine bleach:** Aside from being a toxic skin and eye irritant, chlorine bleach also has the potential to create fatal fumes if mixed with other household cleaners.

**Petroleum derivatives:** Many conventional detergents contain surfactants made from petroleum. These ingredients are byproducts of nonrenewable resources and have the potential to form harmful compounds when combined with other waste.

**Ammonia:** Vapors can cause dizziness and fainting, and it is also a skin irritant.

**A word of caution:** when making the switch to nontoxic cleaning products, don't dump your old ones down the drain. Dispose of them safely; use **Earth911**'s recycling locator to find a hazardous household-waste drop-off site near you.

## Some Awesome Alternatives That Really Work

Environmentally friendly cleaners get a bad rap because they are often accused of being less effective. I have tried many an enviro-cleaner, and I can tell you that while you may not get the same chemically induced "spring fresh" or "line-dried" fragrance, there are many brands of biodegradable cleaners that do the job just as well as conventional ones. Here are some of my favorites.

**Laundry and dish detergent:** My favorite brands are **Biokleen** and **Ecover**. Both make detergents and cleaners that are biodegradable and effective. Biokleen also makes many of its cleaners in concentrated formulas, which reduces packaging significantly.

**Make your own:** Baking soda and white vinegar are very effective multipurpose cleaners. Find do-it-yourself cleaner recipes at **Eartheasy.** As an added bonus, since a gallon of white vinegar and a container of baking soda cost about four dollars total, this cleaning method is lighter on both the environment and your wallet.

**Makeup Madness**  🕐=2  💲=2  🏠=2

Perhaps the most rabidly brand loyal area of our lives is hygiene and beauty products. Americans spend nearly $25 billion in this market every year. That is a ton of buying power, not to mention makeup and cleanser on faces.

So take another few minutes in front of the mirror, and start contemplating exactly what you are putting on your face every day. Chances are, you will find that the ingredient lists are shockingly similar to those of the toxic household cleaners you just replaced—more carcinogens, petroleum byproducts, and hormone disrupters—all spending some not-so-quality time with you before getting washed down the drain for wildlife, fish, and rivers to enjoy.

So turn that toxic-makeup frown upside down! Sure, some natural products are definitely more expensive, but how many tubes of lipstick or bottles of aftershave do you actually need? By factoring in the health benefits to you and the planet, you can easily justify the added expense. Here are some companies that make products you can happily put on your face (or anywhere else for that matter).

## A Few of My Favorite Things

**Alba Botanica**
I don't go anywhere without its garnet lip gloss.

**Dr. Hauschka Skin Care**
Deodorant is tough because nobody wants to be stinky, and this a tough switch for me to make because I am so active (and therefore sweaty). But almost all antiperspirants contain aluminum, which has raised concerns about neurotoxicity (deodorants less so). When I realized how many options were out there (and I have tried

almost all of them), it was easy for me to go au naturel without going all stinky. There are several eco- and armpit-friendly brands that work well including ones made by **Kiss My Face, Alba Botanica, Weleda, and Nature's Gate.** But my favorite is **Dr. Hauschka's Deodorant Fresh.** Admittedly I also have a soft spot for those no-nonsense, semi-lost-in-translation German brand names.

## Hugo Naturals

Hugo's shampoo and body wash smell good enough to eat, and all of its products are made without artificial fragrances, parabens, or alcohols.

## Jäsön Natural Products

Body-wash gel and soap are of special concern because they have so much contact with our bodies on a daily basis (well, most of us, at least), and it needs to be effective without being toxic.

## Nature's Gate

My fave flavors of this company's toothpaste are crème de peppermint and crème de mint, and as an added bonus this all-natural toothpaste doesn't taste like chalk.

## Pangea Organics

I love Pangea's lotion, and as an added bonus, all of the containers are recyclable and the packaging is embedded with seeds of basil or sweet amaranth. Packaging you can garnish your pasta with. Brilliant!

## Preserve

Great recycled toothbrushes and razors. It turns out you can brush your teeth with yogurt containers—another one of life's great mysteries.

## Some Ingredients to Avoid in Your Skin Care

**Formaldehyde:** Yes, the stuff your frogs were suspended in back in high-school biology. Used to make numerous household products and found in some brands of nail polish, formaldehyde has been classified by the International Agency for Research on Cancer as a human carcinogen.[47] Need I say more?

**Phthalates:** Found in cosmetics like nail polish and perfume, phthalates are also widely used as plasticizers for items as varied as PVC piping and toys. Studies have shown potential reproductive hazards, and phthalates are also classified as a water and air pollutant.[48]

**Triclosan:** This antimicrobial agent is found in many "antibacterial" soaps , as well as in some toothpastes and hair products. The concern of triclosan is twofold: it has the tendency to bioaccumulate in humans and animals (which means it continues to accumulate in our bodies and the bodies of any animals we ingest), and studies suggest its prevalent use may be contributing to increasingly potent strains of bacteria, which are resistant to antiseptics and antibiotics.[49]

**Parabens:** Used widely as a preservative in cosmetics, parabens have been shown to accumulate in human tissue and have been found in human breast tumors. While studies have not yet shown that parabens cause cancer, research does show that they act like estrogen and therefore may be a hormone disruptor.[50]

Visit **Skin Deep,** the **Campaign for Safe Cosmetics,** and the **Green Guide** for more buying tips and product updates.

**Give the Gift of Awareness** 🕐=2 💲=2 ▦=1

Presents are a great way to raise awareness about the many responsible, natural, low-impact products available. So why is it that every year many of us find ourselves up until midnight the night before whichever holiday we celebrate wrapping presents? Not just any old presents, either; these are often the gifts that we frantically grabbed at the last minute. Worse still, we find that we are wrapping them in the last of the reindeer wrapping paper that we had to borrow from our roommate.

When you find yourself in a gift-giving pinch, use these festive opportunities to give presents that align with your consumer values. In addition, shop online because not only is it less stressful, it is also more energy efficient. According to **Stop Global Warming**, "E-commerce warehouses use 1/16th of the energy used to operate retail stores. Even overnight air shipping uses 40% less fuel than the average car trip to the store." So chill out, stay home, hang those solar-powered or LED lights, skip the gift wrap (use newspaper or reusable gift wrap like scarves, jars, or reusable boxes), and check out a few of my favorite gift ideas for all of the memorable or obligatory gift-giving moments in your life.

## *WAYS* GUIDE TO GIVING GENEROUSLY

1. **For the person who has everything he or she needs (and really, that's most of us, isn't it?):** Choose a charity that matches your recipient's interests, and make a donation in his or her name. Most charities are ready to help you spread tidings of joy and are set up to send off an email or card to your loved one as soon as they receive your contribution. If you are not sure which charity to choose, **GuideStar** offers a free search service that classifies and rates nonprofit organizations and has recently added a new feature that enables you to donate directly from its site. **JustGive** is another site that facilitates the donation process: you can either donate directly to a charity of your choice in your name or in someone else's. For more ideas, check out the list of "Organizations Making a Difference" at the *Ten Ways* website.

2. **For the kidlets:** If you have been paying attention to the news recently, you are probably as scared as I am that the cute little doll you've been eyeballing for your niece will turn into next year's PVC-laden leadsicle. Lucky for us and all of the wee ones in our lives, we can find gifts ranging from footballs to musical instruments from such responsible purveyors as **Ten Thousand Villages**, **Kidbean**, and **Fair Trade Sports**.[51]

3. **For those who need a little pampering: Pangea Organics** is my favorite company for skin care. All of Pangea's products, from facial scrub to lip balm, are organic and made without synthetic preservatives, fragrances, parabens, or petrochemicals. For a little bit of a splurge, I also love the pricier products from **Dr. Hauschka Skin Care**.

4. **For the mamas and the mamas-to-be: Earth Mama Angel Baby** offers everything from ready-made gift baskets for the new and expectant mama to healing salves and teas—all organic of course. The website also offers a plethora of information, and your expectant mama will be grateful that you introduced her to this company. For more gift ideas, you can also check out **Baby Bunz and Co.** and **Babyworks**.

5. **For the gardeners (and eaters!): Seeds of Change** will send gift boxes of organic apples and pears to your fruit-fanatic friends around the country. You can also order gardening gifts or gift certificates to encourage your friends to plant their own organic bounty.

6. **For the perfect housewarming gift: Big Dipper Wax Works** makes beeswax candles of all shapes, sizes, and scents. While most candles are made with paraffin, which is a petroleum byproduct, Big Dipper uses beeswax, a 100 percent renewable

and natural resource. In addition, paraffin is a pollutant when it burns, and beeswax burns soot free.

7. **For the aspiring greenie:** If you know someone who is just getting started making environmental practices a part of his or her life, send a starter kit from **Greensender.** The box contains a reusable Sigg water bottle, a reusable organic cotton bag, an energy efficient CFL light bulb, and an organic cotton T-shirt.

8. **For those who appreciate the artisans:** If you have decided to eschew the big-box stores in favor of local community artisans, your first option is to go to local shops and markets and ask what is crafted nearby. If you can't find that perfect gift, table, or matching set of candlesticks, you may have to go a bit further afield. If this is the case, check out the websites of businesses like **World of Good,** which is a fair trade–, Green America–certified seller that works with local artisans all over the world to sell artwork at fair-trade wages. What's more, they have developed the "goodprint," which allows the seller to select specific statements about how the goods are produced, like "made in a producer-owned cooperative," "supports education and training," or "supports marginalized ethnic groups." Along those same lines, **Fair Indigo** sells "clothing and gifts made by paying a fair wage to those who make them." Fair Indigo's artisans from around the world produce clothing and accessories for men and women (often made with organic cotton), bath and spa products, gifts for babies, and gift certificates. **Ten Thousand Villages** works with artisan groups in over thirty countries, who make everything from home décor to jewelry. One of my favorite sections on its website is the section of "Recycled Treasures." For a sustainable online store that has everything from designer pillows to pet toys, check out **Branch.**

Still can't find what you are looking for? Visit the *Ten Ways* website for an updated list of "Businesses Making a Difference." You can also search *National Green Pages,* Green America's directory of screened and approved green businesses. Green America also maintains a **Green Gift Guide** with suggestions for everything from diamonds to diapers (I'm not sure who gives diapers as a gift, but it's on there). The list is updated seasonally.

## TOWARD CONSCIOUS COMESTIBLE CONSUMPTION

Speaking of necessities, we all have to eat. All facets of food consumption and production are a vital part of the conversation about how to improve the state of the planet and its inhabitants. As a consumer, you once again hold the key to demanding food that is grown in ethically and ecologically sound ways. **Chapter 7** will explore your role in the food chain and what you can do to ensure that everything on your table is not only healthy but has also had the lowest impact on the planet with regard to both humanitarian and environmental issues.

Chapter 7

# WAYS TO EAT WHAT YOU WANT WITHOUT EATING *THAT*

*The Triumphs of Good Taste for the New Low-Impact, Seasonal Omnivore*

> We could continue to decipher every far-flung product that appeared on our supermarket shelves. Or we could start fresh. We could immerse ourselves in the here and now, and the simple pleasures of eating would become a form of knowing.
>
> *Alisa Smith,* Plenty

## IN THIS CHAPTER

- Food: A Subject Near and Dear to Our Hearts— Like Four Inches
- Getting Started: Baby Carrots and Baby Steps
- Become a Local Gatherer
- Tips on Being a Compassionate Omnivore
- Grow Your Own
- Decisions, Decisions: What to Do with All That Food?
- *Ways* Guide to Canning without Killing Yourself or Your Friends
- Friends Don't Let Friends Eat Alone

## FOOD: A SUBJECT NEAR AND DEAR TO OUR HEARTS—LIKE FOUR INCHES

I'm talking about our stomachs, of course. Start talking to anyone about food, and you will find that it gets very personal very quickly. Food is the conduit that sentimentally whisks us back to the scenes of our life. For me, the perfect breakfast is still the one eaten on a crisp morning in my grandmother's kitchen. It was a simple meal composed of little more than fried farm eggs with orange yolks and steel-cut oats that had been soaked overnight. With a little attention to these simple ingredients over a cast-iron wood stove, both were cooked to perfection, and I hungrily gobbled them up, to my grandmother's delight. I make just as poignant an association with the smell of frying bacon. One whiff and I can see my Slovak father minding the thick slabs of grease-spitting meat on the stovetop while the pastries, with their flaky crusts and molten fruit centers, baked in the oven below.

We embrace food as both a necessity and as a reflection of our cultural and social identities. The establishment and evolution of our eating habits, our likes and dislikes, and the stories of our food are really our stories. Some of you, I'm sure, are looking curiously at your bowl of Froot Loops and wondering what story it tells about you. The answer to that question is more profound than you likely realize.

### Why Food Matters

In the early part of the twentieth century American food culture was still largely agrarian and local in nature. Without widespread conveniences like refrigeration, plastics, or chemical preservatives and with little transportation infrastructure, shipping food over long distances didn't make much sense. Had you lived back then, you would have found your choices much more limited. Fulfilling your daily nutritional requirements would have been much more difficult than it is today. To make a long story extremely short, all of that changed by the time we were born. Today there are some fast-food sandwiches that will provide all your calories, fat, and sodium in one pop.

For those of you who have grown up in the last two or three decades, most of the food you ate was probably prepared based on three main factors: affordability, ease of preparation, and shelf life. From frozen TV dinners to microwavable waffles and from Twinkies that defied the laws of decomposition to instant breakfasts that you simply mixed with milk, convenience was the name of the game. In our parents' increasingly hectic world, preservatives were seen as solutions, not problems. And in the world of upwardly mobile families, the ability to put any food product on the table, regardless of its origin or the costs involved in getting it there, was something to be proud of.

These beliefs were reinforced by school systems and other institutions, most of which served food with suspect nutritional value that only loosely approximated the recommended daily intake of vitamins and minerals. In most colleges, dining consists of whatever the cafeteria serves or whatever you can buy at the campus store or eat at a local restaurant or bar. Living on your own for the first time and without an impetus to do otherwise, most of you will relate to food in the same familiar way you always have.

Sure, when you're young and active and your metabolism is in high gear, there might seem to be few negative ramifications with eating food that lacks nutritional balance. Our supermarkets, with their well-stocked shelves and neat-looking packaging, convey the sense that both the food and the production processes are wholesome and healthy. Yet beneath the well-marketed surface of convenience lies the reality that, from the FDA to fast-food chains, our food priorities are almost completely disconnected from food realities. While the social, environmental, and health-related consequences of this reality are enormous, asking just a few simple questions will go a long way toward correcting our course.

I will tell you from the outset that when it comes to food, I have three main priorities: health, environmental, and social implications. This is not to say that I refuse to eat unhealthy food—believe me, I have my food vices! Instead, I tie health to both nutritional value *and* the production process. So I'm much more likely to eat an apple if it is grown without pesticides and not chemically treated to prolong its life.

My second priority is environmental impact, such as how much energy does it take to get the food to my plate, and how does production affect the environment (i.e., pollution from factories, toxic runoff from fertilizers and pesticides, or water contamination from animal waste, etc.)?

Finally, what are the social implications of our eating habits? Do they support local farms? Do they support the humane treatment of animals? Do they exploit the labor and resources of other countries? Obviously, taste matters, too, and no amount of sound practice can compensate for food that tastes bad; however, I have found that most of the food that aligns with my priorities is also delicious. So even if you do not rethink your eating habits for the many health, environmental, or social reasons given in this chapter, perhaps you will because local, organic, unprocessed foods simply taste better.

I included this chapter in the book because I believe that it is one of the greatest tragedies of modern living that we look at food preparation as more of an inconvenience than a celebration. This chapter offers information that will enable you to consume all kinds of food more responsibly. I encourage you to be curious about the food that you eat—where it comes from, how it is grown, and who is growing it. Like much of this book, this chapter encourages you to view your lifestyle in the context of the big picture. As something that all six billion–plus people in the world need on a daily basis, food—and the global system of production and distribution surrounding it—is one of the most complex systems of interrelationship to envision and understand. You may not like what you learn, but the more you know, the easier it will be to find alternatives and the more you will probably celebrate the food you eat.

## What Is Wrong with Obtaining Our Food from This Global System?

A lot. Obesity rates in the United States have been rising steadily and are correlated to the easy availability of cheap, unhealthy food. The farmers who produce food on a large scale are often underpaid and exposed to chemical pesticides and fertilizers. Additionally, recent food recalls in the United States and China provide ample evidence of the challenge posed in enforcing health and safety standards when food is produced on such a massive scale.

Even if you are comfortable consuming food that has been grown with chemical fertilizers and pesticides, there is the matter of processing, packing, and transporting the food, all of which takes resources and energy. It is estimated that the average meal travels 1,500 miles from farm to table, and the fossil fuels burned to get our food into a shiny package and from point A to B continue to contribute to global warming. Put it on a truck and refrigerate it, and you end up expending even more energy to get, for example, that kiwi from New Zealand into your fruit salad. I was shocked to learn that from farm to table, agriculture represents nearly 20 percent of U.S. energy consumption.[52]

What we put into our bodies is not only complicated from an individual standpoint; it is also a decision that involves all who may touch our food from planting to processing to platter. It is a true world-changing endeavor to make sure that the food we put in our mouths does not cause harm to ourselves, to others, or to the planet's ecosystems. What follow are some practical ways to simplify the process of ethically nourishing ourselves while at the same time eating more delicious meals, regardless of cooking ability.

## GETTING STARTED: BABY CARROTS AND BABY STEPS

### Read the Label 🕐=2 $=1 ▥=1

The first step toward more mindful eating is to just start paying closer attention to the food you buy. Look at nutritional labels and ingredient lists for starters. You may be shocked at, say, the sodium levels in many soups, or the chicken fat in your Doritos. If there's one benefit to supermarkets, it's variety, so compare products. Here are a few general rules to help you decide:

- Choose the one with ingredients that are the least processed. Processed ingredients have been altered in some way from their natural state for convenience or to change taste.
- Choose the one with the fewest ingredients.
- Lastly, if you are not sure what something really is—from what it is derived or how it is produced—then get on the Web and look it up.

There are plenty of chemically and genetically engineered "foods" that have been deemed fit for consumption, but that doesn't mean that we should be eating them or supporting an industrial food system that does not always have our health in mind. Consider olestra, a fat substitute found, until recently, in some low-fat chip products. Olestra was approved by the FDA as a fat substitute, although products containing olestra had to print the following on their packaging:

> **This product contains olestra**. Olestra may cause abdominal cramping and loose stools. Olestra inhibits the absorption of some vitamins and other nutrients. Vitamins A, D, E, and K have been added.

Apparently olestra worked as a fat substitute because it is too large to be digested. Barreling through one's intestinal tract, it had the unfortunate effect of depleting the body of important vitamins. It also caused lots of problems on its way out (including, though it did not end up on the warning label for obvious reasons, "anal leakage"). Setting aside the question of how the FDA could approve such an additive, a quick survey of that chip package would be enough for most of you to take your business elsewhere. So do your best to avoid additives with dubious names and potential side effects.

## Eat Organic Food ●=2 $=2 ▦=1

Just as I am creeped out by the fact that people who use Botox inject a strain of neurotoxin into their faces, I also worry about the fact that many of the pesticides used on my produce today are derived from nerve agents developed during World War II. The EPA sets allowable amounts of pesticide residues in food sold for human consumption, but recent studies suggest that organic foods are better for us in several ways. The obvious reason is that organic food does not contain pesticide residue, which can be especially toxic in infants (who have less-developed immune systems) and pregnant women (who already have organs under extra stress). Certain organic fruits and vegetables have also been shown to contain higher levels of vitamins and antioxidants due to the increased phytochemical production needed to naturally battle pests and weeds. When left to their own devices, these plants make better tasting, healthier fruits and vegetables.

Organic food has been criticized for being more expensive than conventionally grown food. Given the labor and care that goes into those perfect heirloom tomatoes or crisp hand-picked leaves of spinach, the cost usually seems worth it. However, all organic foods are not created equal, and some conventionally grown foods have more of a pesticide residue than others.

## The Dirty Dozen

**The Environmental Working Group (EWG)** puts out an updated list (called the "Dirty Dozen") of produce to avoid because of their high concentrations of pesticides. The information was compiled by the USDA and the FDA, and as of this publication, the twelve on the list were peaches, apples, sweet bell peppers, celery, nectarines, strawberries, cherries, kale, lettuce, imported grapes, carrots, and pears. These fruits and vegetables were tested *after* being washed and peeled, so don't think you can get off that easy. Even if you do not go completely organic overnight due to budget and/or availability, these twelve are a good place to start making the switch. EWG also puts out a list of the "Clean Fifteen" fruits and vegetables with the lowest concentrations of pesticides.

### Start Local with a Few Favorite Foods ●=2 $=2 ▦=2

Like some of you, I know how fortunate I am to live in a place where I *can* make decisions about what food I will eat, because *everything* is available in some nook of each of the cities in which I have lived—New York, Seattle, and Los Angeles have all provided me with a plethora of international culinary opportunities. But no matter where you live, start by making a list of organic foods that you are going to try to purchase as alternatives to nonorganic or processed ones. Of course, there is also the sticky issue of whether it is better to buy local or organic. Ultimately, the hope is that this is not a choice we need to make. However, during the winter months or in a location with a short growing season, it can be difficult to find much local fresh food. Still, products like meat and dairy can be produced year round, and winter in milder climates is a great time for root vegetables; I'm currently in love with the sweet-tasting rutabaga.

Even a partial commitment to eating locally produced foods will go a long way toward reducing the carbon footprint of your meal, so try committing to at least a few foods that you will only obtain seasonally from nearby sources.

## Find Out Where Your Food Comes From 🕐=2 💲=1 ⊞=1

Investigating the origin of a few favorite foods will really get you thinking about the resources required to get your meal from farm to table. For me, one of these gateway foods was baby carrots. I had been eating them for years with peanut butter, with hummus, in salads, and on their own. The whole time, I was patting my beta-carotene-rich back for choosing this snack food over its many less-healthful cousins. And while nutritionally I was making the right choice, there were many more factors that I needed to take into account.

First of all, it turns out that the name "baby carrot" is a misnomer. A true "baby" carrot is pulled from the ground at an early age, while the baby carrots we find in the store are most likely pulled out full size and then whittled down to "baby" size. After a particularly bland batch of my orange pals, I decided to investigate where my carrots actually came from. When I contacted the company that packaged my carrots, I was told by a nice woman that the company has "sources from all over the world" for its vegetables. Okay, so the charming health fable of my baby carrots just got a bit dicier.

This innocent yet eye-opening process got me thinking about the food I eat and how far it must travel to reach me. My usual carrot supply (when I cannot get them at local markets) is the organic, bagged carrots from Trader Joe's. A look at the back of that bag revealed that my peeled carrots (at least Trader Joe's doesn't call them babies) are coming from California. If these carrots are making the trek from California to Seattle, then I am certainly not eating them at the peak of freshness. And what about the fossil fuels used to package and ship my carrots almost a thousand miles? How many eighteen-wheelers on the road at this moment are taking California carrots and other produce to parts north and east? Are there hundreds of carrot trucks passing each other in the night? If two carrot trucks leave, one moving west at 60 mph...well, you get the picture.

By refusing to buy the carrots, lettuce, and other items of produce that come from faraway lands, we can reduce the economic and environmental costs associated with carting them all over the country and the planet. It's kind of simple, especially when you consider the fact that farmers' markets are springing up all over the place, and even "big box" natural food stores like Whole Foods now make a practice of informing customers where the produce has come from. Remember the power of the consumer: the more local food we purchase, the more farmers will produce in order to meet demand. As more businesses produce local food, competition will eventually bring the prices down. For more ideas about ways to harness your buying power, see chapter 6.

## Calculate Your Food Miles 🕐=2 💲=1 🏢=2

The **Natural Resources Defense Council (NRDC)** has a page on its website that allows you to forage for a list of foods that are in season right now near you. Here is a sample of what you will find:

## Washington State in late February?

| | |
|---|---|
| Apples | Onions |
| Carrots | Pears |
| Collard greens | Potatoes |
| Garlic | Rhubarb |
| Mushrooms | Winter squash |

## Connecticut in early August? Cornucopia:

| | |
|---|---|
| Apples | Lettuce |
| Beans | Mushrooms |
| Beets | Nectarines |
| Blueberries | Onions |
| Broccoli | Peaches |
| Cabbage | Pears |
| Cantaloupe | Peppers |
| Carrots | Plums |
| Cucumbers | Potatoes |
| Eggplant | Summer squash |
| Garlic | Sweet corn |
| Greens | Tomatoes |
| Herbs | Watermelon |
| Leeks | Winter squash |

## Frequent Fliers

The NRDC website also has links to help you find farmers' markets near you and a list of "frequent fliers" (fruits and vegetables that travel notoriously long distances from field to plate). Not only will produce from farmers' markets taste better, but they won't produce nearly as many global warming emissions on the way to your table.[53]

- Asparagus (Peru)
- Bell peppers (Netherlands)
- Tomatoes (Netherlands)
- Blackberries (Chile)
- Blueberries (Argentina)
- Cherries (Chile)
- Raspberries (Chile)
- Peaches (Chile)
- Nectarines (Chile)
- Papayas (Brazil)

## BECOME A LOCAL GATHERER

### Make Friends with Your Farmers 🕐=2 💲=2 🏠=2

So where to get all of this local, delectable food? Why not from the ones who grow it? Of course, your own garden is also an option, and tips on starting one can be found later in this chapter. Even if you live in an urban area, you will find that cities are more of a cornucopia than you ever anticipated. Consider the **Stone Barns Center for Food and Agriculture** in Pocantico Hills, New York: it is situated amidst the old Rockefeller estate just thirty-five miles north of New York City. The farm is overseen by Jack and Shannon Algiere, who both started working there when they were in their twenties. When I visited, I was greeted with the surprisingly fresh and crisp scents and sounds of a working farm. Here, the farm's beneficial symbiotic practices extend to all of the flora and fauna that have the privilege of living in this organic oasis.

When I entered the herb gardens where the market is held, I was greeted with the aroma of an herbal medley and the sight of tables loaded high with different varieties of lettuce, Asian braising greens, garlic scapes, herbs, several varieties of meat, and, of course, the vegetable that started my quest for local food: bunches and bunches of carrots!

On a subsequent Saturday morning, I visited the farmers' market in Pleasantville, New York. It is one of nineteen markets run in the New York City area by **Community Markets**. The three driving principles of the markets are "to make fresh produce available to all people, to support local agriculture, and to strengthen local communities." I'm down. A visit to a market with these values also ensures the opportunity to speak with the farmer who is growing the food, which is just what I did.

After a quick scope of the several stands, I met an entire family from Claverack, New York, who farms using "local, humane, sustainable farming and uses organic/biodynamic methods." Their name is pretty cute, too. The **Cowberry Crossing Farm** sells a variety of vegetables and also raises free-range, organically fed farm animals including bees, horses, chickens, and rabbits. The farm is their livelihood, which means that business is a family affair. This is the case for many organic farmers, who, despite the growing demand for their products, still struggle to turn a profit in the shadow of an agrarian system that is still mainly geared toward large-scale farming.

## Resources for Finding a Market Near You

**LocalHarvest**

**USDA Agricultural Marketing Service**

**CSA Center** (Note: CSAs [community-supported agriculture] work by connecting local farms with communities. People buy shares of the farm and receive weekly seasonal portions of whatever the farms produce. The CSA model provides farmers with much-needed steady income, while shareholders receive delicious, locally grown food and support local agriculture.)

# SUCCESS STORY

## A New Generation of Organic Farmers

Twenty-two-year-old Blake Johnston and twenty-five-year-old Julie Bottjen did not set out to try to change the world; they were just trying to grow enough food to sell to keep themselves out of debt and to keep nonorganic pesticides and fertilizers out of the water supply. The result? The best eggs, onions, cucumbers, and kale I have ever eaten. They are currently running Johnston's mother's farm, aptly named Growing Things, but they plan to buy their own farm in the near future.

What draws these young, articulate, introspective people to organic farming? For Johnston it has been a way of life. He grew up helping his mother, one of the pioneering organic farmers in the Seattle area, who first farmed flowers and later expanded to raising chickens and growing vegetables. Bottjen took a more circuitous route: she grew up in North Carolina and earned her bachelor's degree in anthropology and interdisciplinary studies, with a focus on sustainable development. She didn't begin farming until an internship after college. She utilized the **Worldwide Opportunities on Organic Farms (WWOOF) program,** which sets up aspiring organic farmers with internships all over the world, and found a position at the Oxbow Farm, just down the road from Growing Things.

While Bottjen and Johnston certainly have a lot of support within the organic farming community, the life they have chosen is not an easy one. In addition to the usual issues that farmers face (living at the mercy of unpredictable weather patterns, long hours, limited growing seasons), they must research prechemical farming history for clues as to how crop management was achieved naturally. In addition to crop rotation, which allows nutrients in the soil to be restored between plantings, Bottjen and Johnston use decoy crops, which are meant to draw pests away from their marketable crops. They also propagate beneficial plants, which attract useful insects, and they hide crops and insulate them to make them more weather resistant. All of these practices lead to healthy soil and roots. "That's the genius of it," Johnston says of organic farming. "Of course, there are plusses and minuses, and sometimes the weeds will take over, and it is difficult to get everything done, but we work within the seasons, and we are successfully producing food without added chemicals such as pesticides and herbicides."

Bottjen and Johnston believe that it is crucial to establish personal relationships with the people who grow the food we eat. The bigger and more remote your source of food, the less your health and well-being are likely to matter, and the less accountable large food producers are to you as a consumer. "Ask your farmers what they use for fertilizers. Educate yourself so you can ask questions," says Johnston. Ultimately, it is the demand from the consumer that will drive changes in farming practices.

For those who are interested in learning more about organic farming, Bottjen and Johnston encourage getting on-farm experience by visiting a farm or even spending a season living and working on one.

## Brave New World—Get More Than Veggies at the Market
🕐=2 💲=2 🏠=2

In addition to produce, eggs, and meat, many farmers' markets now offer a diverse selection of products. In the cities where I've lived, I have found some of the tastiest organic breads, cheeses, and pasta. And I eat a lot of organic bread and cheese (remember Violet Beauregard from *Charlie and the Chocolate Factory*? That's me, only with cheese). Bread and cheese addictions aside, you can usually feast for days on your farmers' market food, and during the most bountiful months, you can often go weeks without a trip to the supermarket.

While I initially thought that eating locally would require deprivation, the equation seems to work out like this: the more seasonally you eat, the more diversely you eat, and, consequently, the better you eat. The more colorful your plate and the more diverse your culinary palate, the more likely it is that you are getting all of the nutrients you need…from your food. Imagine that.

In the interest of candor, yes, buying local fresh food instead of packaged premade dishes means that you will have to cook. For some of you this may not be big deal, but I recognize that for others, this is like asking you to clone a child. Take it slowly enough to keep the experience enjoyable. Try organic free-range eggs from a local farm for breakfast, or try a salad made from organic fresh vegetables for lunch. Don't try to cook up an organic, grass-fed beef Wellington or local organic fruit tart pastries on your first go 'round.

## Take the Local Challenge ●=4 $=3 ▦=4

Once you have spent a little time eating locally and want to take your commitment even further, consider eating locally for a month, six months, or even a year. Get yourself excited for the project by reading such local-eating primers as *Plenty* and *Animal, Vegetable, Miracle*, and then set down a list of ground rules. Check in over at **Eat Local Challenge**, where you can pick a month when lots of others are also eating locally and perhaps even form a support group. I kid, of course, but you can swap recipe ideas and tips for local eating so that it feels like an adventure rather than an ordeal. Here are a few steps to get started:

- **Choose your "eat local" month(s) ahead of time.** Give yourself time to prepare.

- **Plan ahead.** Get ready by preserving (canning, freezing, drying) other foods that you will want but that may not be available year-round.

- **Research recipes.** This way you'll know what to do with all of these wacky, wonderful new vegetables that have found their way into your crisper. Alice Waters's book *Chez Panisse Vegetables* and Deborah Madison's book *Local Flavors* are great resources on the time of year to find the best vegetables in your region. Both provide delicious concoctions to make once you get your hands on them.

- **Choose a few "cheater goods" that are allowable exceptions.** After all, there are certain items, such as coffee, chocolate, and wine, that would be dangerous (to those around me) for me to go without.

### Drink Local, Too! 🕐=1 💲=2 🏠=1

If you happen to be a caffeine addict like I am, doing without that particular drug is not an option. However there are plenty of sustainably grown, bird-friendly, fair-trade coffee roasts available all over the country. And, of course, if your vices skew more toward spirits, there are local, organic beers and wines available all over the world. Microbreweries are cropping up everywhere, so even if you can't find a good organic wine or beer to suit your fancy, at least make an effort to drink what is produced locally. Liquid is heavy (a single case of beer weighs nearly twenty pounds—and you wonder where beer bellies come from), and the amount of energy needed to cart your booze around is a real buzz kill.

Keep your eyes open, too: as more producers strive for sustainability, more choices will become available. As my quest to eat locally increased in intensity, I often felt a real sense of guilt when it came to the wine I was drinking. In New York, my wine usually came from as far afield as California, Spain, and Argentina—although there were some good wineries out on Long Island, and I tried to drink their wine, too. Now that I live in Seattle, I am surrounded by the Pacific Northwest's wine country. Several local and regional wineries have begun to use organic and biodynamic growing techniques, which take organic farming to another level of purity.

## TIPS ON BEING A COMPASSIONATE OMNIVORE

**Meet Your Meat** 🕐=2 💲=1 🏠=1

Steak used to be my favorite food. The centerpiece of the most delicious meal I could imagine was a juicy slab of rare steak just off the charcoal barbeque. Meat—it's what I wanted for dinner. But those mad cows back in the mid-nineties changed all that. I spent a semester abroad in London during the height of the onset of bovine spongiform encephalopathy (BSE), or mad cow disease. The first case was reported in the United Kingdom in 1986, but the mayhem really started in the mid-nineties. According to the FDA, BSE is caused by feeding infected meat from another animal to a cow. That's how humans catch it, too, although in humans it is called Creutzfeldt–Jakob Disease.[54]

The more research I did on BSE, the more I realized that it wasn't just the meat that stunk; it was the entire food-production industry. It was an industry in which people no longer had a clear relationship with their food. How was it considered normal to feed discarded, processed cow parts, such as brains and blood, back to the cows we eat?

Instead of drowning my sorrows in beer—I was in London, after all—or rolling the dice with inexpensive but potentially BSE-laden cuts of beef, I decided to start researching where my food actually originated. Keep in mind that this was before such compelling exposés as *Fast Food Nation*, *Super Size Me*, or *The Omnivore's Dilemma* were available for consumption. But I knew enough to recognize that if there was a steak out there that could kill me, it was time to reevaluate my food choices.

There are several reasons you may be concerned about beef consumption and production, including the news in early 2008 that downers (cows so sick they are not able to stand on their own) were processed at a California meatpacking plant owned by Westland/ Hallmark Meat Company, which supplies food to school lunch programs.[55] Then there's the disturbing environmental statistic that livestock manure accounts for 25 percent of global methane emissions (a gas that contributes to global warming).[56] Or the fact that roughly 80 percent of our agricultural land and half of our water goes to raising and feeding our livestock population.[57] This is land that could be used to grow food for the nearly one billion people in the world who are undernourished and water that could go back into ecosystems, provide for hydroelectric energy, or support the growing human population.

I am not asking that you abandon your favorite food (even if it happens to be steak), but I do urge you to reconsider your meat consumption for the sake of the intrinsically entwined health of yourself and the planet. Think about how much of it you are eating, how the meat is raised, and what the animal is fed.

If you decide to eat meat, it is critical that you know what happened to your meat before it became that neatly wrapped package in your market. Make sure it meets your requirements, whatever they are. Might I suggest grass fed, free range, humanely raised, and antibiotic and hormone free, for starters?

Here are three easy ways to insure conscientious, compassionate consumption:

1. **Reduce the amount of meat you are consuming.** Try to limit yourself to once a week or less. As environmental author and activist Bill McKibben has suggested, try to think of meat as a condiment rather than as a main dish.

2. **Get to know your local farmers.** No matter where you live, it is now much easier to find grass-fed beef produced under

humane conditions by small farmers. Visit the farm and ask questions.

3. **Educate yourself.** Read some of the books suggested earlier, and for more books on responsible eating, see **page 11 in chapter 1.** Do a little research on the Web, talk to others about their decisions to eat less or no meat, and patronize organic, local restaurants and markets whenever possible.

### Hold Your Horses ●=2 $=1 ▦=3

You don't have to dive into a new diet whole hog, but if you do decide to eat less meat or none at all, take the transition at your own pace. For many vegetarians I have spoken to, their decision to stop eating meat was gradual, while for others it was cold turkey (okay, no more meat puns, I swear). It is important to choose a level of meat consumption that you are comfortable with. If you are worried about losing nutrients such as iron and protein, check with your doctor first to see how to stay healthy on a vegetarian diet.

For those of you who still crave the variety that a diet including animal products provides, or for those of you not yet ready to wear the badge of vegetarian, here are some alternative stops along the non-meat-eating spectrum:

- **Pescatarian:** No mammal meat, but fish is allowed. However, depending on your reasons for becoming a vegetarian (e.g., religious, environmental, health), there are many fish that may be off your list of acceptable foods. See **page 199** for resources to help you in your quest to be a savvy seafood consumer.

- **Vegetarian:** Vegetables, fruits, and legumes along with eggs and cheese are the mainstay of most vegetarian diets.

- **Vegan:** No animal proteins or animal byproducts. A big commitment to whole foods and strong reading glasses for the manufacturers' labels are necessary for this one, because animal products such as milk and eggs are used to make all kinds of food from bread to veggie burgers (oh, the irony).

### Know Your Fish Facts 🕐=2 💲=1 🏠=2

How would you like to do your part in further destroying the health of oceans? How about a side of mercury with that tuna or halibut? If you answered "no" to both of these questions, then read on. The oceans, which are one of the leading indicators of climate health, are not well. Nearly one-third of the world's fisheries have collapsed, and scientists have warned that the other two-thirds may follow by the middle of the century if current trends continue.[58] This decline can be attributed to several factors—overfishing and pollution among them. The choices we make about which fish to eat will have long-lasting effects on the survival of the oceans' creatures.

In addition to reading Taras Grescoe's book *Bottomfeeders*, which includes a list of questions you should ask your fishmonger and server before buying or ordering any fish, there are also several organizations that produce wallet-sized seafood cards to help you make your decision about which types of fish are okay to eat and why.

## If You Seafood on These Lists, It's Okay to Eat

### The Blue Ocean Institute

The institute's color-coded *Guide to Ocean-Friendly Seafood* is a great place to find out whether your fave fish is a victim of overfishing or may contain PCBs or mercury. Blue Ocean offers online lists, wallet cards, and a FishPhone, which gets you immediate information about your seafood choices when you send a text message along with the type of fish your are considering eating. Blue Ocean's methods of ranking are peer-reviewed for accuracy and are easy to understand.

### Seafood Watch

This is a project of the Monterey Bay Aquarium, and along with excellent information about how your seafood choices affect both your health and the health of the planet, Seafood Watch provides many tools to help you make informed seafood choices including a pocket-size guide, regional guides, and even mobile access for the most up-to-date, regional lists.

### The Marine Stewardship Council

The Marine Stewardship Council is an international certification and eco-labeling program. Its website describes standards for sustainable fisheries as well as information about how to find sustainable fisheries and their products in your area.

## GROW YOUR OWN

### How Does Your Garden Grow? Do It Yourself, and You'll Know
🕐=3 💲=2 ▦=2

If you have a tiny patch of land or even a deck or a room that gets a lot of sun, you can start practicing your gardening skills. What better way to ensure that you know where your food comes from then by growing it yourself? Nothing tastes better than a tomato from the vine or lettuce pulled straight from the garden. Start with a few vegetables; it's a small investment—some organic soil, seeds, and a few pots or a little plot of land—and see what grows. Don't be afraid to experiment. As long as you are composting, your "mistakes" will serve to feed next year's delicious take-twos. If you do end up with the mother lode of vegetables, such as beans, tomatoes, or cucumbers, there are several ways of preserving your food so it lasts year-round. This is especially handy if you live in a place where a year-round garden is not possible. For more on methods of preserving, see **page 205**. If you don't have a yard, consider getting a plot in a local community garden or growing your own hardy herbs and greens like rosemary and arugula in the kitchen or on the balcony. Most greens will germinate at a fairly low temperature and will go from seed to plate in about six weeks. Find a local community garden, or get tips on starting your own by visiting the **American Community Garden Association** website. You'll be surprised how much food you can grow with relatively little space.

---

## Gardening Books for Dummies

*Four Season Harvest* by Eliot Coleman

*How to Grow More Vegetables* by John Jeavons

*Eat More Dirt: Diverting and Instructive Tips for Growing and Tending an Organic Garden* by Ellen Sandbeck

*Carrots Love Tomatoes: Secrets of Companion Planting for Successful Gardening* by Louise Riotte

*All New Square Foot Gardening: Grow More in Less Space* by Mel Bartholomew

*The Kitchen Garden: A Passionate Gardener's Comprehensive Guide to Growing Good Things to Eat* by Sylvia Thompson

In addition to the these books, check and see if climate-specific books are available from local gardening associations. For

---

example, for the Northwest region of the United States, Seattle Tilth publishes the *Maritime Northwest Garden Guide*, which is full of seasonal tips for all types of gardening. It is useful to novices and experts alike.

## SUCCESS STORY

### From One to Thirty

Simon and Jane Frost did not plan on becoming farmers. After studying anthropology and architecture at Wesleyan University in Connecticut, Simon got involved with building alternative houses such as straw-clay and straw-bale homes. He even lived off the grid and grew about an acre and a half of vegetables for himself, hauled water from a well, and used firewood for heat. Gradually he began to wonder about the production and energy costs related to his daily food purchases, and he interned at farms in New York and New England. "I wanted to learn about it from people who were actually doing it," he recalls.

In 2004, at the ages of twenty-eight and twenty-five, the Frosts started their own thirty-acre farm in Maine. They now grow vegetables to sell at several farmers' markets, raise pigs that also help to clear the land, and make sauerkraut and other lacto-fermented vegetables, which are produced and sold year-round at natural food stores.

Like Blake Johnston and Julie Bottjen at Growing Things, the Frosts know that they have chosen a difficult way to make a living, but they also know how important it is that organic farmers persist. Simon and Jane work closely with other organic farmers in their area to keep the local food movement viable and healthy. Simon says, "We believe in the local food movement. We can all choose where to put our energy, and the most important thing is to do something positive."

Simon and Jane have just had a baby, and while they are concerned about the environment and the state of the world in general, they also feel that farming has kept them in touch with what is most important while still allowing them to do something tangible to improve the world for their son. "Farming is certainly not a way to get rich," Simon says, "It is a different lifestyle, because I get to work at home at something I want to be doing. I enjoy the spirit of the farm—seeing improvements, getting up early and seeing the sunrise, experiencing the cycles of the seasons—I am more aware of it all. Almost everyone is connected to the earth, but farmers are able to be connected in such a deep way."

## Work on a Farm 🕐=5 💲=1 🏠=5

Do you want to learn how to grow your own food and perhaps even grow food for others? Get thee to a farm! Most organic farms welcome interns, who do everything that the real farmers do (after learning how, of course). Working on an organic farm is the best way to understand how your food is grown, methods of pest control, soil preservation, and protection of diverse crops. And don't forget about all of the incredible, healthy food you'll get to eat. Most farms offer room and board in exchange for your sweat equity, and the organizations listed in the sidebar will help you find the perfect fit.

## Find an Organic Farming Internship Anywhere in the World—Let These Organizations Help

### Worldwide Opportunities on Organic Farms/WWOOF

WWOOF is a network that was started in the United Kingdom to help those who wanted to volunteer on organic farms. It has since expanded into an international organization with chapters all over the globe, which help volunteers find a suitable placement in exchange for food, room, and board.

**ATTRA—National Sustainable Agricultural Information Service**
This website offers a wealth of educational resources.

**Oregon Tilth and Washington State Tilth Associations**
The Oregon Tilth Association advocates, educates, and certifies organic farmers throughout Oregon and the rest of the United States. While Oregon Tilth does not have direct links to organic farming internships, its website has extensive resources for farmers and consumers.

## DECISIONS, DECISIONS: WHAT TO DO WITH ALL THAT FOOD

**Yes, We Can!**  🕐=3 💲=2 🏠=1

Or freeze. Or dry. While the prospect of eating locally seems easy to embrace in the middle of July when the farmers' markets are well-stocked with heads of lettuce as big as your head, it is another thing to think about eating locally during the middle of winter, especially if you live somewhere where winter involves frost or frozen ground. If you are committed to eating locally, however, there are plenty of methods that have gotten people through the non-growing season since before the invention of refrigeration (canning, root cellaring, drying, smoking)—and after, too (freezing). Many people shy away from preserving food because they don't know how to do it, they think it might be too much of a hassle, and/or they are afraid of accidentally ending up with a self-inflicted case of botulism (don't give presents of preserved peppers until you are sure you won't be doing this). Not to worry; there are plenty of good books and websites with step-by-step instructions on how to can, freeze, dry, ferment, and otherwise preserve everything from huckleberries to salmon fillets.

## *WAYS* GUIDE TO CANNING WITHOUT KILLING YOURSELF OR YOUR FRIENDS...A SORT OF SUCCESS STORY

I started my first canning adventure with a quick search on the Internet on how to make blackberry jam; within minutes, I had several natural recipes consisting mostly of the correct ratios of sugar, blackberries, and apples to choose from. Besides, the canning process dates back hundreds of years, so how hard could it be? Oh, what hubris! What naïveté! I invited a friend to join me for the fun. We were both canning rookies, but she had taken a six-hour canning class at a local culinary school, earning her the title of expert. I also called a friend back on the East Coast who "puts up" many bushels of tomatoes a year (we're talking hundreds of pounds here). She was understandably incredulous that our venture didn't include a canning veteran, but nonetheless, she eagerly offered advice.

My friend and I were able to pick a bounty of blackberries at a local park in less than an hour. One of the lessons we learned from our haul was that if you are willing to make the time (and in this case, brave the spiders that like hanging with the berries as well), you can gather enough free fruit for months! We also picked tomatoes from our gardens and supplemented them with a box of "seconds" from a local farmer.

Loaded down with ingredients and ambitious plans and armed with advice from my canning guru and a book called *The Busy Person's Guide to Preserving Food*, we embarked on our canning adventure.

The good news first: we learned a lot. While we were still woefully underprepared for a nuclear winter, we were well stocked for a power outage or snowstorm. Here are the most salient nuggets and a few bad, but not completely rotten, canning puns:

1. **Head into your adventure with a positive outlook.** Like many skills, canning takes a little practice, or in our case, trial and a few errors. Remember, in order to succeed, it is imperative that you have a can-do attitude.

2. **Be sure to enlist the help of a canny canner.** There are a lot of absolutes to canning: you need to know how much space to leave; how much salt to add; and the right moment to take the jam off the stove, or it will burn and become brown sludge (yup, learned the hard way)—so it is a good idea to preserve food with someone who has done it before.

3. **Don't be too ambitious.** For our first time, we tried to do too much. What's too much? Let's see...making jam, freezing berries, canning tomato sauce, and canning whole tomatoes. For first-time preservers, capping your endeavors at two projects will ensure that your experience is much more *can*joyable.

4. **Have all your recipes ready, and understand directions from start to finish.** Since we were trying to use both a pressure canner and a boiling-water bath to preserve our concoctions, we had a hard time transferring directions and figuring out timing. We also did not have exact recipes for everything; in short, "winging it" on your first time is not advisable!

---

### A Few Good Books on Food Preservation

*Putting Food By* by Janet Greene

*The Big Book of Preserving the Harvest: 150 Recipes for Freezing, Canning, Drying, and Pickling Fruits and Vegetables* by Carol Costenbader

*Preserving Summer's Bounty: A Quick and Easy Guide to Freezing, Canning, and Preserving, and Drying What You Grow* by Rodale Farm Center, edited by Susan McClure

*Joy of Cooking All about Canning and Preserving* by Irma S. Rombauer, Marion Rombauer Becker, and Ethan Becker (apparently it takes a family to raise a pickle)

How you eat—the mood or spirit, the beauty of the table, and the company with whom you enjoy a meal—also matters. As a source of satisfaction and renewal, few daily rituals have the extraordinary potential of the act of preparing and sharing a meal. Whether you are feeding your family, friends, or even strangers, cooking can be an expression of affection and connection, both of which are good for the mind and the body. The conversation and social interaction are usually the best part of the meal.

*Irma S. Rombauer*, Joy of Cooking

### Cook Your Own Food   ●=3   $=1   ▦=2

From an organic cheese-and-lettuce sandwich to an elaborate six-course meal, what matters most are the ingredients. One of the best ways to ensure that you are eating exactly what you want without also eating preservatives, chemicals, additives, or pesticides is by purchasing and cooking the food yourself. If you happen to care about money at this point in your life, there are also monetary benefits to cooking for yourself; for the price of having someone at a natural food store or market prepare you a sandwich, you could probably buy the ingredients whole and make three or four at home.

If you haven't done much cooking for yourself or are only

handy with a microwave, the prospect of cooking a meal on your own can be intimidating. And if you are beginning to wean yourself off of meat, learning to cook vegetarian staples like tofu or couscous can be downright frightening. As is the case with most things in this chapter, start out slowly. Buy yourself a rice cooker; those things are idiot proof. Buy a few good, simple cookbooks, and ask friends for suggestions. Almost anyone you ask will have at least one favorite vegetarian or interesting seasonal dish to share.

Of course, this is a great task to take to the Web, which now has recipes for *everything*. A quick search with the name of a dish you would like to try or key ingredients that you have on hand will often yield hundreds of options. Food blogs are especially interesting to look at because readers will usually review posted recipes, and writers often include photos, step-by-step instructions, potential pitfalls to avoid during preparation, and links to some of their favorite recipe websites and blogs. I am especially fond of **Epicurious** because of the reader reviews and photos and of the blogs **Smitten Kitchen** and **Chocolate and Zucchini**. Don't be intimidated by the fact that many of the Epicurious recipes come from *Gourmet* and *Bon Appetit*, but do pay attention to the prep time. If you don't have three hours for a dish, don't start one that requires that much time; and if you're not used to working from a recipe, leave yourself up to 50 percent extra prep time.

Remember to start with easier recipes. You can always work your way up to that elaborate three-layer vegan chocolate cake. Learn how to laugh at experiments gone awry. After all, when you consider the garbage you have eaten on those late-night snack runs or backcountry road trips, your less-than-perfect pasta won't seem so bad. And who knows? You just might turn out to be a budding culinary genius. For now, though, I consider my meals successful if they don't send my friends to the hospital—and by that measure, I am a pretty successful cook.

# A Few Good Books and Websites for Beginners

*How to Cook Everything Vegetarian: Simple Meatless Recipes for Great Food* and *How to Cook Everything: Simple Recipes for Great Food* by Mark Bittman

*Vegetarian Cooking for Everyone* by Deborah Madison (she has a lot of other excellent cookbooks, too, but this is a good one to start with)

*Moosewood Restaurant Cooks at Home: Fast and Easy Recipes for Any Day* by the Moosewood collective

*Joy of Cooking* by Irma S. Rombauer, Marion Rombauer Becker, and Ethan Becker

*The New Vegetarian Epicure* by Anna Thomas

*Blue Eggs and Yellow Tomatoes: Recipes from a Modern Kitchen Garden* by Jeanne Kelley

**All Recipes**—a nicely organized and detailed recipe website with useful features, such as the ability to select recipes according to budget, ease of preparation, or healthfulness

**Culinate**—a lovely blend of magazine, blog, cookbook, discussion forum, and news site for all things food; its big-picture approach to how food is raised and prepared is seamlessly integrated into the site's content

## Take It Slow  🕐=2  💲=1  🏠=2

The **Slow Food** movement was started in 1986 by Carlo Petrini and a merry band of protestors who did not want a McDonald's in Rome. The international Slow Food movement was founded in 1989, and since then it has grown into a worldwide organization with over seventy-five thousand members. The movement is centered on the idea that all of our food should be prepared with care, with attention to our communities, and with a connection to its source. The slow foodies want people to view food preparation as an integral part of preserving not only the environment but also a quality of life. Additionally, there is a movement within the movement that focuses on mentoring and encouraging younger generations. Events for all ages take place all over the country, and they are a great place to meet like-minded people. My husband, who has never made a meal in under an hour, loves this movement.

## Let Someone Else Do the Cooking  🕐=2  💲=3  🏢=1

Many still believe that a good restaurant meal must contain a combination of the following: fat and lots of calories, exotic dishes, and at least one unexpected and out-of-season ingredient. So the conversation about the meal goes something like this: "Aren't we lucky to have this chutney of kiwis from New Zealand?" or "This cheese from the French countryside is so creamy," or "I just love Italian tomatoes."

Indeed, you may be right in your comments, but there is a problem with this scenario: these items will have spent many days traveling and will consume much fossil fuel in order to get to your plate. As demand for fuel rises and supplies begin to dwindle, we will have to make more sensible decisions about how we are going to use what fuel remains. Do we really want to find ourselves facing the catastrophic effects of global warming, not to mention gas lines in fifty years, because we just had to have those grapes from Chile or those avocados from Mexico? Of course it's necessary to ship food around the world in some cases, but the more you develop an appreciation for the flavors of your region, the more you'll be supporting a system that can last over the long run.

So why not jump-start your commitment to local, sustainable eating with a trip to a restaurant where the chefs prepare food with these values in mind? Many restaurants are making the shift to local ingredients in order to meet customer demand and also because local tomatoes generally cost less and taste better than those shipped or trucked in over a period of days. A night out at such an establishment is also a good place to get ideas about what you might be able to make in your own kitchen. Simple recipes with high-quality ingredients often produce the best food you have ever eaten. For very special occasions, I keep a list of local, sustainable restaurants that I want to try all over the country (as you've no doubt gathered, I love lists). This list of delicious restaurants with sustainable values just keeps on growing. Many restaurants will even take the feast to you by catering special events, allowing you to open up the world of local organic cuisine to others. For more ideas about how to raise awareness about issues of food and more at any social occasion, see **page 227 in chapter 8.**

## A Few of My Favorites

There are incredible sustainable restaurants with an emphasis on seasonal ingredients springing up all over the country. Here is a sampling of my favorites from some of the places I have lived:

**Seattle:** Stumbling Goat, Canlis, Le Pichet, Tilth, Crush, Homegrown

**New York:** Blue Hill at Stone Barns, Cookshop, Marlow and Sons, Quartino Bottega Organica, Café Habana, Candle Cafe

**Los Angeles:** Lou Wine Bar, Akasha, Elf Café, Lucques, Urth Caffé

Check out the *Ten Ways* blog and website for more of my restaurant recommendations and to add yours!

## FRIENDS DON'T LET FRIENDS EAT ALONE

As you progress through your twenties, your idea of a great evening might begin to shift from the expensive nights out getting elbowed in crowded bars to a night spent at home with music of your choosing, wine by the bottle, and the opportunity to prepare a delicious feast with your close friends. This, of course, brings us to one of the best parts of being in your twenties: all of those chances to throw or attend a party! Now that you have mastered the fine art of cooking—or at least figured out how to find and prepare some delicious, sustainable nachos and wings—it's time to show off those skills. **Chapter 8** will help you combine your love of local cuisine with your love of parties and your desire to raise awareness about the causes you believe in. Who knew multitasking could be so much fun?

# WAYS TO THROW (OR ATTEND!) A PARTY WITH A PURPOSE

*A Step-by-Step Guide to Throwing Parties That Can Change the World*

Remind me tomorrow that I helped someone today!
*Society of Mature Adults Seeking to Help, Entertain,*
*and Donate (SMASHED)*

## IN THIS CHAPTER

- Cause(s) for Celebration

- Ideas for a Few Good Parties

- *Ways* Guide to Throwing Your Own Bash

- Crash a Bash

- Let's Eat! Food and Drink for the Big Party

- The World Is Your Oyster. Explore Your Oyster.

## CAUSE(S) FOR CELEBRATION

Let's face it: partying is a fact of life when you are in your twenties. According to the United States Department of Labor's Bureau of Labor Statistics, the average twenty-five- to thirty-four-year-old spends 4.3 hours a day on leisure and sports activities.[59] Why not capitalize on all this leisure time by also giving to a worthy cause or learning more about an important social issue? What's more, if you have already found a cause to support, a party is a great place to share your commitment and to recruit your friends.

So stop worrying so much about making something of yourself, and keep partying—these are your twenties after all, an important time to enjoy life, let loose, and live a little. If your twenties are anything like mine were, there is probably much time devoted to work *and* play. Here are some easy ideas to help you make the most of your parties while making life better for others in the process.

In college or at gatherings with friends, it may be all about beer pong, scavenger hunts, card-game tournaments, or costume parties. Before and after graduation, you have the opportunity to take those "skills" and use them to announce your decision to make the world a better place, raise money for a cause you believe in, hold a phone party urging registered voters to get out to the polls, or screen a documentary to shed light on an environmental or humanitarian cause. Get inspired, excited, and creative as you plan your world-changing kick-off party!

If you are not sure where to get started, don't worry; this chapter includes step-by-step directions on planning a party to suit your budget and interests. There are also tips on how to find socially conscious catering companies, organic restaurants, beer, wine, and party victuals.

## IDEAS FOR A FEW GOOD PARTIES

The difficulties of hosting a benefit largely depend on how long it takes you to put together your party, how much money you spend, how much money you would like to raise, what entertainment you provide, and where you host it. Remember, your party should reflect your interests, so be as creative as you can! A charity bash is a fun way to raise money and awareness about your favorite (or latest) organization, cause, or candidate. Don't be afraid to ask your guests to grow their facial hair, dress up in funny costumes, play dodge ball, or just sit on the couch and drink beer. Just make sure you choose activities that suit the interests of you and your friends, and everyone will have a great time. Once you throw a party with a purpose, you will never want to throw a regular party again!

## *WAYS* GUIDE TO THROWING YOUR OWN BASH

1. **Decide on a cause and a charity that will receive the proceeds.** There are nonprofit organizations profiled throughout this book, and an updated list of worthwhile organizations making a difference can be found on the *Ten Ways* website.

2. **Send out an email invitation, and request that your guests RSVP.** This way you'll know how many snackables and drinkables to have on hand. Be sure to explain to your prospective guests the premise of the party, the importance of the cause, and how their donation will support it. If you want to send a paper invitation, be sure to use ones made with recycled paper.

3. **Find a location.** If you are on a tight budget, chances are the location will be your apartment. You also should consider

asking friends with a bigger place to let you use it or asking a local bar to donate space (and possibly even drinks). If your friends with the sweet pad need convincing, you can tell them that their donation of location will count as their contribution. Also assure them that you have very responsible friends—and be prepared to help clean up the next day!

4.  **Get busy buying the goodies.** Buy in bulk—i.e., a big wedge of cheese, oversized bags of chips, jars of salsa, and a bunch of celery and carrots. People aren't looking for gourmet food; they know that you are on a budget and that the less money you spend on goodies, the more money you'll spend on the charity. Also, this type of bulk entertainment "cuisine" is better for the environment (less packaging) and better for your wallet. Try to buy local and/or organic goods whenever possible. There are suggestions for organic food and drink in this chapter as well as in **chapter** 7. You can also ask each guest to bring a dish, and you may be able to get a beer company or local store to sponsor you, so ask around.

5.  **Accept help from guests.** Some of your friends may offer to bring a donation and a bottle of wine, etc., and others may be so excited about the concept that they offer to pitch in by helping you with the food, the setup, or even the cleanup. Whatever the offer to help is, say yes. After all, the more you can make the charity party feel like a community effort, the more likely your guests will be to invest their time and money in future events.

## Ten Sustainable Beers and Wines Worth Toasting

- Wolaver's Organic Ales
- Bison Brewing

- North Coast Cru D'Or Belgian Style Ale
- New Belgium Mothership Wit
- Lamar Street Organic Pale Ale
- Bonterra Vineyards
- Mas de Gourgonnier
- Quivira
- Ceàgo Vinegarden 2007
- Fetzer
- Sokol Blosser

## Host a Benefit on Your Budget  🕐=3 💲=2 ⊞=2

After the devastation of Hurricane Katrina, my husband and I decided that it was important for us to help. He is a teacher and I am a writer, so the amount of money that we could contribute on our own was negligible. However, we were not alone in that many of our friends expressed an interest in finding ways to make a tangible, immediate impact with a financial donation.

We decided to make it easy for our friends to contribute by throwing the appropriately alliterative low-budget benefit bash. We told everyone to bring the money they would have spent on a bottle of wine or a six-pack of beer and donate it instead to the victims of the hurricane. Our friends and acquaintances (we wanted to seem quite popular) loved the idea, and by pooling our donations, we were able to raise much more for the hurricane relief effort than we could have on our own. We found that people wanted to be generous and give to a worthy cause; we just made it easy for them to do so.

The best part of this kind of party is that you will see immediate results! We raised a sizeable donation toward the hurricane relief effort, and the party rolled on into breakfast the next morning.

If you find yourself with more money and a worthy cause to support, consider throwing a benefit with a higher budget. You will still supply the food and drink (which will be an upgraded version of the low-budget benefit previously described), and you may want to sell tickets and extend the invitations beyond your circle of friends. Consider partnering with a local nonprofit or asking friends to become sponsors and agree to bring at least ten people to your bash. Keep in mind that your expenses should be less than 50 percent of the amount of money you gross, so be on the lookout for in-kind donations of goods and services as well as free publicity. Some municipalities also require that you register your benefit before you publicize it, so check with your town or city first.

## Five Websites Every Green Party Animal Should Know

**Evite**—paperless invitations
**Organic Bouquets**—organic flowers
**Epicurious and Culinate**—delicious recipes
**Green America**—directory of socially and environmentally responsible businesses; start here when looking for party supplies

## SUCCESS STORY

### $20,000 of Lemonade

After the loss of her beloved aunt to breast cancer, twenty-nine-year-old Sheila Paule decided to throw a benefit party in New York City to raise money for a cancer support center. She wanted to find a way to honor her aunt's memory by raising money to help both those living with cancer and their loved ones. Sheila is an event planner, so she knows how to bring people together for a good cause. The cost of admission to the party was $75; she rented out a bar, served free drinks, held two auctions, and played great music all night. Sheila's advice for those interested in hosting a benefit is to "choose an organization that will work with you to help send out invitations to its members." With a little help from her friends, the DJ, and the bartender, she raised $20,000 for Gilda's Club, a cancer support network.

## Hold a Screening 🕐=3 💲=2 🏠=2

Many not-for-profits have adopted the brilliant idea of asking supporters to throw parties in their homes to introduce new people to their organization, to educate the public about a cause such as youth development, arts, education, or health care, or to alert them to a social or environmental injustice. Often the sponsoring organization will send a kit with step-by-step instructions, so this kind of party is easy to organize and a good excuse to get together with friends. Here are some ideas for ready-made presentations:

- **The New Heroes:** The New Heroes motto is "Have a party and change the world." Robert Redford and the **Skoll Foundation** teamed up to promote a series of documentaries about young men and women who tackled serious social issues such as poverty and illness by using "business skills coupled with passion and determination." Each documentary draws attention to a specific plight and to the ways in which ordinary men and women are using their ingenious ideas to do something about it. Here are some of the featured stories:

  - Two men in Africa who are bringing new technology to African farmers
  - A group of women in India who are teaching impoverished children at ad hoc schools housed in train stations

- Women in Brazil who are earning a fair wage for their sewing skills through a women's cooperative

By throwing a house party, you not only shed light on these inspiring people and their causes, but you also inspire others to come up with their own creative solutions for social problems closer to home or further afield. Although the New Heroes official campaign has ended, you can still go to the New Heroes website for tips on throwing the parties, suggestions for discussion, and links to the PBS website where you can order a DVD of the entire series.

- **Sierra Club Chronicles—Spotlight on Environmental Issues:** The *Sierra Club Chronicles* is a DVD series produced by Brave New Films in association with Sierra Club Productions. Each thirty-minute episode explores a current environmental situation, such as the effects of the air quality on 9/11 rescue workers, the 1989 Exxon Valdez oil spill off of Prince William Sound and its ongoing effect on local residents, and the fight to protect the Gulf Islands National Seashore from drilling. As the host of the house party, you choose which episode you would like to show, and you offer your guests specific suggestions for actions to take in order to help alleviate each featured environmental problem. You can also order the entire series for $10 from the Sierra Club website.

You can also customize your party by choosing to screen a documentary that made an impact on you. For the cost of a case of beer and some microwave popcorn, you can begin to educate your friends about an important cause. Believe me, there are movies out there about almost every subject, and you have the freedom to explore any issue that interests you. Simply choose a film to share that changed the way you think about a topic, and invite some friends over to watch it. Check out the list on **page 17 in chapter 1** for many movie suggestions.

## Swanky Stuff Swap 🕐=2 💲=1 🏠=1

One of the best ways to raise a little awareness about the high cost of a disposable lifestyle—and to acquire some new-to-you belongings—is to hold a "swanky stuff party." If you would like to attend a party instead of hosting, find a swap near you at **Swap-O-Rama-Rama.**

A swap works something like this:

1.  **Invite a few friends over to refresh your wardrobe and theirs.** These types of parties are also a great opportunity to catch up with friends and discuss current issues. A friend of mine calls her party "Bitch and Swap."

2.  **Ask them to bring clothes, CDs, DVDs, books**—basically your typical yard-sale fare, minus the garden gnomes.

3.  **Ask a friend who loves to cook (or owes you a favor) to make some yummy hors d'oeuvres.** I usually ask my husband to do it (he almost always owes me a favor).

4.  **Start the evening off with a little "junk education."** I recommend showing *The Story of Stuff with Annie Leonard*, a twenty-minute video about "the underside of production and consumption habits."

5.  **Let the games begin!** Have everyone display what he or she has brought and start swapping goods with each other. You might want to break stuff into lots—like the kitchen lot, the bathroom lot, or the coveted "everything drawer" lot—or you can just have everyone rummage and rumble. Try to limit alcohol consumption if you choose the latter.

6. **Bag up all unwanted leftovers, and donate them to a local thrift store.**

My husband and I started this tradition on our second long-haul move from Los Angeles to New York. At that point, we were all about "net reduction," and we only wanted the "swap" to go one way, so this particular party worked more like a "give." Of course at the end of the night, anyone who felt burdened by our fabulous stuff was encouraged to leave it behind (we didn't want anything "accidentally" making its way into the local landfill). Any of the fabulous goods left behind—I mean, who wouldn't want the seashell ashtray I made in seventh grade? (don't ask why I was making ashtrays in seventh grade)—was donated to a local Goodwill. The net result was that many of our friends left with "new" stuff, and to this day, we have visitation rights with many of our former belongings still residing on the West Coast. For more ideas about ways to reduce, reuse, and recycle, check out **chapters 4 and 5**.

## Set Up the Home Soapbox 🕐=2 💲=2 🏢=1

If you would rather have someone speak in person to your group of friends, throw a "We Give a Damn: Good Party." Many organizations will send local representatives to offer firsthand accounts of how they have served others, or they will help you invite a board member or other advocate to come and speak. These community representatives can offer quick highlights about the organization, answer questions, and prep the party planner (you!) with material and talking points. Most people are much more likely to get involved with an issue or cause when they meet someone who has been directly affected, so having someone speak about why an issue is important to him or her is an effective way to encourage activism. If you are not sure how to contact the local chapter or representative of your favorite organization or charity, contact the national chapter and explain that you are trying to throw an awareness party. Most will gladly put you in touch with someone locally. Many organizations are already set up with outreach networks, so it will only take a phone call or two to find someone near you.

## Phone It In   🕐=2  💲=1  🏢=2

Speaking of the phone, if you and your friends like to talk on the phone and have unlimited cell minutes on the weekends or more rollover minutes than you could ever use, then this is the party for you. If you are trying to raise awareness about a referendum or political candidate, mobilizing voters by calling them and asking them to vote is a great way to start. Individual campaigns as well as political action organizations like **MoveOn** organize voter call parties all over the country for elections and referendums, and those on its email list will always get notified when a gathering is brewing. You can also contact your local political party or favorite candidate's headquarters during the next election season and ask how you can help organize a phone party. No matter what your political affiliation, these types of gatherings are also great places to network with like-minded people.

## Serve a Meal, Serve a Cause   🕐=3  💲=3  🏢=2

**Epicurious** and **Feeding America** (formerly America's Second Harvest) have teamed up to offer Wine. Dine. Donate charity dinner menus and a "host kit" to help you organize your very own event. Each dinner party is a powerful opportunity to raise awareness about poverty and to raise money to feed your hungry neighbors. Menus from many famous chefs are available online, and each dinner item comes with a suggested wine pairing. The online party guide gives you time lines for food preparations, a list of the cookware you'll need, and a link to **Evite** to help you send out the invitations. It even gives you place-card templates and printable menus. Each guest brings a donation for Feeding America, and assuming you know which end of a knife to hold, everyone enjoys a "professional" meal. You don't have to be a top chef or a sommelier to throw an amazing dinner party that will benefit the nation's largest hunger relief organization; you just have to enjoy a hearty dinner gathering.

## CRASH A BASH

If you are not really into the whole organizing thing, the good news is that the party couldn't happen without attendees like you! Whether your tastes are clambake or gala, if you are interested in putting some of the money that you spend on partying anyway toward supporting an important cause, attending a charity function may be your golden ticket. Even as you read this, there are well-established groups throughout the country whose goals are to provide creative entertainment and to raise money for their cause. Many organizations are looking for a few good partiers like you to boost their attendance, cool factor, and, of course, revenues.

## SUCCESS STORY

### Sweet 'Stache!

**Mustaches for Kids** started in Los Angeles and, because goofball ambassadors are irresistible, now has chapters throughout North America. The basic premise is that a bunch of guys get together and grow wacky mustaches. Each competitor finds friends to sponsor him, and the contest takes place over a period of several weeks, giving the organizers lots of excuses to get together for growth checks, parties, and general tomfoolery. At the end of the four weeks, there is a final competition, and the guy with the best 'stache wins. All of the proceeds go to children's charities. The organization now has chapters all over the United States and a few in Canada. Its website also offers a complete guide to starting your own chapter.

## Attend a Benefit for Grown-Ups 🕐=2 💲=2 🏢=1

If getting your face in the style section of the *New York Times* appeals to you, step out and attend a benefit party thrown by your favorite charity, organization, or art institution. These types of events are also an excellent place to network with potential employers or socialites who otherwise wouldn't give you the time of day, so don't be shy. It's easier to snag an invite than you think—get on their mailing/emailing lists and ask them to keep you informed of upcoming events. If you throw them a little cash (or a lot, depending on the charity), you will probably make the cut. If the ticket price is too steep for you, most of these functions also need volunteers to help staff the event. Volunteering your time also means you will probably get to attend some or all of the gala.

If you still can't find a party, concert, or event near you, you can also search the Internet under "benefit parties," "benefit concerts," or "charity dinners/events," along with the name of your city or town. For example, entering "upcoming benefit parties Columbus, Ohio" turned up links to Columbus Running Company charity races, a March of Dimes chef's auction, and a charity challenge to raise money for the Mid-Ohio Food Bank.

## Start Your Own Charity 🕐=5 💲=3 🏢=4

If you love to party and are good at organizing events, why not start your own charity party group? This is exactly what Ellen Shortill, a professional meeting planner, and Christine Kohlmeyer, a Washington, D.C., legal pro-bono program coordinator, decided to do. In lieu of making a New Year's resolution in 2006, Shortill decided that she wanted to raise $5,000 for charity. She had been raising money for charities by participating in kickball tournaments, but she wanted to do more. After a few evenings of brainstorming over happy-hour cocktails, **SMASHED** (the Society of Mature Adults Seeking to Help, Entertain, and Donate) was born.

Each person on the SMASHED board contributes a specific skill to the cause. There's a writer and editor who writes the website's text and marketing materials, and a group of self-titled "geeks" not only maintains the SMASHED website but also lives in the self-titled "geek pad." Shortill and Kohlmeyer, meanwhile, use their planning skills to make the parties happen. As an added bonus, these eligible male computer experts were featured in *People* magazine as sexy, single bachelors. Geek pad aside, their charitable work also seems to have improved their love lives.

## SUCCESS STORY

### Getting SMASHED with No Regrets

So far, SMASHED has sponsored such events as the urban Idiotarod, where contestants race around the city in shopping carts, the ManPageant, and an *Amazing Race* Scavenger Hunt. According to co-founder Ellen Shortill, "We usually come up with a stupid, crazy idea first, then we find a charity that fits it."

Since its inception, SMASHED has raised thousands of dollars for charities benefiting pediatric cancer patients, homeless children, war veterans, and food banks. This charity has earned a reputation for throwing good parties and for offering twentysomethings and beyond an easy way to donate to charity by doing something they would probably be doing anyway. Ninety percent of the proceeds from each event goes directly to charity (the other 10 percent likely goes to Advil and cold compresses). This successful formula may even result in the participants having such a good time that competitors can't remember their acts of philanthropy the next day! As their website says, "Remind me tomorrow that I helped someone today." SMASHED is based in Washington, D.C., but visit its website to get ideas about how to start a similar organization in your area.

## LET'S EAT! FOOD AND DRINK FOR THE BIG PARTY

If you are serving food, try to use a catering company that uses organic and local food and/or donates money to a charitable cause. If you are cooking for the party yourself, the same rules apply. Either way, be sure to drink organic beer and wine! Here is a simple guide for ideas on finding sustainable and/or organic food and drink for all of your charity events and special celebrations.

### Use a Caterer  ⏱=2  💲=3  🏠=1

Here is a regional sampling of the many socially responsible and/or organic catering options available:

- **National:** Start with your local greenmarkets. Depending on where you live, many farmers' markets are now open year-round, and with a bit of notice, many farmers would be happy to provide extra ingredients for your party and/or direct you to a local organic caterer. To find a farmers' market or organic grocery store or co-op near you, visit the **LocalHarvest** website. **Whole Foods Markets** is another option, with hundreds of stores in North America and the United Kingdom. They have a lot of organic prepared foods, and they are a good bet if you are looking for organic food year-round.

- **New York City:** Check out **The Works Catering**—operated by Housing Works, which is a nonprofit organization dedicated to providing social services to New Yorkers who are homeless or living in poverty.

- **Seattle: Heroes Catering with a Cause** is a nonprofit subsidiary of **Bread of Life Mission,** which works to break the cycle of homelessness for people who are trying to transition from rehabilitation to independent living. **FareStart** has a similar mission to Heroes Catering and offers job training to employees.

- **Indiana:** All profits from **Just 'Cause Catering** go to **Second Helpings,** which works to "eliminate food waste, train people in meaningful careers, and eliminate hunger in Indianapolis."

- **Chicago: First Slice** allows you to buy subscriptions to a local chef's home-cooked, organic meals. The subscriptions not only feed you, but the extra money goes toward providing the same nutritious meals to those in need. Those interested can also volunteer to help make the meals in the community kitchen.

The previous list of catering suggestions is just a tiny sample of the many community-minded options available. To find a caterer near you, ask friends for recommendations, and do an Internet search for "organic" or "sustainable" caterers. I also invite you to add your own local catering favorites by emailing me your suggestions for inclusion on the *Ten Ways* website resource pages.

### DIYummy  🕐=3  💲=3  🏠=2

If you decide to cook the food yourself, try to buy as much seasonal, organic produce as you can from your local organic co-op or farmers' market. Also try to choose a cookbook tied to your geographic area to get party menu ideas that are local and tap into cultural wisdom.

For many more tips on low-impact, delicious cooking, see chapter 7.

# More Recipe Resources

In addition to the book and website recommendations on **page 209 of chapter 7,** here are some suggestions for places to find recipes for your parties:

*Moosewood Restaurant Celebrates: Festive Meals for Holidays and Special Occasions* by the Moosewood collective: The name says it all, and the Moosewood crew never disappoints. This cookbook has vegetarian menus for all sorts of holidays and party treats for anytime.

*A Year in a Vegetarian Kitchen: Easy Seasonal Dishes for Family and Friends* by Jack Bishop: Bishop is also the executive editor of *Cook's Illustrated*. The book is divided into sections based on the seasons and focuses on simplicity and taste.

*The New England Cookbook* by Brooke Dojny: Dojny is a regular contributor to *Bon Appetit* and a well-known food writer. This book features recipes for dishes from around the Northeast, from native favorites to those brought across the Atlantic from Portuguese, Greek, and other immigrant communities. Her Peabody cheddar wafers alone will become an easy favorite for noshing on with drinks.

*Essentials of Classic Italian Cooking* by Marcella Hazan: The Godmother of Italian cooking in America provides classic recipes for all skill levels, as well as informative lessons on seasonings and ingredients. Besides, everyone knows how a nice pasta dish is the perfect menu item for large parties.

No matter what type of benefit or bash you decide to throw, remember to have fun and party like you care what happens in 2099!

## THE WORLD IS YOUR OYSTER. EXPLORE YOUR OYSTER.

If you have experimented with some of the suggestions in the first eight chapters, you may have discovered a new favorite seasonal food, found new ways to save energy, or volunteered with a local political campaign. All of these worthy ventures at home may spark an interest to explore issues further afield. Perhaps you have thrown a party to benefit a humanitarian organization, and now you want to see the work you are supporting firsthand; or maybe you want to understand more directly why it is so important that those producing your fair-trade chocolate are paid a living wage. Travel is the key to opening many more arenas of exploration, and **chapter 9** not only offers ideas and resources to guide you on your way, but it also includes suggestions for making all of your journeys environmentally savvy and respectful.

# Chapter 9

# WAYS TO TRAVEL LIGHTLY (AND CHEAPLY!) EVERYWHERE YOU GO

*Expand Your Horizons by Heading for...Well, the Horizon*

Sometimes you have to act as if acting will make a difference, even when you can't prove that it will.

*Michael Pollan*

## IN THIS CHAPTER

- **Embark on a Quest for Knowledge**

- **Travel Lightly Everywhere You Go**

- *Ways* **Guide to a Great, Green Move**

- **Ideas for Inspiring Travel**

- **Now about That Job...**

## EMBARK ON A QUEST FOR KNOWLEDGE

Travel—it's good for us all. Whether you are exploring parts unknown to gain a deeper understanding of cultures, experience rich biodiversity, volunteer, or just have a good time, traveling makes you a richer person. Of course, anyone who's been abroad or even on a long road trip could fairly argue that travel makes you a much poorer person, and the environmental footprint of travel can be staggering. Three things to keep in mind: First, if ever there was a time to blow your savings on adventure, this is it (do NOT sink hopelessly into debt, but few beyond their twenties can live with as little as you can). Second, there are many ways to travel in an eco-responsible and economical manner. Finally, the realities of life creep right up on you, so seize the day! Talk to people in their thirties and forties or beyond, and many will tell you their biggest regret is not traveling while they had the chance. Travel is priceless because it helps us to form opinions, understand issues, and appreciate firsthand the diverse cultures and environments of other parts of our country as well as the rest of the world. It often serves as a poignant reminder of just how lucky (and in some cases wasteful) we are in the United States.

By paying attention to your means of travel and your daily commuting choices, you can easily reduce the amount of carbon emissions your explorations may entail. Whether you are traveling with briefcase or backpack, this chapter will offer tips for reducing your travel emissions before sending you packing to parts unknown.

## TRAVEL LIGHTLY EVERYWHERE YOU GO

### Lower Your Octane Output  🕐=2  💲=1  🏠=3

The United States is responsible for nearly a quarter of the world's carbon emissions from fuel use. You can easily help to lower this staggering statistic by using less gas. Pay attention to how much time you spend in a car. Keep a log for at least a week of how many trips you take each day. Add up the mileage, gas money, and/or hours you are spending in your car. Then think honestly about alternatives. Could you ride a bike to the grocery store or the library? Could you walk to the post office or the coffee shop? Could you take the bus to yoga class or your basketball game? What irony that we drive to the gym to work out! Assess which trips could be accomplished on a fuel-saving bus or subway ride or a calorie-burning walk or bike ride. Make a commitment to take some form of alternative transportation and/or reduce the number of car trips you make every week.

Whether it is buying a bike designed for commuting—replete with pedal-powered headlights and a briefcase holder—or approaching your boss about telecommuting a few days a week (more and more companies are allowing it), there is a fuel-saving solution for you. Try consolidating your errands or carpooling with co-workers. And if the idea of public transportation intimidates you, don't be afraid to look for a little guidance from the bus driver, a friendly looking passerby, or a map (these don't talk yet, but stay tuned).

---

## Organizations to Help You with That *Car*less Habit of Yours

**Adventure Cycling Association**
**Bicycle for a Day**
**League of American Bicyclists**
**MapMyRide**

**Google Maps**—note: this has a feature that lets you find directions by bus or as a pedestrian

Some bike organizations will also set you up with a bike buddy to ride with you on your commute to help you get used to the route and learn safety tips. Check with your local bike club to see if it offers this type of service.

## Step Softly upon Thy Gas Pedal 🕐=1 💲=1 ▦=2

When you must drive, be sure you are driving the most fuel-efficient vehicle possible. Here's how:

- **Know your mileage.** If your car isn't getting over 30 mph, then you should consider driving a different car. To find the most fuel-efficient cars, check out the list of the "greenest" and "meanest" over at **Greenercars.org**.

- **Drive a fuel-efficient vehicle.** When you finally decide that it is time to buy, make the switch to a hybrid or similarly lean model; you will find more and more efficient options as car manufacturers work to meet the demands of fuel-savvy travelers (supply and demand at work again). Besides such able vehicles as the Honda Civic Hybrid (40 mpg city/45 hwy) or the Toyota Prius (40 mpg city/45 hwy),[60] there are also exciting advances being made in the development of even more fuel-efficient electric, hybrid, and diesel vehicles.

- **Don't take the scenic route.** Plan out and consolidate trips to ensure that you are always driving the shortest distance between two destinations.

- **Don't drive angry.** Relaxing behind the wheel is not only good for your blood pressure and the safety of your passengers, it is also a more efficient way to motor. Both speedy accelerations and sudden stops contribute to decreased fuel efficiency.

- **Don't idle.** Idling is never necessary. It gets a less-than-impressive 0 mpg.

- **Pump it up.** Your car will operate at its fuel-efficient best with a little help from you, the environmentally (and fiscally) responsible car owner who takes good care of your vehicle.

---

## Can't Afford a New Car Just Yet?

Here's how to get the most out of every gallon of gas:[61]

- **Get frequent checkups.** Good maintenance includes using the recommended type of motor oil and regularly replacing air and engine filters.
- **Be sure your tires are properly inflated.**[62]
- **Carry a light load.** Less weight equals better fuel efficiency.
- **Remove all bike/ski racks when they are not in use**—they cause more drag. (Hey! What is your bike doing up on the top of your car anyway?)
- **Use air-conditioning sparingly.** Aim for enough to keep you from overheating, but there should never be sweaters and scarves worn in mid-July.

---

### Crash a Carpool  🕐=2 💲=1 🏢=2

Who are those magical people who zip happily past with a few pals at the height of a rush-hour commute? What have they got that you don't? The answer is simple: passengers. They have discovered the secret magic of the carpool, and you can, too.

## Carpool Matchmakers

**Carpoolworld.com**—matches riders all over the world and offers tools for starting your own carpool

**eRideShare.com**—offers a similar service, offering rideshares by category: daily carpools, cross-country trips, errands, and groups such as churches and clubs

### Be a Part-Time Lover 🕐=2 $=2 ▦=2

If you can easily commute to work on your bike or the bus and it is possible to walk, bike, or take the bus to all other day-to-day locales, why do you still have that car anyway? Perhaps you are nervous about giving up the possibility of a last-minute getaway weekend or an impromptu visit to the in-laws upstate. Thanks to car-sharing companies like **Zipcar**, you can reserve cars all over the country for less than the cost of a rental. Find more car-sharing programs at **Car Sharing**.

### Flying Leaves a Huge Footprint—Reduce Yours 🕐=2 $=1 ▦=3

Flying takes a lot of fuel. We're talking over 3,300 gallons per hour for a 747-400 aircraft, according to British Airways. If you have flown in the last year or so, you have probably noticed that the airlines, which know better than anyone how much fuel they are using, are already doing a lot to be more efficient with space. Less legroom, fully packed flights, and a charge for that extra bag, anyone? While you may have initially balked at these "inconveniences," considering that each pound of weight costs (or saves) airlines $14,000 a year in fuel,[63] many of these changes are not only good for the airline's bottom line, but they are also good for the environment. Thanks to the affordable cost of airfare, we have been lulled into taking airline travel for granted—when in fact it really is a luxury in this carbon-overloaded, oil-depleted world. So before you take a flight, be sure that it is absolutely necessary. If it is for a meeting, is there a way to teleconference instead? If it is for pleasure, is there a way to consolidate the trip to see more than one person or sight at the same time? I am not advocating grounding yourself permanently, but I am suggesting that it is a good idea to assess whether or not the flight you would like to take is worth the fuel it will burn. When you do take to the "friendly" skies, do everything you can to reduce your flying footprint by following these simple steps:

- **Offset your travel.** Be sure that you are offsetting the carbon emissions created by your travel. Check out the **Conservation Fund,** which will plant trees as offsets, or **Carbonfund.org, LiveNeutral, TerraPass,** or *Native*Energy, which will use your offset money to invest in clean energy technology such as wind, solar, or hydroelectric.

- **Take only what you need.** Like many of you, I used to be a card-carrying member of the overpacker's club, but when I learned about the fuel costs per pound of luggage, I started to forego that extra pair of shoes or the "just in case I need something superfancy" outfit.

- **Once you land, try using public transportation to get around in your new locale.** It's a great way to save fuel and get to know your surroundings. If you find that you have landed in a place with limited bus, subway, or train options, try to rent a hybrid vehicle or a small, fuel-efficient vehicle to get around.

## *WAYS* GUIDE TO A GREAT, GREEN MOVE

For many twentysomethings, moving is a rite of passage undergone not once but often several times. Many in our demographic—youngish, no kids, a few moves already under our belts (even though Mom and Dad helped, those moves in and out of dorms and campus housing count)—find that we have a common problem: we have once again managed to accumulate too much stuff, despite our vows to do otherwise.

Especially if you are covering a great distance, the prospect of moving every last mismatched sock and high-school yearbook is not only overwhelming, it is also a drag—for both you and the environment. However, as you haul your stuff from point A to B, remember that when you lighten your load, you reduce your costs as well. Consider also that your net reduction of former prized possessions need not be a net gain for the landfill. Whether you face the prospect of a cross-country move or a move around the corner, or you are just looking to reclaim some much-needed closet space, here are some creative ways to reduce and reuse before, during, and after your move.

### Lighten Your Load 🕐=3 💲=1 ▦=3

Why is a light load so important? Whether you are renting space on a moving trailer, using an entire truck, putting your possessions on Amtrak, or driving them yourself, the equations are simple: stuff equals fuel and fuel equals money; therefore, stuff equals money. There are a lot of things in my apartment that I don't mind having around but would not pay a penny to move someplace else, and I bet the same is true in most places (though I know better than to underestimate the strange sentimentalities that move us to hoard every crappy memento we've ever been given). Once you have had a moving sale, made several trips to Goodwill, and given away stuff to friends, use the reduction and recycling resources in **chapters 4 and 5** to get rid of the last of those tough-to-recycle items.

**Get Going Already!** 🕐=2 💲=2 🏠=2

Net reduction is just the first part of the efficiency plan. *How* you go about packing and moving makes a big difference with regard to your environmental impact as well. Here are some tips when it comes time for the actual move:

1. **Pack it in recycled boxes.** Despite your best efforts to recycle, regift, and sell, you will still have plenty of stuff left over that you actually want to keep. Before acquiring any boxes, stash your stuff in anything that remotely resembles a box. This can include various duffels from college sports, bureaus, laundry hampers, or even magazine baskets. After this creative use of space, you may find that you still need boxes. Before heading over to your local packing store to *buy* new boxes, ask around. Chances are you will be able to get boxes from neighbors and friends who have moved within the last few months or from supermarkets and other stores (so I dumpster dive—sue me).

2. **Don't let the boxes die with you!** Once you get to your destination, don't forget to pass those boxes along for further reuse. All U-Haul locations have a free box-exchange program where used boxes can be dropped off or picked up for reuse. Try to reuse or give away leftover packing peanuts and bubble wrap as well. Since polystyrene packing peanuts will never biodegrade, we may as well keep them in use above ground for as long as possible. Many UPS locations and pack-and-ship stores will accept packing peanuts for reuse. Also be on the lookout for packing alternatives such as biodegradable cornstarch packing peanuts and EcoCradle compostable packaging material, whose youthful founders are profiled on **page 140 of Chapter 5**.

3. **Pack it tightly.** Use all possible space. Think of each box as a 3-D jigsaw puzzle of your belongings.

4. **Throw a last-minute giveaway bonanza.** You can bet that everyone who entered our apartment in that final week before our most recent cross-country move was showered with an array of last-minute detritus. One of my friends was very excited about my collection of Sunday *New York Times* (they will supply her rabbit with bedding for months to come), and several jars of pickles went to my in-laws (my father-in-law shares my pickle addiction). And despite our commitment to drink as much as possible in the weeks leading to our departure, our leftover liquor cabinet was a boon to thirsty friends.

5. **Leave a housewarming gift.** And no, I don't mean your old toilet brush. But if you are making a longer trek, consider leaving behind for the new tenants some nice items (wine, olive oil) that won't travel well and are heavy, as well as some cleaning supplies, which are always useful when moving in or out.

6. **Let your boxes ride the rail.** Another environmentally and economically sound way to move belongings around the country is on Amtrak. This is a great option for those of you who own a car and don't want to cross the country in a U-Haul. Keep in mind that there are restrictions on box sizes and weights, but those I know who have used this service highly recommend it—and it is a bargain compared to other moving services.

## IDEAS FOR INSPIRING TRAVEL

Now that you have a plethora of ideas about ways to transport, move, and travel with minimal environmental impact, it is time to hit the road. Short of putting yourself into bankruptcy, do whatever it takes to make travel possible in your twenties. If you are in school and your college or university offers a study abroad program, take advantage of it. Even schools that do not run programs directly (or don't have among their offerings the country that you would like to visit) will usually be able to direct you to other programs that they partner with. If you have graduated and are not yet sure what to do, traveling can be a great way to help you figure it out. Many in their twenties feel the urge or the pressure to get out of college and find that perfect job. This rarely happens, and a year or so spent taking stock of your situation and goals can offer a whole new perspective. Just don't expect Mom and Dad to understand—or fund—your adventures.

I lived the proverbial rat race briefly, with a good portion of that time spent in the film industry, where moving from job to job was the name of the game. Now, over a dozen jobs later, I wish someone had told me to relax, enjoy, and explore. I'm not suggesting that you don't work (your parents will probably flog me and/or you), but keep in mind that now is the time to open yourself to exploration, either through travel or through jobs or internships in a field you are curious about, or both. Even if your college loans aren't going anywhere, you should be. As you travel and gain a deeper understanding and appreciation for the world around you, the suggestions and resources in the next section will help you on your way.

## Ask for Time Off  🕐=3 💲=3 🏢=2

If you find yourself in a job that you love, good for you! You can still travel, explore, and volunteer during your time off. An increasing number of companies are even offering paid time off to employees who want to work for a nonprofit organization or volunteer locally or abroad. These companies range from the usual progressive suspects like outdoor outfitter Patagonia to women's clothing purveyor Eileen Fisher, which has teamed up with several other companies like Timberland to start In Good Company, a collaborative volunteer program for their employees.

Even if your company does not currently offer time off for such ventures, it can't hurt to ask if this type of model is something the company may consider sponsoring. For more information about how such a program might work, visit the **Patagonia** website and check out the information on environmental internships.

## SUCCESS STORY

### Making a Serious Business of Child's Play

As a college student, Kristen Eddings was already involved with short-term volunteering gigs like planting trees and serving food at the local homeless shelter, but she was also on the lookout for a travel opportunity that matched her interests. She serendipitously found a flyer about a student group that was traveling to volunteer at an orphanage in Sierra Leone on the same day she learned that it was one of the poorest countries in the world. Eddings interviewed and went on the trip, which she says profoundly changed her. "I was working with a three-year-old girl named Phoebe who couldn't walk or talk, and it was moments with her that made me realize that I could *do* something as an individual, whether it was working to end malaria or putting a smile on this little girl's face." While she knew her trip would come to an end, her commitment to helping others in the future had grown markedly.

No longer a faraway, imagined place, Sierra Leone is where Eddings first connected to orphaned children, and she now has a deep concern for the fate of Phoebe and the millions of other children worldwide who suffer due to inadequate care. When she returned home, she found a way to stay connected with children through Bridges to Understanding, an organization that connects local students with international pen pals of the same age using email and video. Eddings facilitated conversations about cultural similarities and differences between groups of third-graders in

Seattle and Tibetan students of the same age in India. "With so many indigenous cultures out there that are in danger of dying out, it is crucial that we give them a way to tell their stories and draw attention to their plight," she says.

After graduating from college, Eddings entered and won the Miss Washington contest, which meant that in addition to the scholarship money she received, she got to travel all over the country. She used the opportunity to speak about international education. She was also able to lobby on behalf of the Abraham Lincoln Study Abroad Act and even met several senators, including then Senator and now President Barack Obama.

When her reign ended, Eddings was determined to continue the meaningful work she had grown to love. She applied at nonprofits that had a global focus, and she asked every organization she contacted for an informational interview. Once on the radar, she was able to land a job as a program assistant within the Washington Global Health Alliance, a consortium of ten organizations that are working to find solutions to such global health issues as malaria and tuberculosis. She is contemplating earning her master's degree in global health, and she is excited to be working with people who are making groundbreaking policy regarding the future of global health.

## Take a Hike  🕐=2  💲=2  🏠=2

You need not travel far to have a life-changing experience. One of the best ways to become a conservationist is to see firsthand why forests, oceans, and open spaces are worth preserving. One glance up at the mountains from Yosemite's valley, and you will understand why Ansel Adams devoted his life to documenting and protecting wild places. From atop a vista in Glacier National Park, you will understand why it is so important to protect not only the glaciers that give this breathtaking park in northwestern Montana its name but also the grizzly bears that roam freely throughout. A trip to a national park is much more than an inexpensive way to travel and connect with nature; it is a trip back in time where you can witness the grandeur of biodiversity with little or no interference from man. It is also one of the only times in our "connected" lives when we can turn off all of the usual electronic stimulation.

Some of the most profound, peaceful, and memorable trips in my life have been camping and hiking trips throughout the country, from Rainier National Forest in Washington to the northern reaches of the Appalachian Trail in Maine. It is these moments that reenergize me, and I return from these trips more determined than ever to work to preserve habitats and species that could soon be jeopardized, or even destroyed, without action from us all. For more information on visiting and getting involved with national parks conservation work, visit the **National Parks Conservation** website. You can view current and past advocacy campaigns, find ways to take action, and, of course, plan your trip to a park using the organization's database, which offers links to each national park. You can search by name, location, or category (seashores, scenic trails, parks, etc.).

## SUCCESS STORY

### Explore What You Love

Marah Hardt has always had an innate affinity for the oceans. From visits to aquariums and playing in tide pools at a young age to traveling around the globe to study the health of the world's water today, she has jumped at every opportunity to be close to the sea. As she began to scuba dive and learn more about the science of the oceans, she also started to realize how fragile and endangered they are. "I wasn't really an environmentalist as a kid," she says. "We recycled at home and turned off the water, but when I learned how bad things were with the oceans, I took it as a personal affront. I was probably thirteen or fourteen at the time, so I was old enough to get what was going on, but I was not really sure what to do about it."

After a earning a BA in the history of science from Harvard and then a year of teaching yoga in Australia, Hardt was accepted into a prestigious graduate marine biology program at the Scripps Institution of Oceanography in San Diego. Hardt knew that she could successfully share her excitement for the oceans as well as her knowledge of why they are so crucial for all of us to protect. "The oceans are in a really bad spot, and we basically only have about ten to twenty years to take drastic action to reverse the current course, especially with climate change, or we're going to lose some species and fundamentally change ocean ecosystems. If we just keep reporting the science in scientific journals without communicating these critical findings to the public, then the scientific record is basically just the oceans' obituary."

Knowing all of this, Hardt turned her sights on transforming all of the research about global warming and oceans in peril into articles for mainstream publications and creative presentations that would inspire adults and children to take action. "There are many good people studying the science of the oceans but not enough people getting the science where it needs to go," she says. As a staff member at the **Blue Ocean Institute,** Hardt focuses on trying to build awareness about how climate change impacts oceans. "I look for new studies that are coming out and topics where I don't see much public awareness, and I try to take the scientific information and come up with stories that will be more palatable and inspiring for the general public," she explains. Perhaps most importantly, she organizes coalitions between scientists and leaders in other sectors because, as she puts it, "When it comes to caring for the planet, everybody has the same goal."

Aside from having "to unlearn talking like a scientist and learn how to talk like a normal person," Hardt also has to balance her sense of urgency about the state of the planet with hope and creativity. She takes time every day to observe nature and stay in touch with what she is fighting for. "We can't give up hope," she says. "Nature is so resilient and so surprising. This is a human behavior issue—we have the technology to make the necessary changes, so we can change if we choose to. I believe my job is to inform people in a way that inspires them to make the efforts to change their actions to ones that are low-impact and renewable." For more tips on what you can do to protect the ocean, see Hardt's recommendations in on **page 104 in chapter 4** and visit the **Blue Ocean Institute** website.

## Take Economical and Eco-savvy Trips 🕐=3 💲=4 🏢=3

Many of the best trips happen when you embrace each outing with spontaneity. Pack up your fuel-efficient car and head across the country with friends. Get a Eurail pass and stay in youth hostels throughout Europe. Strap on your pack and head to the mountains of Appalachia for a long-term, long-distance hike.

If you want your adventure to be a bit more planned, there are websites like **Couchsurfing** devoted to helping you find a roommate, an apartment to swap or rent, or a couch to surf. You can also look on the international section of websites like **Craig's List** for help finding a job or an apartment before you land. If you want to volunteer or work with an organization abroad, check out the job listings over at **Idealist** as well as the many volunteering suggestions in **chapter 2**. You can also look into which airlines travel most frequently from your city and sign up for their frequent-flyer programs and credit cards. When you are shopping for flights, be sure to check several websites and always look at the airline's site as well. I have often found the best deals on the airline's own website. With a little shopping around, I was able to afford many a trip in my twenties, often on a minuscule budget. Here are some web tools to help you get out there and explore.

# Travel on the Cheap

### Camping USA

The perfect summer activity for college students: grab some friends, pack your things in the trunk, and cruise the country during the summer months. Campgrounds are one of the most affordable options for overnight stays, and they are often located at or near the most spectacular national parks and monuments.

### Eurail/Busabout Explorer

If you are traveling through Europe, both the Eurail train system and the Busabout coach bus system offer inexpensive ways and a variety of options to see over twenty-five different countries. Both types of travel are affordable (the Busabout more so), and travelers have the option of purchasing several different types of passes that offer flexibility in the length of your stay in each country.

### Farecast

This website offers predictions about which direction your chosen fare is going. For example, on a recent search for my Turkey Day travels, I was advised that my fare from Seattle to New York was holding steady or rising. Farecast's confidence level in its prediction was 80 percent or higher, and it told me to buy. This service is especially helpful if you are on a budget and want to be sure you are getting the best deal possible because it compares fares from all over the Web.

### Hiking and Backpacking

Use this website to find the hiking clubs in your area. The website offers a directory by state with external links to each group.

### Hostelling International

Use this website to get a youth hostel membership card, and find and reserve a youth hostel anywhere in the world.

**Hotwire/Kayak**

These are great websites for hotels, car rentals, and flights because they search multiple sites. While Hotwire does not tell you the name of the hotel or car rental agency before you agree to purchase, the site gives you enough information to find a hotel at a reduced rate in the area of the city where you want to be and only deals with reputable car rental agencies, so you won't end up with a wreck.

**TripAdvisor/Hotels.com**

When I need to find a place to stay, I go here first to see what is available in the area where I am traveling and what other travelers are saying about the accommodation options in my budget.

## Get the Real Deal on Eco-friendly Trips 🕐=2 💲=1 🏨=2

While "environmentally friendly" has sometimes become synonymous with luxury, it certainly does not have to be. Sustainable tourism allows intrepid travelers to respectfully explore new surroundings without tarnishing the landscape for the next visitors. Yet "eco-friendly" and "green" have become marketing buzzwords of late, and the travel industry's vernacular certainly reflects this trend, too. In order to discern what "green" really means, some organizations and alliances have begun to establish rating systems to help the prospective traveler sort the eco-friendly from the greenwashed. For more information on what makes a trip or locale sustainable, visit the website for the **Partnership for Global Sustainable Tourism Criteria**, which is a coalition of over thirty organizations. Started by the Rainforest Alliance, United Nations Foundation, and United Nations World Tourism Organization, the partnership evaluates hotels, restaurants, and resorts based on criteria including recycling and reuse policies, water and electricity use, and the impact of a property on the surrounding environment and communities.

## Websites to Help Guide You on Your Great, Green Travels

**Sustainable Travel International**
**"Green" Hotels Association**
**responsibletravel.com**
**Natural Habitat Adventures**
**International Ecotourism Club**

## SUCCESS STORY

### Bringing Ubuntu around the World

For most people, a visit to South Africa would be a life-changing experience; and for most people, the memories, photos, and stories would be enough. But Jacob Lief was so affected by his experiences and interactions with his mentor and students that he started his own organization even before graduating from the University of Pennsylvania. While living and teaching at a local school with Banks Gwaxula, a teacher in the New Brighton township during his junior year, Lief witnessed firsthand the lack of basic necessities that made teaching much more difficult. When he returned to the University of Pennsylvania, he started fundraising for sustainable development in the communities he visited. Six months after meeting Gwaxula, the two founded the **Ubuntu Education Fund**, which now helps over forty thousand children, youth, and families through its education and health-care programs.

Founding and running an organization of this size and scope has taken Lief's almost constant attention, but he has a very compelling motivation. "The work never ends because there are always more children to help," he says. Following the philosophy of Ubuntu, which means "a universal bond of sharing that connects all of humanity," Lief and his staff of more than 80 (many native South Africans) focus their efforts in four main areas: empowerment, HIV prevention, clinical care, and support. The latter encompasses such services as legal advocacy and counseling services. To learn more about the Ubuntu Education Fund and how you can get involved, visit the organization's website.

## NOW ABOUT THAT JOB...

Whether you have traveled far and wide in order to discover your passion or you have always known what you wanted to be when you grew up, at some point you will need to actually start searching for a job. While your path may not necessarily be linear, the same characteristics that are necessary to implement many of the other ways suggested in this book—persistence, integrity and passion—will also serve you well in a job search. Let the stories in **chapter 10** inspire you, and use the resources to help you in your search. And no matter what you do, remember that employment and exploration need not be mutually exclusive.

# Chapter 10

# WAYS TO TURN YOUR PASSION INTO PROMISE

*Turn Your Interests into Your Vocation*

How we spend our days is, of course, how we spend our lives.

*Annie Dillard*

## IN THIS CHAPTER

- Time to Show You the Money...Well, Some of It at Least

- *Ways* Guide to Finding the Perfect World-Changing Job for You (or at Least One to Try Out for a While)

- Ten under Thirty Who Turned Their Passion into Promise

## TIME TO SHOW YOU THE MONEY...WELL, SOME OF IT AT LEAST

Getting paid to make a meaningful difference in the lives of others is about as good as it gets professionally, so when you are ready to step into a career that will provide you with both money and a warm, fuzzy feeling, this chapter is ready to help.

Perhaps you have perused some of the other chapters and tried some of the suggested *Ways*. Maybe you have volunteered, organized events, or even spent a summer interning with an organization you love. Or maybe you skipped right to the last chapter because you just couldn't wait to see how the story ends. Either way, here you are, ready to figure out how to find a job that matches your skills and interests in making the world a better place. You've looked around at the state of the world today and concluded that there must be some real dunces in charge, and you know just the person to get things on the right track at this critical juncture (yes, you). The world is counting on us to roll up our sleeves, raise our voices, and start doing what young people do (no, not drink our worries away until 4 a.m.—unless it's at a charity party!): be the innovators who leave a legacy of hope for our generation and those that follow. Besides, toasting to success is much more fun than drinking out of despair.

Many of us have already experienced the weightiness of war, the burden of climate change, or the devastation of poverty. The time has come to choose: we can either retreat into our comfort zones, in which case we're pretty much screwed, or we can evolve to face the challenges of the twenty-first century with the energy and innovation of youth.

## Get Thee to Work

This chapter is different from all other chapters, especially in its layout. There are no levels of difficulty because, let's face it, finding a job when you get out of college, especially one where you are fulfilled, making a difference, and not subsisting on mac and cheese and ramen noodles, is a tall-enough order.

Instead of ways to change the world, you will find suggestions for finding a job to help you do just that. While many of these tips pertain to finding a job in the nonprofit or social entrepreneur sectors, you can make a difference anywhere you go, and major corporations are some of the most important stakeholders to bring on board when it comes to investing in the future. Strides are already being made, as more and more companies are eager to go green and cultivate an image of social responsibility. Just don't be disheartened if the altruistic motive isn't the driving impetus for change. Sustainable practices are good for the bottom line and great PR—and yes, they are better for the planet, too.

No matter what drives corporations and governmental agencies to become more socially and environmentally aware, the end result is that these changes are better for us all. Many of these companies and agencies are on the lookout for bright, eager, and talented millennials who want to bring their enthusiasm to the workplace, and many of the success stories in this chapter and throughout the book are based on people working within the private sector. According to Meg Busse, co-author of *The Idealist Guide to Nonprofit Careers*, "An ideal career can be an elusive thing, and it depends on where a job seeker is in a particular stage of life. There are many ways and many sectors in which to find a meaningful career. And for many people it may not be a career; it may be what they do with their family or what they do after work, but the most important thing to determine is what you are passionate about.

It's not unusual to be twenty-five and realize that 'this is not what I want to be doing the rest of my life.' People change so much from the first years of their career, and this is normal and exciting."

Advice for jobseekers abounds no matter your interests, but so often we hear about ways to negotiate the best salary or get the best perks. And while you may be comfortable now trading the soul-crushing tedium of a thankless job for that sweet parking space and big check, there is certainly a case to be made for finding happiness and fulfillment in your career as well. For those looking to earn more than just a paycheck, here are some suggestions for finding the right job now.

## *WAYS* GUIDE TO FINDING THE PERFECT WORLD-CHANGING JOB FOR YOU (OR AT LEAST ONE TO TRY OUT FOR A WHILE)

1. **Do your research.** Whether you are looking for a job, internship, or volunteer opportunity, **Idealist** is the place to start. There are a variety of different ways to search for positions (type of organization/geographic region/type of work, etc.), and the website is geared to be a resource for those interested in finding opportunities to make a difference. It is a great place to see the range of possibilities that exist (almost ninety thousand organizations maintain profiles on the site), and the career center resources and videos are designed to appeal to the seasoned social networker. You can also check out organizations doing highly rated work at **Charity Navigator**. In addition, pay attention to the for-profit companies that are working toward sustainability and fair trade and are committed to transparent business practices. Many companies that fit this profile will issue a corporate sustainability report, which you can usually find on the company's website or at **CSRwire**.

2. **Become a member.** Once you find a few organizations or businesses that might be good potential employers, visit their websites often and sign up for email action alerts and updates. If you can afford it, consider becoming a donor. Doing so not only guarantees that you will stay informed, but your membership will show a tangible commitment to their cause when a job does become available.

3. **Network, network, network.** Put the word out to anyone who asks (and even those who don't) about the kind of work that you would like to do. Check in with friends, acquaintances, former bowling league buddies, and anyone who might know someone at the type of organization that you would like to be involved with. Attend mixers like the **Green Drinks** parties, and don't be shy about asking for help. Many people find their job through someone they know, and it only takes one good connection to turn you on to that perfect job!

4. **Get in the door with informational interviews.** Even if you can't immediately find an organization that has a job opening to match your skill set (expert hacky sacker, soap-opera-trivia genius, nap master, to name a few), many will be more than willing to sit down with you for an informational interview. These types of conversations are an excellent way to learn more about an organization, express your interest when something does open up, and make a good first impression on someone influential within the company. Treat these discussions like real interviews, and schedule as many as you can.

5. **Name those skills!** While it is great to be passionate about a cause and to convey your passion in a job interview or well-crafted cover letter, it is important that you can also

enumerate the specific skills that you bring to the table. Perhaps you are great with people, a technological wizard, a lightning-fast learner, or the oft-used "people person." No matter what kinds of magic you work, be sure you are your own biggest advocate when it comes to wowing potential employers.

6. **Persistent and patient—learn to be both.** If you just sit home after sending out your cover letters and wait for the phone to ring, you may be disappointed. Don't forget that you are competing with lots of other people who think that they too are the perfect candidate for the job. Continue to set yourself apart with timely follow-up calls and/or emails. That said, you don't want to be a pest, so try to respect the parameters for contact that a prospective employer has laid out in the job announcement; late-night phone calls and obsessive emails are deal breakers. Once you have been thorough with your follow-ups, be patient: the job-search process can sometimes take months, and you have to trust that you will be able to convey your passion to someone who can give you a job.

7. **Be willing to work for free.** The more glamorous name for this, of course, is an internship. No matter how you label your position, it may not feel like the best use of your time, and it may squeeze the old budget. But if it is an organization or company you really want to be involved with, sometimes the best way in is to show them what you've got without expecting any compensation. When a paid position does come up, you'll be sitting pretty to move on up, having already demonstrated your talents.

8. **Apply for fellowships.** If you have an innovative research project or idea that would benefit from funding, consider

researching and applying for appropriate fellowships. The amount of funding varies greatly, but often it is possible for a frugal grad to live on a fellowship budget while carrying out the project. Fellowships are available for almost every discipline from environmental research to journalism, and they are an excellent way to pursue studies and research that you might not be able to finance on your own.

9. **Be okay with a not-so-perfect fit.** Think of your job like a girlfriend or boyfriend. Some are fun but shallow, some are demanding but meaningful, and some will set fire to your clothes and throw your favorite furniture out the window. That's cool…it is your twenties after all, and you shouldn't rush to marry yourself to the first paid gig that rolls along. Get your foot in the door at an organization doing whatever it is they need you to do, and determine to work your way up, or out, from there. If you are as fantastic as your parents keep telling their friends you are, you will find the right fit for your energy and talents.

10. **Give it all you've got.** Whether you have landed your dream job, a solid entry-level position, an internship, or a fellowship, approach your new challenge with energy and excitement. First, you'll have plenty of time to be jaded and unmotivated in your fifties, and second, whether you love or hate what you're doing, hard work is the best path to bigger and better things.

11. **Read all about it.** For many more tips on finding a job in the nonprofit world, check out *The Idealist Guide to Nonprofit Careers for First-Time Job Seekers*, which is available for free at the Idealist website.

The one thing you can't do anymore is to say, "There's nothing I can do about this."

*Bill Clinton*

## TEN UNDER THIRTY WHO TURNED THEIR PASSION INTO PROMISE

Like the other success stories interspersed throughout this book, the people profiled in this section are devoted to shaping a better future. They are visionaries who understand the importance of learning how to transform our present circumstances through creativity, compassion, and diligence. While none of these stories holds the magic formula for how to live a meaningful life, I hope what follows inspires you to continue to make decisions that will give you room to dream, innovate, and act. These people are changing the world, and you can, too.

### Kali Lindsey—Encouraging Education and Teaching Compassion

Twenty-eight-year-old Kali Lindsey grew up in a traditional middle class family in Detroit, Michigan, with close ties to a prominent Baptist church. "I sometimes compared my family to the Cosbys," he recalls. "My parents were professionals and were together, and this was during a time when many of my friends came from an increasingly large number of single-parent households." Lindsey's childhood was not always idyllic, though, especially as he reached adolescence and began to realize an attraction to the same sex. "My family is so religious, and therefore I didn't have anyone to talk to about my feelings. It was an isolating time," he recalls.

Although he did meet a few other peers who were also coming to terms with their sexuality, it was not until college that Lindsey was able to find a stronger sense of belonging. He got involved with gay advocacy groups and took part in organizing a queer-student leadership summit. He eventually told his parents that he was gay, but their responses were more of disbelief than acceptance.

Despite all of these internal struggles, he graduated in 2001 from Eastern Michigan University with a degree in psychology and began working at a bank. After a bout of shingles and nearly fatal viral meningitis, Lindsey was diagnosed with HIV. In order to bring his T-cell count back up, he needed to take aggressive drugs that came with severe side effects. Still afraid of rejection and discrimination, Lindsey hid his suffering and diagnosis from everyone, including his family. It took months for him to talk to anyone about his HIV status. "When I started talking to someone else who was HIV-positive about my situation, I finally began to heal," he says.

Remembering how crucial it was for Lindsey to have someone to talk to after his diagnosis, he began to volunteer with the Michigan AIDS hotline as soon as he was healthy. He helped callers find a place to get tested, answered questions about care and prevention, and gave HIV-prevention trainings and talks in the community. He realized quickly that he had a talent for connecting with others and decided to sell everything he owned and make the move to Washington, D.C., where he could pursue advocacy work. He quickly landed a job with the **Human Rights Campaign** before moving on to work for the **National Association of People with AIDS**. The twenty-eight-year-old is now the vice president for federal government affairs, and he regularly meets with political and social action groups to try to improve HIV care and research and to remove some of the stigma associated with HIV.

Lindsey is a proponent of calm, deliberate action and education. "I often go into rooms with people who represent very different viewpoints, and it is our job to reach a consensus. The person who enters the room screaming rarely wins. Most people don't realize how much of a utility conversation has. Just try talking to people about who you are and what you believe," he advises. Lindsey has seen a wave of people making their careers out of their passions, and he has great hope for the America of the future. "As a country, it is so important that we appreciate the full color that we have to offer," he says.

For those wanting to get more involved with HIV education and outreach, Lindsey recommends looking for grassroots organizations in your community, like the **One campaign** or the **Community HIV/AIDS Mobilization Project**, which address the root causes of the disease, such as poverty, inadequate education, and joblessness.

## Maisha Everhart—Finding Consensus When It Matters Most

After graduating from Spelman College with a degree in political science, Maisha Everhart decided to work before going to graduate school. "I highly recommend taking time off between degrees because school doesn't necessarily prepare you for the real world. It's important to go out and get some work experience and explore what you might want to study," she explains.

Everhart worked for a law firm and eventually went to law school at Rutgers. Her favorite part of earning her law degree was working at law clinics, where she was able to get some hands-on experience as a public defender. In 2004, she was asked to do some advocacy work on political campaigns in Pennsylvania. From there she worked on campaigns in several different states and was eventually called to work on Senator Clinton's campaign. After Clinton's 2008 presidential bid ended, Everhart was offered a job at the **Alliance for Climate Protection**. This latest job was a bit of a surprise, considering that she doesn't consider herself an environmentalist and her experience has been mainly political, but she says, "I believe that we should take care of the environment because it is the right thing to do, and it will solve a lot of our country's problems."

Everhart advises jobseekers to network by finding people in fields that they are interested in pursuing—but also to be open to opportunities, however unlikely, when they present themselves. "The majority of the time, the best way to get an interview is through someone you know, so you have to be really proactive. If you just email your résumé out, it is hard to separate yourself from the pack. Don't be embarrassed to ask for help, and remain open-minded. By no means would I have predicted that I would end up where I am. Sometimes life points you in a different direction, and you have to be open and embrace it."

Everhart's work in politics and with the Alliance has also shown her how important it is to form unlikely coalitions with unlikely collaborators. She cautions those interested in effecting change to "be careful not to spend too much time talking to ourselves." Everhart also points out that young people have often led the way in implementing bold changes. "It is important to educate yourself, stay engaged, and hold your elected officials accountable. Also, make sure that you are active in your local community, and remember that there is such a thing as positive peer pressure," she adds. When faced with those who disagree with your point of view, Everhart recommends listening and attempting to find common ground. If she and the Alliance can get enough people on board with significant carbon emissions reductions, the somewhat nomadic Everhart will once again be looking for a job. "If we do our jobs right, we can happily close up shop within the next three years," she says.

## Concerned about Climate Change? So Are They

**1Sky**
**350.org**
**Alliance for Climate Protection**
**Green for All**
**Power Vote**
**Stop Global Warming**

## Sarah Kalloch—Working for Justice, Not Charity

When Sarah Kalloch graduated from Harvard in 2000, she, like many college graduates, was facing a mound of student debt. However, she also wanted to find out more about urban poverty, so she applied for and received a fellowship to work in Uganda. She says of her decision, "I knew I could pay my loans off over time, and I didn't want to get a job for the sake of getting a job and then find myself miserable. Time is what you don't have when you get older, and the twenties are the exciting time to figure out what you want to do."

So at the age of twenty-two, Kalloch went to Africa to work at the Uganda Fisheries Research Institute, which is dedicated to helping communities responsibly manage resources. She took the opportunity to travel around East Africa and was transformed by what she saw. "My time in Africa opened my eyes, and I realized I don't know anything," she recalls. "There were challenges there that I wanted to be a part of figuring out. We are all responsible as global citizens, but if something is in your backyard, the problem is more pronounced," she says.

After her time in Uganda, Kalloch returned home determined to go back to Africa as soon as possible. After a brief stint in the Bahamas at a resort job, she found a paid internship in Boston at a philanthropic family foundation. Although this position wasn't going to get her back to Uganda, she knew she could learn valuable fundraising skills, and the position was flexible enough that she could continue to search for a position in Africa. When a friend sent her a posting for a job working with **Physicians for Human Rights** in Africa, she recalls thinking, "This is my dream job." The organization hired Kalloch to work with the Health Action AIDS campaign, which was dedicated to starting advocacy networks to fight the spread of AIDS in East Africa.

Now the director of outreach of campaigns and constituency organizing for Physicians for Human Rights, Kalloch believes in the potential for millennials to effect change. "Our generation wants to look at the root causes, and we want to find jobs that both make an immediate impact and allow us to fix structures that are flawed. We can have the most impact by working with the voiceless to amplify their voice. It is justice, not charity, that is wanted in the world."

## Web Resources for the World-Changing Job Seeker

### Idealist
Idealist is one of the best places to search for nonprofit jobs. If you missed this chapter's *Ways* Guide, see **page 254** for more details.

### Craig's List
With a Craig's List for almost every city in United States and many international pages as well, a visit here is a good way to get an idea of the opportunities that may exist throughout the country and the world. Since there are apartment listings, too, you can also get a sense of cost of living, how hard it is going to be to score that free couch, and even your dating prospects. The job listings, on the other hand, while abundant, tend to be limited in scope and will probably have many applicants. I recommend using this site as a starting point to see which companies and organizations are hiring in a given region.

### Environmental Career Opportunities/Environmental Jobs and Careers/Stop Dodo
As their names imply, all three of these websites maintain databases of job listings with an environmental focus. From renewable-energy development to outdoor education, there are thousands of jobs in dozens of industries that fall under the large umbrella of environmental pursuits.

**Future5000**—Future 5000 is an online directory of over 700 progressive youth organizations throughout the United States. Their goal is to someday reach 5,000, but you don't have to wait until that happens to utilize their resources. You can browse through participating organizations by topic and contact those that interest you, or check their announcements section for job openings and internship opportunities.

**Each Organization's Own Website**
Nothing beats pounding the virtual pavement, so once you have identified some organizations and/or businesses and regions where you would like to work, make frequent visits to individual websites to search for potential jobs.

### Janelle Robbins—Working for 186 Bosses

As a teenager growing up in a rural area of New York, Janelle Robbins got her first lesson in environmental science from her father. When she expressed an interest in the environment as a teenager, her father brought her to a large dairy farm and said, "See that cow standing in the middle of the creek? That is where a lot of pollution comes from, but people don't often think of this as a source. It is important that whatever you do, you educate people about the root causes of problems."

Robbins kept her dad's advice in mind and went on to major in agricultural and biological engineering at Cornell. While in college, she had a three-month internship with **Hudson Riverkeeper**, an advocacy group devoted to protecting the Hudson River in New York. She went on to earn her master's in biological systems engineering from Virginia Tech, all with the idea that she would eventually be an advocate and educator on behalf of the environment. As part of her degree program, she was able to do fieldwork with farmers who were trying to find best land-use practices with regard to water- and soil-pollution issues. While her work with the farmers reaffirmed Robbins's inclination not to remain in research, she had reached a professional crossroads of sorts, because many people with her degree go on to work as consultants for agribusiness or for the Army Corps of Engineers. "I knew that I would need to be a good advocate, not just a good scientist," she recalls. "In the nonprofit world, I could translate the scientific facts into something that was protective for the environment and useful to people trying to understand the complex issues surrounding pollution sources and solutions."

During her time at Virginia Tech, Robbins did some pro bono research work for Riverkeeper and the **Waterkeeper Alliance,** which is the umbrella organization for the individual Waterkeeper organizations all over the world. Her commitment to their cause paid off with a job offer. "They asked me one day when I was close to finishing my degree if I wanted to be paid for answering all of the questions I had been answering for free for the last two years," Robbins recalls.

As a staff scientist at the Waterkeeper Alliance, Robbins now spends her days working as a consultant for the 186 (and growing) Waterkeeper organizations across six continents. "Many of our Waterkeepers have really unique pollution problems in their watersheds, and one of the great things about my job is that no two days are the same," she says. Robbins also coordinates Waterkeeper Alliance's anti-coal campaign and assists other campaign staff working on such issues as safe seafood and anti-CAFO (concentrated animal feeding operations, which are a huge source of pollution) campaigns. Robbins says that one of the strengths of Waterkeeper is its commitment to community engagement. According to her, "The individual Waterkeepers are there to serve their own communities, and it is such a good model for environmental protection, because each watershed and each community faces unique challenges that have to be addressed at the local level."

### Ben Jervey—Big Ideas in the Big Apple

The author of *The Big Green Apple* is ironically not from New York at all but rather a rural town in Massachusetts. What's more, he became interested in environmental planning while studying environmental studies and geography at Middlebury College in Vermont. After graduating, he moved to New York City to pursue his interest in the city's ecosystem and moved to New York City. His first job was doing advocacy work with a nonprofit partner of the City Parks Department. "I was looking for ways to reconcile my environmental ethics with my new urban lifestyle," he recalls. His curiosity about the topic gave him the idea for a book, and he soon found a wealth of topics to cover. Jervey says, "There were many people trying to live an environmentally conscious lifestyle, and I was impressed by how much was going on."

Determined to spread the word about the innovative initiatives he had found, Jervey went to the library, took out books on how to write a proposal, and began to craft his book idea. After nine months refining his pitch in his spare time, he had a proposal ready to send to prospective publishers. "I had a hard time getting publishers to understand that there is anyone in New York that cares about the environment, but I knew this was the case because I was immersed in it," he says.

Jervey persisted, and his book was released in 2006. He continues to work as a freelance writer, and he has also turned his sights to the Web, curating **sustaiNYC**, a "reblog covering NYC's sustainability scene," and writing a weekly web column on energy and climate change for *Good* magazine.

### Rachel Meeropol—Watchdog for the Accused

Rachel Meeropol was twenty-six when she started working for the **Center for Constitutional Rights** (CCR) shortly after graduating from the NYU School of Law. Before enrolling in law school, she studied cultural anthropology at Wesleyan. She knew that she was interested in law with a focus on public interest, and NYU had a good loan-repayment program for those practicing public interest law after graduating. "If you are earning below a certain salary, NYU makes all of your loan payments; the program is generous enough that I was able to graduate with a shocking amount of debt and still live in New York City and work for CCR," she says.

While at NYU, Meeropol prepared for her current job by working on a death penalty case in Alabama, at legal services for **Prisoners with Children** in San Francisco, and as an intern at CCR. She was also able to secure an **Equal Justice Works** Fellowship to work at CCR after graduation.

Since joining CCR, Meeropol has co-authored an updated version of the *Jailhouse Lawyer's Handbook*, an easy-to-use handbook for prisoners who are trying to advocate for their rights. CCR combines litigation efforts with education and outreach programs, and Meeropol finds her work extremely rewarding. "People need to think really carefully about the kind of work that is going to make them happy. There are so many ways to make a difference, and there is a role for all of us to play. Ask yourself, what do I want to do on a daily basis that is going to make me fulfilled and happy?" she says. What is the key to finding happiness if you have chosen a potentially stressful, politically active career? According to Meeropol, it is feeling passionate about what you are doing. "I work in an excellent environment with highly motivated people who love their work."

### Nancy Diaz Bain—A Role Model for Success

Nancy Diaz Bain always knew that she wanted to be an educator, but her field experience at a local middle school during her practicum in college almost discouraged her from the field entirely. "Nobody wanted to be there," she recalls, "It was a sad, dark environment for kids and staff." A chance meeting with Dennis Littky, one of the founders of the Met School in Providence, Rhode Island, and two of his high-school students would offer her the chance to experience an entirely different model of education.

The Met, one of the **Big Picture** schools, was started by educators Dennis Littky and Elliot Washor, who believe in a holistic approach to learning. The schools are based in low-income neighborhoods, and students have an advisor, rather than a teacher, who works closely with them through all four years of high school. The advisors are involved with every facet of a student's individualized educational plan, which is geared toward his or her unique skills and interests. The model is clearly working too, as over 90 percent of graduating seniors head to college.

After meeting Littky, Bain volunteered at the Met and encountered a completely different learning environment. "The kids and the staff were happy, and there was an energy that was unlike anywhere I had ever been in my life." She went on to serve as an advisor at the school, became principal of one of the campuses in 2002, and now serves as the co-director of the entire school.

According to Bain, the Met's educational model works because "everything we do is about creating a respectful, encouraging, happy, passionate, and inviting environment with high expectations." Bain also feels like she can relate to many of the students because they have gone through similar experiences. "I feel very lucky because I have worked hard, taken advantage of opportunities, and because of that I have been able to move ahead and be successful, and I am constantly encouraging my students to do the same."

## Learn More about Alternative Education Models

**Alternative High School Initiative**
**Big Picture Schools**
**Met Center**

## Elizabeth Robinson—A Benevolent Army of One

When Elizabeth Robinson graduated from college in 2001, the twenty-two-year-old religion major knew that she wanted to find a job that would enable her to give back, since she had had a childhood blessed with opportunity. Her interest in the African continent had been piqued during her last year in school, when her studies branched into sociology, anthropology, and French. Several classes touched on different African cultures and belief systems. She looked into international volunteer organizations and decided to volunteer with WorldTeach in Namibia.

Her first foray into the realm of fundraising arose when she set out to raise $6,000 to cover the cost of her trip and living expenses for the year. While in Namibia, she worked as an English and HIV-prevention teacher. She extended her contract to stay an extra year, immersing herself in the community and HIV-prevention efforts. She and her colleague Geoffrey Silver developed and filmed an educational video about HIV with students from her HIV and AIDS awareness club.

To get the educational video into the hands of Namibian teachers and to help train teachers in HIV-prevention education, she founded a nonprofit, **Sekolo Projects, Inc.,** in 2004. Robinson has been working to train teachers and educate young people about HIV ever since. She uses the educational video and teachers' guide that she put together and works in conjunction with the Namibian education sector to raise awareness and teach prevention and care. "It only takes one mistake to contract HIV and anyone can get HIV, not just prostitutes or drug users. We are working to fight stigmas about HIV infection and foster awareness, understanding, and acceptance," she says. Sekolo also promotes the "combined HIV ABC" of "Abstinence, Be faithful, and Correct condom use."

Robinson travels back and forth between Namibia and the United States and works hard while in the United States to raise money in support of her work. Many countries have been able to reduce their infection rates by teaching the combined HIV ABC, and Robinson knows her work has made a difference. Her next goal is to expand her work into more parts of Namibia. Her advice to those interested in getting involved in similar work is simple: "Immerse yourself in the culture and know that you are not going to change things overnight. But if you are committed to a grassroots effort, you will eventually be able to impress upon people that they have a choice," she says.

In 2008, the Namibian Ministry of Health released statistics showing that the HIV infection rate in fifteen- to nineteen-year-olds, Sekolo's target age group, dropped by half in the two years after Sekolo implemented the *Our HIV ABC* program. The Ministry of Education in Namibia, in conjunction with UNICEF, developed and is now implementing its own HIV-prevention training program for teachers called Windows of Hope. The program is more holistic and extensive than Sekolo's program, though it incorporates similar concepts. Now that HIV prevention is available in schools, Sekolo works to ensure that children are able to attend school in a healthy state of mind that encourages learning. To that end, the organization supports after-school programs, extra meals, and dormitories where marginalized children can stay. Robinson's goal is to turn Sekolo over to her Namibian partners so that it is a fully sustainable, local effort.

It may seem like Sekolo is a one-woman show, and it is certainly Robinson's full-time job to run both the education and fundraising projects. Yet she is also adamant that she could never do all of the work without the hundreds of people in the United States who help raise money or those in the Namibian education system who help bring her curriculum into the schools. "What one person can do is amazing," she explains. "But one person never stands alone."

### Stacie Okosky—First-Generation Green

Twenty-five-year-old Stacie Okosky has always been interested in the environment, but it wasn't until she started taking classes in business that she realized how intertwined business and environmental issues could be. While studying for a business marketing degree at the University of Vermont, she took advantage of every opportunity to learn more about the balance between the planet and the bottom line. One of her most memorable experiences was taking a class in Costa Rica taught by John Todd, inventor of the **Living Machine** (a filtration system that uses only natural biological processes to treat wastewater). Okosky was so inspired that she decided to take classes outside of the business curriculum and opted for a self-designed major titled Business Administration: Marketing and the Environment.

Within the course of her college studies, she became aware of the corporate sustainability work that green-cleaning and paper producer **Seventh Generation** was doing, and she set her sights on a job with the company after graduation. While she met with some resistance from her parents, who assumed she would take a more traditional route as a salesperson, she held firm to her principles and interests. According to Okosky, "I always knew that I would work for a company whose values were aligned with my own." Despite her determination, it wasn't easy for her to get a call back from her ideal employer. "I applied three times before I even got an interview, so you can imagine how excited I was to be offered a position," she says.

Okosky now spends much of her time communicating with consumers, answering questions, and fielding suggestions, which she compiles for some of the company's executives. However, unlike a more traditional corporation, Seventh Generation is not big on hierarchy, and Okosky is regularly invited to cross-functional, high-level meetings where her participation is greatly valued. "I can bring any feedback to anyone in the company, and we often have meetings with our president where input about company decisions is welcome."

Okosky's commitment to the environment doesn't stop at her day job. She is also involved with the Green Team at Seventh Generation, which asks all employees to lower their carbon footprint 20 percent by 2010. New employees are given mentors to help them meet this goal, and the company also offers monetary incentives toward expenses like the purchase of a more fuel-efficient vehicle or energy-efficient upgrades in the home.

To learn more about bringing sustainability to the workplace, visit the Seventh Generation website and download the company's *Corporate Consciousness Report.*

## Daniel Lurie—Tipping the Scales against Poverty

Daniel Lurie grew up with money and a sense of obligation to do something good with it. After graduating from Duke with a degree in political science, his first foray into the nonprofit world was at the **Robin Hood Foundation** in New York, which supports 240 poverty-fighting nonprofits throughout the city. The organization raises its more than $100-million budget through donations and allocates the funds to nonprofits in the form of cash, management, and technical assistance. Robin Hood's model is unusual because board members fund the entire overhead of the organization, which allows 100 percent of every donation to go to funding foundation programs.

Lurie's project at the Robin Hood Foundation was to find architects to do pro bono work to put top-notch libraries in existing elementary schools. According to Lurie, "This was a way to impact 100 percent of the school by changing 5 percent of the real estate." Lurie was so inspired by the foundation's work that he decided to start the same type of community in the San Francisco Bay Area, where he is originally from. In 2003 he went to UC Berkeley's public policy school with the intention of acquiring the skills necessary to start his own foundation. He took classes in social entrepreneurship and financial management for nonprofits and began making connections with people in the community to see if he could generate financial support.

Many of those he approached agreed to help, and the **Tipping Point Community** launched in 2005. Based on Robin

Hood's model, Tipping Point funds anti-poverty organizations throughout the Bay Area. Lurie's careful planning did not stop with his academic preparation. "We do our due diligence on an organization before we give them a grant, and we view the relationships with these nonprofits as partnerships; we are with them for the long haul." Lurie continues to raise money by hosting philanthropic gatherings, and he relies on prominent board members to help with fundraising and PR efforts. In the organization's first three and a half years, they have raised over $10 million and supported the work of twenty-two groups.

While fighting poverty may seem like a daunting task, Lurie is confident that his organization is making a difference by immediately putting 100 percent of its donations to work. As the Tipping Point continues to grow, Lurie remains firm in his belief that "poverty can be preventable instead of inevitable."

# CONCLUSION

## START MAKING WAVES

We are coming of age in one of the most challenging moments in history, yet time and again, extraordinary people have emerged capable of the innovation and compassion needed to meet the diverse challenges of living with six billion other people. I challenge you—our circumstances challenge you—to use your curiosity, creativity, and energy to discover how to make the world a place we will be proud to hand over to our children.

No one expects one person to tackle all of these issues at once, especially since the path to becoming a world changer is a deeply personal one. You don't have to feel guilty about choosing one cause over another. There are, after all, millions of you, and for every one of you who is committed to fighting the spread of HIV, there is another ready to teach underprivileged children and yet another who is fired up about alternative energy solutions. I hope that the suggestions in this book have whetted your appetite and empowered you to explore and discover the possibilities and that by the time you put this book down, you will believe in your powerful potential to make a difference.

While belief is the first critical step, action is the only way to create change. Do not consider a three-month volunteering trip to Africa or a radical career change, decide it's impossible, and abandon the idea of making a difference. Rather, start by going on a hike at a local park, buying a batch of organic blueberries, or donating a few dollars to a cause that matters to you. When you consciously choose to act in the interest of your future, you will begin to feel that your actions have the power to shape all that lies ahead of you. And when you believe in that kind of power, it will be easy for you to do your part to change the world, no matter how old you are. Working together, we will create the world we wish to see.

## PERSONAL AFTERWORD

By now, I hope you've marked several sections in this book that appeal to you, and perhaps you have already made a pledge to reduce your plastic use or to go on a volunteering trip to Bolivia. Maybe your next party will be one that raises money for your favorite new cause, or you have decided to purchase local, organic food whenever possible. No matter what decisions you make about how you will try to change the world, I hope you see these commitments as part of an exciting new adventure. I have provided these pages at the end of the book to serve as a place for you to keep track of resources, plans, ideas, and of course, accomplishments.

I encourage you to visit the *Ten Ways* website and blog to share your experiences and to connect with other members of the vibrant community of young, energetic, and effective leaders who are already hard at work changing the world. Enthusiasm is contagious, and making the world a better place is a cause we can all rally behind. As you meet people who have embarked upon similar paths, and as you share your ideas and achievements, your network of fellow world changers will grow, and you will realize that your potential for making the world a better place is as boundless as your creativity.

| WAYS I PLAN ON MAKING A DIFFERENCE | PAGE NUMBERS |
|---|---|
| | |
| | |
| | |
| | |
| | |
| | |
| | |
| | |
| | |
| | |
| | |

| USEFUL RESOURCES AND ORGANIZATIONS | PAGE NUMBERS |
|---|---|
| | |
| | |
| | |
| | |
| | |
| | |
| | |
| | |
| | |
| | |

| NEW IDEAS/CONTACTS | PAGE NUMBERS |
|---|---|
| | |
| | |
| | |
| | |
| | |
| | |
| | |
| | |
| | |
| | |
| | |

| NOTES | PAGE NUMBERS |
|---|---|
|  |  |
|  |  |
|  |  |
|  |  |
|  |  |
|  |  |
|  |  |
|  |  |
|  |  |
|  |  |

# APPENDIX

## CHAPTER 1 APPENDIX (TIME)

| ICON | PAGE | 🕐 | $ | 🏢 |
|------|------|-----|-----|-----|
| Get the Ball Rolling | 3 | **1** | 1 | 1 |
| Listen | 7 | **1** | 1 | 1 |
| Moving Pictures, Please! | 16 | **1** | 1 | 1 |
| Don't Just Take My Word for It | 12 | **2** | 1 | 1 |
| See What Those Pundits Have to Say | 15 | **2** | 1 | 1 |
| Become a Blog Hog | 15 | **2** | 1 | 1 |
| Read the Charity Cliff Notes | 19 | **2** | 1 | 1 |
| Dare to Dream…with Your Dollars | 20 | **2** | 3 | 1 |
| Okay, I'm Hooked. What about a Book? | 8 | **3** | 2 | 1 |
| Go on Some Charity Speed Dates | 19 | **3** | 1 | 1 |

## CHAPTER 1 APPENDIX (MONEY)

| ICON | PAGE | $ | 🕐 | 🏛 |
|---|---|---|---|---|
| Get the Ball Rolling | 3 | **1** | 1 | 1 |
| Listen | 7 | **1** | 1 | 1 |
| Don't Just Take My Word for It | 12 | **1** | 2 | 1 |
| See What Those Pundits Have to Say | 15 | **1** | 2 | 1 |
| Become a Blog Hog | 15 | **1** | 2 | 1 |
| Moving Pictures, Please! | 16 | **1** | 1 | 1 |
| Go on Some Charity Speed Dates | 19 | **1** | 3 | 1 |
| Read the Charity Cliff Notes | 19 | **1** | 2 | 1 |
| Okay, I'm Hooked. What about a Book? | 8 | **2** | 3 | 1 |
| Dare to Dream…with Your Dollars | 20 | **3** | 2 | 1 |

## CHAPTER 1 APPENDIX (LIFESTYLE)

| ICON | PAGE | 🏛 | 🕐 | $ |
|---|---|---|---|---|
| Get the Ball Rolling | 3 | **1** | 1 | 1 |
| Listen | 7 | **1** | 1 | 1 |
| Okay, I'm Hooked. What about a Book? | 8 | **1** | 3 | 2 |
| Don't Just Take My Word for It | 12 | **1** | 2 | 1 |
| See What Those Pundits Have to Say | 15 | **1** | 2 | 1 |
| Become a Blog Hog | 15 | **1** | 2 | 1 |
| Moving Pictures, Please! | 16 | **1** | 1 | 1 |
| Go on Some Charity Speed Dates | 19 | **1** | 3 | 1 |

| | | 🕐 | 💲 | 🏨 |
|---|---|---|---|---|
| Read the Charity Cliff Notes | 19 | **1** | 2 | 1 |
| Dare to Dream…with Your Dollars | 20 | **1** | 2 | 3 |

## CHAPTER 2 APPENDIX (TIME)

| ICON | PAGE | 🕐 | 💲 | 🏨 |
|---|---|---|---|---|
| Join the Ranks of Volunteers | 28 | **2** | 1 | 2 |
| Start the Search | 29 | **2** | 1 | 1 |
| Think Big. Start Small. | 30 | **2** | 1 | 2 |
| Count on the Kindness of Strangers and the Advice of Friends | 32 | **2** | 1 | 1 |
| Virtual Volunteering | 33 | **2** | 1 | 1 |
| Go With God and/or a Group | 34 | **2** | 1 | 2 |
| Change Lives – Take a Vacation | 35 | **3** | 4 | 3 |
| Toughest Job You'll Ever Love | 44 | **5** | 1 | 5 |

## CHAPTER 2 APPENDIX (MONEY)

| ICON | PAGE | 💲 | 🕐 | 🏨 |
|---|---|---|---|---|
| Join the Ranks of Volunteers | 28 | **1** | 2 | 2 |
| Start the Search | 29 | **1** | 2 | 1 |
| Think Big. Start Small. | 30 | **1** | 2 | 2 |
| Count on the Kindness of Strangers and the Advice of Friends | 32 | **1** | 2 | 1 |
| Virtual Volunteering | 33 | **1** | 2 | 1 |

| | | 🏠 | 🕐 | $ |
|---|---|---|---|---|
| Go With God and/or a Group | 34 | **1** | 2 | 2 |
| Toughest Job You'll Ever Love | 44 | **1** | 5 | 5 |
| Change Lives – Take a Vacation | 35 | **4** | 3 | 3 |

## CHAPTER 2 APPENDIX (LIFESTYLE)

| ICON | PAGE | 🏠 | 🕐 | $ |
|---|---|---|---|---|
| Start the Search | 29 | **1** | 2 | 1 |
| Count on the Kindness of Strangers and the Advice of Friends | 32 | **1** | 2 | 1 |
| Virtual Volunteering | 33 | **1** | 2 | 1 |
| Join the Ranks of Volunteers | 28 | **2** | 2 | 1 |
| Think Big. Start Small. | 30 | **2** | 2 | 1 |
| Go With God and/or a Group | 34 | **2** | 2 | 1 |
| Change Lives – Take a Vacation | 35 | **3** | 3 | 4 |
| Toughest Job You'll Ever Love | 44 | **5** | 5 | 1 |

## CHAPTER 3 APPENDIX (TIME)

| ICON | PAGE | 🕐 | $ | 🏠 |
|---|---|---|---|---|
| Make Friends with Your Candidates | 56 | **1** | 1 | 1 |
| Make a Political Fashion Statement | 59 | **1** | 2 | 1 |
| Just the Facts | 54 | **2** | 1 | 1 |
| Dip into the Issues on the Internet | 57 | **2** | 1 | 1 |
| Get In on the Vote | 60 | **2** | 1 | 2 |
| Get Involved in State and Local Elections Too | 61 | **2** | 1 | 2 |

| | | | |
|---|---|---|---|
| Become a Laptop Lobbyist | 62 | **2** | 1 | 2 |
| Party with Your Party | 69 | **2** | 2 | 2 |
| Enter the Blogosphere | 58 | **3** | 1 | 2 |
| Send Your Own Message | 64 | **3** | 1 | 2 |
| Not Getting a Response? Storm the Capitol | 67 | **4** | 2 | 2 |
| Hit the Campaign Trail | 71 | **4** | 1 | 2 |
| Go to Camp | 72 | **4** | 1 | 3 |
| Make It Your Job | 73 | **5** | 4 | 5 |

## CHAPTER 3 APPENDIX (MONEY)

| ICON | PAGE | $ | 🕐 | 🏛 |
|---|---|---|---|---|
| Just the Facts | 54 | **1** | 2 | 1 |
| Make Friends with Your Candidates | 56 | **1** | 1 | 1 |
| Dip into the Issues on the Internet | 57 | **1** | 2 | 1 |
| Enter the Blogosphere | 58 | **1** | 3 | 2 |
| Get In on the Vote | 60 | **1** | 2 | 2 |
| Get Involved in State and Local Elections Too | 61 | **1** | 2 | 2 |
| Become a Laptop Lobbyist | 62 | **1** | 2 | 2 |
| Send Your Own Message | 64 | **1** | 3 | 2 |
| Hit the Campaign Trail | 71 | **1** | 4 | 2 |
| Go to Camp | 72 | **1** | 4 | 3 |
| Not Getting a Response? Storm the Capitol | 67 | **2** | 4 | 2 |
| Make a Political Fashion Statement | 59 | **2** | 1 | 1 |
| Party with Your Party | 69 | **2** | 2 | 2 |
| Make It Your Job | 73 | **4** | 5 | 5 |

## CHAPTER 3 APPENDIX (LIFESTYLE)

| ICON | PAGE | 🏛 | 🕐 | $ |
|---|---|---|---|---|
| Just the Facts | 54 | **1** | 2 | 1 |
| Make Friends with Your Candidates | 56 | **1** | 1 | 1 |
| Dip into the Issues on the Internet | 57 | **1** | 2 | 1 |
| Make a Political Fashion Statement | 59 | **1** | 1 | 2 |
| Enter the Blogosphere | 58 | **2** | 3 | 1 |
| Get In on the Vote | 60 | **2** | 2 | 1 |
| Get Involved in State and Local Elections Too | 61 | **2** | 2 | 1 |
| Become a Laptop Lobbyist | 62 | **2** | 2 | 1 |
| Send Your Own Message | 64 | **2** | 3 | 1 |
| Not Getting a Response? Storm the Capitol | 67 | **2** | 4 | 2 |
| Party with Your Party | 69 | **2** | 2 | 2 |
| Hit the Campaign Trail | 71 | **2** | 4 | 1 |
| Go to Camp | 72 | **3** | 4 | 1 |
| Make It Your Job | 73 | **5** | 5 | 4 |

## CHAPTER 4 APPENDIX (TIME)

| ICON | PAGE | 🕐 | $ | 🏛 |
|---|---|---|---|---|
| Be a Bag Lady or Lad | 91 | **1** | 2 | 1 |
| Break the Bottled Water Habit | 92 | **1** | 1 | 2 |
| Think outside the Bin | 85 | **2** | 1 | 2 |
| Put Away the Plastics | 88 | **2** | 2 | 3 |
| Complete the Cycle with Compost | 94 | **2** | 2 | 2 |

## CHAPTER 4 APPENDIX (MONEY)

| | PAGE | 🏠 | 🕐 | $ |
|---|---|---|---|---|
| Work with Your Favorite Environmental Organization | 113 | **1** | 3 | 2 |
| Put Away the Plastics | 88 | **2** | 2 | 3 |
| Be a Bag Lady or Lad | 91 | **2** | 1 | 1 |
| Complete the Cycle with Compost | 94 | **2** | 2 | 2 |
| Swap Your Books | 98 | **2** | 2 | 1 |
| Be a Paperwise Post-Consumer | 101 | **2** | 2 | 1 |
| Hire Mother Earth a Good Lawyer | 113 | **2** | 2 | 1 |
| Launch Your Own Campaign | 114 | **3** | 4 | 4 |

## CHAPTER 4 APPENDIX (LIFESTYLE)

| ICON | PAGE | 🏠 | 🕐 | $ |
|---|---|---|---|---|
| Be a Bag Lady or Lad | 91 | **1** | 1 | 2 |
| Swap Your Books | 98 | **1** | 2 | 2 |
| Yard Sale | 99 | **1** | 3 | 1 |
| Become a Treehugger | 101 | **1** | 2 | 1 |
| Be a Paperwise Post-Consumer | 101 | **1** | 2 | 2 |
| Tell Them about It | 112 | **1** | 3 | 1 |
| Hire Mother Earth a Good Lawyer | 113 | **1** | 2 | 2 |
| Think outside the Bin | 85 | **2** | 2 | 1 |
| Break the Bottled Water Habit | 92 | **2** | 1 | 1 |
| Complete the Cycle with Compost | 94 | **2** | 2 | 2 |
| Invest in Ocean Stocks | 103 | **2** | 2 | 1 |
| Bring Your Eco-friendly Ideas to Work Day | 109 | **3** | 2 | 1 |
| Work with Your Favorite Environmental Organization | 113 | **2** | 3 | 1 |
| Put Away the Plastics | 88 | **3** | 2 | 2 |

## CHAPTER 5 APPENDIX (TIME)

| | | | | |
|---|---|---|---|---|
| How Many Politicians Does It Take to Get Us to Change Our Light Bulbs? | 126 | **3** | 1 | 2 |
| Hang Them Out to Dry | 129 | **3** | 1 | 2 |
| Avoid Appliance Apathy | 130 | **3** | 1 | 2 |
| Keep a Dump Diary | 137 | **3** | 1 | 2 |

## CHAPTER 5 APPENDIX (MONEY)

| ICON | PAGE | $ | 🕐 | 🏭 |
|---|---|---|---|---|
| Join a Club Dedicated to Helping the Earth Chill Out | 122 | **1** | 1 | 1 |
| Know Your Number | 123 | **1** | 2 | 1 |
| Know Your Other Number | 125 | **1** | 2 | 1 |
| How Many Politicians Does It Take to Get Us to Change Our Light Bulbs? | 126 | **1** | 3 | 2 |
| Use a Clirty Hook | 128 | **1** | 1 | 2 |
| Hang Them Out to Dry | 129 | **1** | 3 | 2 |
| Avoid Appliance Apathy | 130 | **1** | 3 | 2 |
| Calculate Your Thirst | 133 | **1** | 1 | 1 |
| Be a Discriminating Flusher | 135 | **1** | 2 | 2 |
| Do Fewer Dishes | 136 | **1** | 2 | 2 |
| Don't Throw Good Water down the Drain | 136 | **1** | 1 | 2 |
| Keep a Dump Diary | 137 | **1** | 3 | 2 |
| Ditch the Dump | 138 | **1** | 2 | 3 |
| Go Digital | 141 | **1** | 1 | 1 |
| Buy Less Stuff | 143 | **1** | 1 | 3 |
| Unplugged is Not Just for MTV Anymore | 128 | **2** | 1 | 1 |
| Deal with a Dual Climate | 129 | **2** | 1 | 2 |

| | | | | |
|---|---|---|---|---|
| Power Your Home with the Green Stuff | 131 | **2** | 1 | 1 |
| Shorter Showers under the Low Flow | 135 | **2** | 1 | 2 |
| Start New Trends with Thrift | 144 | **2** | 2 | 2 |
| Get Out the Gadgets | 128 | **3** | 1 | 2 |
| Be Truly Energy Independent | 131 | **3** | 2 | 3 |

## CHAPTER 5 APPENDIX (LIFESTYLE)

| ICON | PAGE | 🏠 | 🕐 | $ |
|---|---|---|---|---|
| Join a Club Dedicated to Helping the Earth Chill Out | 122 | **1** | 1 | 1 |
| Know Your Number | 123 | **1** | 2 | 1 |
| Know Your Other Number | 125 | **1** | 2 | 1 |
| Unplugged is Not Just for MTV Anymore | 128 | **1** | 1 | 2 |
| Power Your Home with the Green Stuff | 131 | **1** | 1 | 2 |
| Calculate Your Thirst | 133 | **1** | 1 | 1 |
| Go Digital | 141 | **1** | 1 | 1 |
| How Many Politicians Does It Take to Get Us to Change Our Light Bulbs? | 126 | **2** | 3 | 1 |
| Get Out the Gadgets | 128 | **2** | 1 | 3 |
| Use a Clirty Hook | 128 | **2** | 1 | 1 |
| Hang Them Out to Dry | 129 | **2** | 3 | 1 |
| Deal with a Dual Climate | 129 | **2** | 1 | 2 |
| Avoid Appliance Apathy | 130 | **2** | 3 | 1 |
| Shorter Showers under the Low Flow | 135 | **2** | 1 | 2 |
| Be a Discriminating Flusher | 135 | **2** | 2 | 1 |

| | | | | |
|---|---|---|---|---|
| Do Fewer Dishes | 136 | **2** | 2 | 1 |
| Don't Throw Good Water down the Drain | 136 | **2** | 1 | 1 |
| Keep a Dump Diary | 137 | **2** | 3 | 1 |
| Start New Trends with Thrift | 144 | **2** | 2 | 2 |
| Ditch the Dump | 138 | **3** | 2 | 1 |
| Buy Less Stuff | 143 | **3** | 1 | 1 |
| Be Truly Energy Independent | 131 | **3** | 2 | 3 |

## CHAPTER 6 APPENDIX (TIME)

| ICON | PAGE | 🕐 | $ | ▥ |
|---|---|---|---|---|
| Save Packaging, Money, and Oh Yeah, the Planet | 161 | **1** | 1 | 2 |
| Learn the Lingo | 149 | **2** | 1 | 1 |
| Look for the Triple Bottom Line | 149 | **2** | 1 | 2 |
| Commit to Being a Compassionate Consumer | 156 | **2** | 2 | 2 |
| Put Your Money Where Your Heart Is | 156 | **2** | 3 | 2 |
| Become a Shareholder | 158 | **2** | 2 | 2 |
| Write a Letter | 158 | **2** | 1 | 1 |
| Have the Big Boxes Do Your Bidding | 161 | **2** | 1 | 1 |
| Time to Buy | 164 | **2** | 3 | 3 |
| Wear Eco-chic Clothing on Any Budget | 165 | **2** | 2 | 2 |
| Make Your Home a Green Haven | 168 | **2** | 4 | 3 |
| Keep it Clean and Green | 170 | **2** | 2 | 1 |
| Makeup Madness | 172 | **2** | 2 | 2 |
| Give the Gift of Awareness | 174 | **2** | 2 | 1 |

| | | | | |
|---|---|---|---|---|
| Research, Rank, and Reward Companies | 151 | **3** | 2 | 2 |
| Start a Boycott | 159 | **4** | 1 | 5 |

## CHAPTER 6 APPENDIX (MONEY)

| ICON | PAGE | $ | 🕐 | ⊞ |
|---|---|---|---|---|
| Learn the Lingo | 149 | **1** | 2 | 1 |
| Look for the Triple Bottom Line | 149 | **1** | 2 | 2 |
| Write a Letter | 158 | **1** | 2 | 1 |
| Start a Boycott | 159 | **1** | 4 | 5 |
| Have the Big Boxes Do Your Bidding | 161 | **1** | 2 | 1 |
| Save Packaging, Money, and Oh Yeah, the Planet | 161 | **1** | 1 | 2 |
| Research, Rank, and Reward Companies | 151 | **2** | 3 | 2 |
| Commit to Being a Compassionate Consumer | 156 | **2** | 2 | 2 |
| Become a Shareholder | 158 | **2** | 2 | 2 |
| Wear Eco-chic Clothing on Any Budget | 165 | **2** | 2 | 2 |
| Keep it Clean and Green | 170 | **2** | 2 | 1 |
| Makeup Madness | 172 | **2** | 2 | 2 |
| Give the Gift of Awareness | 174 | **2** | 2 | 1 |
| Put Your Money Where Your Heart Is | 156 | **3** | 2 | 2 |
| Time to Buy | 164 | **3** | 2 | 3 |
| Make Your Home a Green Haven | 168 | **4** | 2 | 3 |

## CHAPTER 6 APPENDIX (LIFESTYLE)

| ICON | PAGE | 🏢 | 🕐 | 💲 |
|---|---|---|---|---|
| Learn the Lingo | 149 | **1** | 2 | 1 |
| Write a Letter | 158 | **1** | 2 | 1 |
| Have the Big Boxes Do Your Bidding | 161 | **1** | 2 | 1 |
| Keep it Clean and Green | 170 | **1** | 2 | 2 |
| Give the Gift of Awareness | 174 | **1** | 2 | 2 |
| Look for the Triple Bottom Line | 149 | **2** | 2 | 1 |
| Research, Rank, and Reward Companies | 151 | **2** | 3 | 2 |
| Commit to Being a Compassionate Consumer | 156 | **2** | 2 | 2 |
| Put Your Money Where Your Heart Is | 156 | **2** | 2 | 3 |
| Become a Shareholder | 158 | **2** | 2 | 2 |
| Save Packaging, Money, and Oh Yeah, the Planet | 161 | **2** | 1 | 1 |
| Wear Eco-chic Clothing on Any Budget | 165 | **2** | 2 | 2 |
| Makeup Madness | 172 | **2** | 2 | 2 |
| Time to Buy | 164 | **3** | 2 | 3 |
| Make Your Home a Green Haven | 168 | **3** | 2 | 4 |
| Start a Boycott | 159 | **5** | 4 | 1 |

## CHAPTER 7 APPENDIX (TIME)

| ICON | PAGE | 🕐 | 💲 | 🏢 |
|---|---|---|---|---|
| Drink Local, Too! | 195 | **1** | 2 | 1 |
| Read the Label | 184 | **2** | 1 | 1 |

## CHAPTER 7 APPENDIX (MONEY)

| | PAGE | 🏠 | 🕐 | $ |
|---|---|---|---|---|
| Work on a Farm | 203 | **1** | 5 | 5 |
| Cook Your Own Food | 207 | **1** | 3 | 2 |
| Take It Slow | 209 | **1** | 2 | 2 |
| Eat Organic Food | 185 | **2** | 2 | 1 |
| Start Local with a Few Favorite Foods | 186 | **2** | 2 | 2 |
| Make Friends with Your Farmers | 190 | **2** | 2 | 2 |
| Brave New World—Get More Than Veggies at the Market | 193 | **2** | 2 | 2 |
| Drink Local, Too! | 195 | **2** | 1 | 1 |
| How Does Your Garden Grow? Do It Yourself and You'll Know | 200 | **2** | 3 | 2 |
| Yes, We Can! | 204 | **2** | 3 | 1 |
| Take the Local Challenge | 194 | **3** | 4 | 4 |
| Let Someone Else Do the Cooking | 210 | **3** | 2 | 1 |

## CHAPTER 7 APPENDIX (LIFESTYLE)

| ICON | PAGE | 🏠 | 🕐 | $ |
|---|---|---|---|---|
| Read the Label | 184 | **1** | 2 | 1 |
| Eat Organic Food | 185 | **1** | 2 | 2 |
| Find Out Where Your Food Comes From | 187 | **1** | 2 | 1 |
| Drink Local, Too! | 195 | **1** | 1 | 2 |
| Meat Your Meat | 196 | **1** | 2 | 1 |
| Yes, We Can! | 204 | **1** | 3 | 2 |
| Let Someone Else Do the Cooking | 210 | **1** | 2 | 3 |
| Start Local with a Few Favorite Foods | 186 | **2** | 2 | 2 |
| Calculate Your Food Miles | 188 | **2** | 2 | 1 |
| Make Friends with Your Farmers | 190 | **2** | 2 | 2 |

| | | ● | $ | ⌂ |
|---|---|---|---|---|
| Brave New World—Get More Than Veggies at the Market | 193 | **2** | 2 | 2 |
| Know Your Fish Facts | 199 | **2** | 2 | 1 |
| How Does Your Garden Grow? Do It Yourself and You'll Know | 200 | **2** | 3 | 2 |
| Take It Slow | 209 | **2** | 2 | 1 |
| Cook Your Own Food | 207 | **2** | 3 | 1 |
| Hold Your Horses | 198 | **3** | 2 | 1 |
| Take the Local Challenge | 194 | **4** | 4 | 3 |
| Work on a Farm | 203 | **5** | 5 | 1 |

## CHAPTER 8 APPENDIX (TIME)

| ICON | PAGE | ● | $ | ⌂ |
|---|---|---|---|---|
| Swanky Stuff Swap | 221 | **2** | 1 | 1 |
| Set Up the Home Soapbox | 222 | **2** | 2 | 1 |
| Phone It In | 223 | **2** | 1 | 2 |
| Attend a Benefit for Grown-Ups | 225 | **2** | 2 | 1 |
| Use a Caterer | 227 | **2** | 3 | 1 |
| Host a Benefit on Your Budget | 217 | **3** | 2 | 2 |
| Hold a Screening | 219 | **3** | 2 | 2 |
| Serve a Meal, Serve a Cause | 223 | **3** | 3 | 2 |
| DIYummy | 228 | **3** | 3 | 2 |
| Start Your Own Charity | 225 | **5** | 3 | 4 |

## CHAPTER 8 APPENDIX (MONEY)

| ICON | PAGE | $ | ● | ⌂ |
|---|---|---|---|---|
| Swanky Stuff Swap | 221 | **1** | 2 | 1 |
| Phone It In | 223 | **1** | 2 | 2 |
| Hold a Screening | 219 | **2** | 3 | 2 |

| | PAGE | 🏢 | 🕐 | $ |
|---|---|---|---|---|
| Set Up the Home Soapbox | 222 | **2** | 2 | 1 |
| Attend a Benefit for Grown-Ups | 225 | **2** | 2 | 1 |
| Host a Benefit on Your Budget | 235 | **2** | 3 | 2 |
| Serve a Meal, Serve a Cause | 223 | **3** | 3 | 2 |
| Start Your Own Charity | 225 | **3** | 5 | 4 |
| Use a Caterer | 227 | **3** | 2 | 1 |
| DIYummy | 228 | **3** | 3 | 2 |

## CHAPTER 8 APPENDIX (LIFESTYLE)

| ICON | PAGE | 🏢 | 🕐 | $ |
|---|---|---|---|---|
| Swanky Stuff Swap | 221 | **1** | 2 | 1 |
| Set Up the Home Soapbox | 222 | **1** | 2 | 2 |
| Attend a Benefit for Grown-Ups | 225 | **1** | 2 | 2 |
| Use a Caterer | 227 | **1** | 2 | 3 |
| Host a Benefit on Your Budget | 217 | **2** | 3 | 2 |
| Hold a Screening | 219 | **2** | 3 | 2 |
| Phone It In | 223 | **2** | 2 | 1 |
| Serve a Meal, Serve a Cause | 223 | **2** | 3 | 3 |
| Start Your Own Charity | 225 | **2** | 4 | 3 |
| DIYummy | 228 | **4** | 5 | 3 |

## CHAPTER 9 APPENDIX (TIME)

| ICON | PAGE | 🕐 | $ | 🏢 |
|---|---|---|---|---|
| Step Softly upon Thy Gas Pedal | 234 | **1** | 1 | 2 |
| Lower Your Octane Output | 233 | **2** | 1 | 3 |
| Crash a Carpool | 235 | **2** | 1 | 2 |
| Be a Part-Time Lover | 236 | **2** | 2 | 2 |

| | | | | |
|---|---|---|---|---|
| Flying Leaves a Huge Footprint—Reduce Yours | 236 | **2** | 1 | 3 |
| Get Going Already | 239 | **2** | 2 | 2 |
| Take a Hike | 243 | **2** | 2 | 2 |
| Get the Real Deal on Eco-friendly Trips | 248 | **2** | 1 | 2 |
| Lighten Your Load | 238 | **3** | 1 | 3 |
| Ask for Time Off | 241 | **3** | 3 | 2 |
| Take Economical and Eco-savvy Trips | 246 | **3** | 4 | 3 |

## CHAPTER 9 APPENDIX (MONEY)

| ICON | PAGE | $ | 🕐 | 🏢 |
|---|---|---|---|---|
| Step Softly upon Thy Gas Pedal | 234 | **1** | 1 | 2 |
| Lower Your Octane Output | 233 | **1** | 2 | 3 |
| Crash a Carpool | 235 | **1** | 2 | 2 |
| Flying Leaves a Huge Footprint—Reduce Yours | 236 | **1** | 2 | 3 |
| Lighten Your Load | 238 | **1** | 3 | 3 |
| Get the Real Deal on Eco-friendly Trips | 248 | **1** | 2 | 2 |
| Be a Part-Time Lover | 236 | **2** | 2 | 2 |
| Get Going Already | 239 | **2** | 2 | 2 |
| Take a Hike | 243 | **2** | 2 | 2 |
| Ask for Time Off | 241 | **3** | 3 | 2 |
| Take Economical and Eco-savvy Trips | 246 | **4** | 3 | 3 |

## CHAPTER 9 APPENDIX (LIFESTYLE)

| ICON | PAGE | 🏨 | 🕐 | $ |
|---|---|---|---|---|
| Step Softly upon Thy Gas Pedal | 234 | **2** | 1 | 1 |
| Crash a Carpool | 235 | **2** | 2 | 1 |
| Be a Part-Time Lover | 236 | **2** | 2 | 2 |
| Get Going Already | 239 | **2** | 2 | 2 |
| Ask for Time Off | 241 | **2** | 3 | 3 |
| Take a Hike | 243 | **2** | 2 | 2 |
| Get the Real Deal on Eco-friendly Trips | 248 | **2** | 2 | 1 |
| Lower Your Octane Output | 233 | **3** | 2 | 1 |
| Flying Leaves a Huge Footprint— Reduce Yours | 236 | **3** | 2 | 1 |
| Lighten Your Load | 238 | **3** | 3 | 1 |
| Take Economical and Eco-savvy Trips | 246 | **3** | 3 | 4 |

# WEBSITE APPENDIX
## Around the Home

| TITLE | WEBSITE ADDRESS | CHAPTER | PAGE |
|---|---|---|---|
| NRDC's Paper Product Guide | www.nrdc.org/land/ forests/gtissue.asp | 4 | 103 |
| Project Laundry List | laundrylist.org | 5 | 129 |
| Green Fiber | greenfiber.com | 6 | 168 |
| Carpet America Recovery | carpetrecovery.org | 6 | 169 |
| Shaw Floors | shawfloors.com | 6 | 169 |
| EPA Energy Star | energystar.gov | 6 | 169 |
| Eco-Green Living | eco-greenliving.com | 6 | 169 |
| Equita | shopequita.com | 6 | 169 |
| Greener Lifestyles | greenerlifestyles.com | 6 | 169 |
| Modernlink | modernlink.com | 6 | 169 |
| VivaTerra | vivaterra.com | 6 | 169 |
| Green Sleep | greensleep.com | 6 | 170 |
| Gaiam | gaiam.com | 6 | 170 |
| Anna Sova | annasova.com | 6 | 170 |
| Loop Organic | looporganic.com | 6 | 170 |
| Biokleen | biokleenhome.com | 6 | 171 |
| Ecover | ecover.com | 6 | 171 |
| Green Guide | greenguide.com | 6 | 174 |
| Seventh Generation | seventhgeneration.com | 10 | 271 |

## Consumer Information and Protection

| TITLE | WEBSITE ADDRESS | CHAPTER | PAGE |
|---|---|---|---|
| Fair Trade Certified | transfairusa.org | 6 | 149 |
| Green Seal | greenseal.org | 6 | 149 |
| Forest Stewardship Council | fscus.org | 6 | 149 |
| CSR wire | csrwire.com | 6 | 150 |
| Green America | coopamerica.org | 6 | 150 |

## Education

## Environment

## Events and Hosting

## Fashion

## Food and Gardening

| TITLE | WEBSITE ADDRESS | CHAPTER | PAGE |
|---|---|---|---|
| Equal Exchange | equalexchange.com | 1 | 6 |
| NRDC Eat Local | nrdc.org/health/foodmiles/ | 6 | |
| Seeds of Change | seedsofchange.com | 6 | 176 |
| NRDC Seasonal Food List | nrdc.org/health/foodmiles | 7 | 188 |
| Stone Barns Center | stonebarnscenter.org | 7 | 190 |
| Community Markets | communitymarkets.biz | 7 | 191 |
| Cowberry Crossing Farm | cowberrycrossing.com | 7 | 191 |
| LocalHarvest | localharvest.org | 7 | 191 |
| USDA List of Farmers'Markets | ams.usda.gov/farmersmarkets | 7 | 191 |
| CSA Center | csacenter.org | 7 | 191 |
| Worldwide Opportunities on Organic Farms | wwoof.org | 7 | 192 |
| Eat Local Challenge | eatlocalchallenge.com | 7 | 194 |
| Blue Ocean Institute Safe Seafood List | blueocean.org/seafood | 7 | 199 |
| Seafood Watch | seafoodwatch.org | 7 | 200 |
| Marine Stewardship Council | msc.org | 7 | 200 |
| American Community Garden Association | communitygarden.org | 7 | 201 |
| National Sustainable Agricultural Information Service (ATTRA) | farmattrainternships.ncat.org | 7 | 204 |
| Oregon Tilth Association | tilth.org | 7 | 204 |
| Epicurious | epicurious.com | 7 | 208 |
| Smitten Kitchen | smittenkitchen.com | 7 | 208 |
| Chocolate and Zucchini | chocolateandzucchini.com | 7 | 208 |
| All Recipes | allrecipes.com | 7 | 209 |

| | | | |
|---|---|---|---|
| Culinate | culinate.com | 7 | 209 |
| International Slow Food Movement | slowfood.com | 7 | 209 |
| Slow Food National Events | slowfoodnation.org/ events/special- programming/ youth-program/ | 7 | |
| Feeding America | feedingamerica.org | 8 | 223 |

## Health and Beauty Products

| TITLE | WEBSITE ADDRESS | CHAPTER | PAGE |
|---|---|---|---|
| Alba Botanica | albabotanica.com | 6 | 172 |
| Dr. Hauschka | drhauschka.com | 6 | 172 |
| Hugo Naturals | hugonaturals.com | 6 | 173 |
| Jäsön | Jason-natural.com | 6 | 173 |
| Kiss My Face | kissmyface.com | 6 | 173 |
| Nature's Gate | natures-gate.com | 6 | 173 |
| Pangea Organics | pangeaorganics.com | 6 | 173 |
| Preserve | preserveproducts.com | 6 | 173 |
| Weleda | usa.weleda.com | 6 | 173 |

## Humanitarian and Social Issues

| TITLE | WEBSITE ADDRESS | CHAPTER | PAGE |
|---|---|---|---|
| One Campaign | One.org | 1 | 4 |
| Genocide Intervention Network | genocideintervention. net | 1 | 13 |
| Global Exchange | globalexchange.org | 1 | 21 |
| Charity: Water | charitywater.org | 2 | 40 |
| Human Rights Campaign | hrc.org | 3 | 79 |
| National Gay and Lesbian Task Force | thetaskforce.org | 3 | 80 |

| Witness | witness.org | 3 | 80 |
|---|---|---|---|
| UNICEF | unicef.org | 5 | 133 |
| Ubuntu Education Fund | ubuntufund.org | 9 | 249 |
| National Association for People with AIDS | napwa.org | 10 | 259 |
| Community HIV/AIDS Mobilization Project | champnetwork.org | 10 | 260 |
| Physicians for Human Rights | physiciansforhuman rights.org | 10 | 262 |
| Center for Constitutional Rights | ccrjustice.org | 10 | 266 |
| Prisoners with Children | prisonerswithchildren. org | 10 | 267 |
| Equal Justice Works Fellowship | equaljusticeworks.org | 10 | 267 |
| Sekolo Projects Inc. | sekoloprojects.org | 10 | 269 |

## Information and Inspiration

| TITLE | WEBSITE ADDRESS | CHAPTER | PAGE |
|---|---|---|---|
| Weekly Way | weeklyway.blogspot. com | 1 | 3 |
| Ten Ways | tenways.org | 1 | 7 |
| Goodreads | goodreads.com | 1 | 12 |
| Daily Beast | thedailybeast.com | 1 | 16 |
| Huffington Post | huffingtonpost.com | 1 | 16 |
| Sightline Institute | sightline.org | 1 | 16 |
| Charity Navigator | charitynavigator.org | 1 | 20 |
| Technorati | technorati.com | 3 | 57 |
| Blogtrepreneur | blogtrepreneur.com | 3 | 58 |
| GuideStar | guidestar.org | 6 | 175 |
| Just Give | justgive.org | 6 | 175 |

| | | | |
|---|---|---|---|
| Green America Gift Guide | coopamerica.org/pubs/<br>greengifts | 6 | 178 |
| Environmental Career<br>Opportunities | ecojobs.com/<br>ecoemploy.com/ | 10<br>10 | 263<br>263 |
| Idealist | idealist.org | 10 | 254 |
| Stop Dodo | stopdodo.com | 10 | 263 |
| SustaiNYC | sustainyc.com | 10 | 266 |

## Investments

| TITLE | WEBSITE ADDRESS | CHAPTER | PAGE |
|---|---|---|---|
| Kiva | kiva.org | 1 | 20 |
| Ashoka | ashoka.org | 1 | 21 |
| Morningstar | morningstar.com | 6 | 157 |
| Social Funds | socialfunds.com | 6 | 157 |
| Community Investing<br>Resource Center | communityinvest.org | 6 | 157 |
| Calvert Investments | calvert.com | 6 | 157 |
| Domini Social Investments | domini.com | 6 | 157 |
| Pax World Mutual Funds | paxworld.com | 6 | 157 |
| Winslow Management<br>Company | winslowgreen.com | 6 | 157 |

## Political Activism

| TITLE | WEBSITE ADDRESS | CHAPTER | PAGE |
|---|---|---|---|
| Constitution Party | constitutionparty.com | 3 | 55 |
| Democratic Party | democrats.org | 3 | 55 |
| Green Party | gp.org | 3 | 55 |
| Independent American Party | usiap.org | 3 | 55 |
| Libertarian Party | lp.org | 3 | 55 |
| Reform Party | reformparty.org | 3 | 55 |

| | | | |
|---|---|---|---|
| Republican Party | gop.com | 3 | 55 |
| GovSpot | govspot.com | 3 | 55 |
| White House | whitehouse.gov | 3 | 55 |
| U.S. House of Representatives | house.gov | 3 | 55 |
| U.S. Senate | senate.gov | 3 | 55 |
| C-SPAN | c-span.org | 3 | 55 |
| Future Majority | futuremajority.com | 3 | 57 |
| Rock the Vote | rockthevote.com | 3 | 57 |
| Bother Voting | | | |
| FiveThirtyEight | fivethirtyeight.com | 3 | 57 |
| Politico | politico.com | 3 | 57 |
| The Democratic Daily | thedemocraticdaily.com | 3 | 57 |
| Little Green Footballs | littlegreenfootballs.com | 3 | 57 |
| Daily Kos | dailykos.com | 3 | 58 |
| MyDD | mydd.com | 3 | 58 |
| Open Left | openleft.com | 3 | 58 |
| Pam's House Blend | pamshouseblend.com | 3 | 58 |
| TPM Café | tpmcafe.com | 3 | 58 |
| Declare Yourself | declareyourself.com | 3 | 60 |
| Vote411.org | vote411.org | 3 | 60 |
| Bother Voting | bothervoting.org | 3 | 61 |
| Resources for the Future | rff.org | 3 | 61 |
| Fact Check | factcheck.org | 3 | 61 |
| Project Vote Smart | votesmart.org | 3 | 61 |
| Drinking Liberally | drinkingliberally.org | 3 | 69 |
| Equal Justice Works | equaljusticeworks.org | 3 | 73 |
| Center for American Progress Action Fund | americanprogressaction.org | 3 | 75 |
| Citizens for Responsibility and Ethics in Washington/ CREW | citizensforethics.org | 3 | 75 |
| Common Cause | commoncause.org | 3 | 76 |

| | | | |
|---|---|---|---|
| Democracy 21 | democracy21.net | 3 | 76 |
| Generation Engage | generationengage.org | 3 | 76 |
| MoveOn | moveon.org | 3 | 76 |
| Center for Constitutional Rights | ccr-ny.org | 3 | 77 |
| FairVote | fairvote.org | 3 | 77 |
| League of Conservation Voters | lcv.org | 3 | 79 |

## Reduce, Reuse, Recycle

| TITLE | WEBSITE ADDRESS | CHAPTER | PAGE |
|---|---|---|---|
| EcoExpress | ecoexpress.com | 1 | 6 |
| Earth 911 | earth911.com | 4 | 85 |
| Real Simple | www.realsimple.com | 4 | 85 |
| Steel Recycling Institute | recycle-steel.org | 4 | 86 |
| Call to Protect | ce.org/about/cea/ceainitiatives/3687.asp | 4 | 87 |
| CollectiveGood | collectivegood.com | 4 | 87 |
| Greendisk | greendisk.com | 4 | 87 |
| Recycleplace | recycleplace.com | 4 | 87 |
| SwapaCD | swapacd.com | 4 | 87 |
| SwapaDVD | swapadvd.com | 4 | 87 |
| Freecycle | freecycle.org | 4 | 88 |
| Goodwill | goodwill.org | 4 | 88 |
| BioBag | biobagusa.com | 4 | 91 |
| Envirosax | envirosax.com | 4 | 91 |
| Reusable Bags | reusablebags.com | 4 | 91 |
| Container Recycling Institute | container-recycling.org | 4 | 92 |
| EarthLust | earthlust.com | 4 | 93 |
| EcoUsable | ecousable.com | 4 | 93 |
| Klean Kanteen | kleankanteen.com | 4 | 93 |

## Socially Responsible Gifts

| TITLE | WEBSITE ADDRESS | CHAPTER | PAGE |
|---|---|---|---|
| World of Good | worldofgood.ebay.com | 4 | 94 |
| Kidbean | kidbean.com | 6 | 176 |
| Fair Trade Sports | fairtradesports.com | 6 | 176 |
| Earth Mama Angel Baby | earthmamaangelbaby. com | 6 | 176 |
| Baby Bunz | babybunz.com | 6 | 176 |
| Babyworks | babyworks.com | 6 | 176 |
| Big Dipper Wax Works | bigdipperwaxworks. com | 6 | 176 |
| Branch | branchhome.com | 6 | 177 |
| Ten Thousand Villages | tenthousadnvillages. com | 6 | 176 |
| Greensender | greensender.com | 6 | 177 |
| Fair Indigo | fairindigo.com | 6 | 177 |

## Travel and Transportation

| TITLE | WEBSITE ADDRESS | CHAPTER | PAGE |
|---|---|---|---|
| Adventure Cycling Association | adventurecycling.org | 9 | 233 |
| Bicycle for a Day | bicycleforaday.org | 9 | 233 |
| League of American Bicyclists | bikeleague.org | 9 | 233 |
| Map My Ride | mapmyride.com | 9 | 233 |
| Google Maps | googlemaps.com | 9 | 234 |
| Greener Cars | greenercars.org | 9 | 234 |
| Carpool World | carpoolworld.com | 9 | 236 |
| eRideShare | erideshare.com | 9 | 236 |
| Zipcar | zipcar.com | 9 | 236 |
| Car Sharing | carsharing.net | 9 | 236 |

| | | | |
|---|---|---|---|
| Carbonfund | carbonfund.org | 9 | 237 |
| Conservation Fund | conservationfund.org | 9 | 237 |
| LiveNeutral | liveneutral.org | 9 | 237 |
| *Native*Energy | nativeenergy.com | 9 | 237 |
| TerraPass | terrapass.com | 9 | 237 |
| Patagonia | Patagonia.com | 9 | 242 |
| National Parks Conservation | npca.org | 9 | 244 |
| Couch Surfing | couchsurfing.com | 9 | 246 |
| Busabout | bussabout.com | 9 | 247 |
| Camping | camping-usa.com | 9 | 247 |
| Eurail | eurail.com | 9 | 247 |
| Farecast | farecast.com | 9 | 247 |
| Hiking and Backpacking | hikingandbackpacking .com | 9 | 247 |
| Hostelling International | hihostels.com | 9 | 247 |
| Hotels | hotels.com | 9 | 248 |
| Hotwire | hotwire.com | 9 | 248 |
| Kayak | kayak.om | 9 | 248 |
| Trip Advisor | tripadvisor.com | 9 | 248 |
| Global Partnership for Sustainable Tourism Criteria | sustainabletourismcri- teria.org | 9 | 248 |
| Sustainable Travel International | sustainabletravel international.org | 9 | 249 |
| Green Hotels Association | greenhotels.com | 9 | 249 |
| responsibletravel.com | responsibletravel.com | 9 | 249 |
| Natural Habitat Adventures | nathab.com | 9 | 249 |
| International Ecotourism Club | ecoclub.com | 9 | 249 |

## Volunteering

| TITLE | WEBSITE ADDRESS | CHAPTER | PAGE |
|---|---|---|---|
| VolunteerMatch | volunteermatch.org | 2 | 29 |
| Women's Expressive Theater | wetweb.org | 2 | 31 |
| Ambassadors for Children | ambassadorsforchildren.org | 2 | 40 |
| Cross-Cultural Solutions | crossculturalsolutions.org | 2 | 41 |
| Global Service Corps | globalservicecorps.org | 2 | 41 |
| Global Volunteers | globalvolunteers.org | 2 | 42 |
| International Volunteer Programs Association (IVPA) | volunteerinternational.org | 2 | 42 |
| Projects Abroad | projects-abroad.org | 2 | 42 |
| Peace Corps | peacecorps.gov | 2 | 44 |
| American Red Cross | redcross.org | 2 | 46 |
| Big Brothers/Big Sisters | bbbs.org | 2 | 46 |
| Citizen Schools | citizenschools.org | 2 | 47 |
| Habitat for Humanity | habitat.org | 2 | 47 |
| Student Conservation Association | thesca.org | 2 | 47 |
| AmeriCorps | americorps.org | 2 | 47 |
| City Year | cityyear.org | 2 | 48 |
| Youth Service America | ysa.org | 2 | 48 |
| Doctors Without Borders | doctorswithoutborders.org | 2 | 48 |
| Mercy Ships | mercyships.org | 2 | 49 |
| Right to Play | righttoplay.com | 2 | 49 |
| WorldTeach | worldteach.org | 2 | 49 |

## Wildlife and Habitat Conservation

| TITLE | WEBSITE ADDRESS | CHAPTER | PAGE |
|---|---|---|---|
| Blue Ocean Institute | blueocean.org | 4 | 104 |
| National Marine Sanctuaries | sanctuaries.noaa.gov | 4 | 104 |
| NOAA's Fisheries Management Council | nmfs.noaa.gov/councils.htm | 4 | 104 |
| Partnership for Interdisciplinary Studies of Coastal Oceans | piscoweb.org | 4 | 104 |
| OceanConservancy | oceanconservancy.org | 4 | 105 |
| Heal the Bay | healthebay.org | 4 | 106 |
| Monterey Bay Aquarium | mbayaq.org | 4 | 106 |
| Defenders of Wildlife | defenders.org | 4 | 113 |
| Rainforest Alliance | rainforest-alliance.org | 4 | 117 |
| World Wildlife Fund | worldwildlife.org | 4 | 117 |

## Youth Action

| TITLE | WEBSITE ADDRESS | CHAPTER | PAGE |
|---|---|---|---|
| Future5000 | future5000.com | 1 | 20 |
| Power Shift | powershift09.org | 3 | 68 |
| Advocates for Youth | advocatesforyouth.org | 3 | 77 |
| YouthActionNet | youthinactionnet.org | 3 | 77 |
| Youth in Focus | youthinfocus.net | 3 | 78 |
| Power Vote | powervote.org | 10 | 261 |

# NOTES

1.  U.S. Environmental Protection Agency and Department of Energy, "Compact Fluorescent Lights," *Energy Star*, http://www.energystar.gov/index.cfm?c=cfls.pr_cfls.

2.  Arthur C. Brooks, "The Poor Give More," *Condé Nast Portfolio*, March 2008, http://www.portfolio.com/news-markets/national-news/portfolio/2008/02/19/Poor-Give-More-to-Charity.

3.  Mark Hugo Lopez and others, "The Youth Voter 2004: With a Historical Look at Youth Voting Patterns 1972-2004," CIRCLE Working Paper 35, July 2005.

4.  Tara Parker-Pope, "Panel Rebukes F.D.A. on Plastic Safety," Well, *New York Times,* sec. d, October 29, 2008, http://well.blogs.nytimes.com/2008/10/29/panel-rebukes-fda-on-plastic-safety/.

5.  Thomas Kostigen, "The World's Largest Dump: The Great Pacific Garbage Patch," *Discover*, July 10, 2008, http://www.discovermagazine.com/2008/jul/10-the-worlds-largest-dump.

6.  Container Recycling Institute, "Bottled Water," http://www.container-recycling.org/plasfact/bottledwater.htm.

7. Janet Larsen, "Bottled Water Boycotts: Back-to-the-Tap Movement Gains Momentum," Earth Policy Institute, December 7, 2007, http://www.earth-policy.org/Updates/2007/Update68.htm.

8. Lloyd Alter, "Pablo Calculates the True Cost of Bottled Water," *TreeHugger*, February 2, 2007, http://www.treehugger.com/files/2007/02/pablo_calculate.php.

9. U.S. Environmental Protection Agency, "Basic Information about Food Scraps," http://www.epa.gov/osw/conserve/materials/organics/food/fd-basic.htm.

10. Thomas Kostigen, "Want to Save the Trees? Try Paying People Not to Chop Them Down," *Discover*, August 20, 2008, http://www.discovermagazine.com/2008/sep/20-want-to-save-the-trees.

11. UN-REDD Programme Fund, "Secretary-General and Prime Minister of Norway Launch UN-REDD Programme," http://www.undp.org/mdtf/un-redd/overview.shtml.

12. Natural Resources Defense Council, "A Shopper's Guide to Home Tissue Products," http://www.nrdc.org/land/forests/gtissue.asp.

13. Washington Toxics Coalition, "Persistent Toxic Chemicals: Dioxin," http://www.watoxics.org/homes-and-gardens/fastfacts/fastfacts-ptc-dioxin.

14. Lea Hartog, "Cool Crowd," *Sierra Club Magazine*, September/October 2008.

15. Global Climate Change Impacts in the United States, Thomas R. Karl, Jerry M. Melillo, and Thomas C. Peterson (eds), *A Report from the U.S. Global Change Research Program*, Washington D.C., USA. Cambridge University Press, 2009.

16. Olive Heffernan, "Foreboding Forecast," *Nature Reports Climate Change*, October 2008, http://www.nature.com/climate/2008/0811/full/climate.2008.111.html.

17. 350.org, "350 Science," http:// www.350.org/about/science.

18. David Gershon, *Low Carbon Diet: A 30 Day Program to Lose 5000 Pounds—Be Part of the Global Warming Solution!* (Woodstock, New York: Empowerment Institute, 2006).

19. U.S. Department of Energy, "Appliances and Electronics," http://www.energy.gov/applianceselectronics.htm.

20. Project Laundry List, "Top Ten Reasons to Air Dry Your Clothes," http://www.laundrylist.org.

21. World Water Council, "Water Crisis," http://www.worldwatercouncil.org/index.php?id=25.

22. Peter H. Gleick, "Water Program," Pacific Institute, http://www.pacinst.org/topics/water_and_sustainability/index.php.

23. Thomas Kostigen, "Everything You Know about Water Conservation Is Wrong," *Discover*, May 28, 2008, http://www.discovermagazine.com/2008/jun/28-everything-you-know-about-water-conservation-is-wrong/article_view?searchterm=coffee&b_start:int=0.

24. Water Footprint Network, "Product Gallery," http://www.waterfootprint.org/?page=files/productgallery.

25. Alliance for Water Efficiency, "Household Leak Detection and Mitigation Introduction," http://www.allianceforwaterefficiency.org/Household_Leaks.aspx.

26. U.S. Environmental Protection Agency, "Municipal Solid Waste in the United States: 2007 Facts and Figures," http://www.epa.gov/osw/nonhaz/municipal/msw99.htm#links.

27. 41pounds.org, "About Us," http://www.41pounds.org/about.

28. Hazardous Substance Research Centers/South and Southwest Outreach Program, "Environmental Update no. 24: Environmental Hazards of the Textile Industry," June 2006, http://www.hsrc-ssw.org/update24.pdf.

29. Ylan Q. Mui, "Wal-Mart to Pull Bottles Made with Chemical BPA," *Washington Post*, sec. d, April 18, 2008.

30. Chris Laszlo, *Sustainable Value: How the World's Leading*

*Companies Are Doing Well by Doing Good* (Stanford, California: Stanford Business Books, 2008).

31. Natalie Thomas (CSRwire sales and client relations), in telephone interview with author, July 11, 2008.

32. Carol Sanford (InterOctave Development, CEO), interview with the author, October 1, 2008.

33. Clorox Company, "Working Together for an Environmentally Sustainable World," *The Clorox Company Corporate Social Responsibility*, http://www.thecloroxcompany.com/community/ourenviropgs/partners_affl.html.

34. Diane MacEachern, *Big Green Purse* (New York: Avery, 2008).

35. Fidelity Investments, "Reasons to Start Early," http://personal.fidelity.com/planning/retirement/saving/content/reasons.shtml.

36. Tracy Fernandez Rysavy, "Responsible Credit Cards: Myth or Reality?" *Real Green*, Nov/Dec 2005, http://www.coopamerica.org/pubs/realmoney/articles/creditcards.cfm.

37. Clifford Krauss, "Exxon Rejects Proposal Backed by Rockefellers," *New York Times*, May 29, 2008, http://www.nytimes.com/2008/05/29/business/29exxon.html?_r=1&oref=slogin.

38. Marc Gunther, "Are Kleenex Tissues Wiping Out Forests?" *Fortune*, September 27, 2006, http://money.cnn.com/2006/09/26/magazines/fortune/pluggedin_gunther.fortune/index.htm.

39. Global 100, "The Global 100: Most Sustainable Corporations in the World," http://www.global100.org.

40. Climate Counts, "Climate Counts Company Scorecard," http://www.climatecounts.org/scorecard_overview.php.

41. U.S. Department of Agriculture, "Food Budget Shares for 114 Countries," http://www.ers.usda.gov/Data/InternationalFoodDemand/StandardReports/Foodbudgetshares.xls.

42. Parker-Pope, *New York Times*, October 29, 2008.

43. BottledWaterBlues.com, "Bottled Water Facts," http://www.bottledwaterblues.com/bottled_water_facts.php.

44. Kostigen, *Discover,* May 28, 2008.

45. U.S. Department of Labor, "Consumer Expenditures in 2006,"*Bureau of Labor Statistics*, October 26, 2007, http://www.bls.gov/news.release/cesan.nr0.htm.

46. www.AboutOrganicCotton.org, "Cotton Is Woven Through Your World," http://www.aboutorganiccotton.org/woven-world.html.

47. National Cancer Institute, "Formaldehyde and Cancer: Questions and Answers," http://www.cancer.gov/cancertopics/factsheet/risk/formaldehyde.

48. Environmental Working Group, "Down the Drain: Phthalates," http://www.ewg.org/node/21838.

49. Environmental Working Group, "Down the Drain: Triclosan," http://www.ewg.org/node/21840.

50. MacEachern, *Big Green Purse.*

51. Green America, "Ten Green Toys for 2008," http://www.coopamerica.org/programs/shopunshop/10greentoys.cfm.

52. David Pimentel and Mario Giampetro, "Food, Land, Population and the U.S. Economy" (executive summary published online, November 21, 2004, http://dieoff.org/page40.htm).

53. Natural Resources Defense Council, "Frequent Fliers,"http://www.nrdc.org/health/foodmiles/results.asp?season=15&state=8.

54. U.S. Department of Health and Human Services, "Federal Agencies Take Special Precautions to Keep Mad Cow Disease Out of the United States," August 23, 2001, http://www.hhs.gov/news/press/2001pres/01fsbse.html.

55. Editorial, "The Biggest Beef Recall Ever," *New York Times*, February 21, 2008.

56. Michael Hawthorne, "Raising a Global Stink," *Chicago*

*Tribune*, July 31, 2008, http://www.chicagotribune.com/features/lifestyle/green/chi-cow-gas-31-jul31,0,4233617.story.

57. People for the Ethical Treatment of Animals, "Vegetarian Diets: Healthy and Humane," *PETA Media Center*, http://www.peta.org/mc/factsheet_display.asp?ID=137.

58. Richard Black, "'Only 50 Years Left' for Sea Fish," BBC News, November 2, 2006, http://news.bbc.co.uk/2/hi/science/nature/6108414.stm.

59. Bradley Johnson, ed., "Day in the Life: How Consumers Divvy Up All the Time They Have," *Advertising Age*, May 2, 2005.

60. U.S. Department of Energy Energy Efficiency and Renewable Energy, "Find and Compare Cars," http://www.fueleconomy.gov/feg/findacar.htm.

61. U.S. Department of Energy Energy Efficiency and Renewable Energy, "Driving More Efficiently," http://www.fueleconomy.gov/feg/driveHabits.shtml.

62. U.S. Department of Energy Energy Efficiency and Renewable Energy, "Keeping Your Car in Shape," http://www.fueleconomy.gov/feg/maintain.shtml.

63. Ben Mutzabaugh, "CNBC: America Spends $20,000 a Minute on Jet Fuel," Today in the Sky blog, *USA Today*, July 13, 2008, http://www.usatoday.com/travel/flights/item.aspx?type=blog&ak=52545752.blog.

# ABOUT THE AUTHOR

Josie St. Peter

Libuse Binder's work has appeared in *Earth911*, *Weekly Way*, *Fit Yoga*, and *Worldchanging*. Formerly in film production in Los Angeles and a middle school English teacher in New York, she is now focused on energizing the next generation of adults for a life of engagement in the social and environmental issues that matter most. Her passions include the environment, sustainable living, volunteerism, public policy, and social networking technology. She currently lives in Seattle with her husband, where they enjoy exploring the natural beauty that surrounds them.